DESIGNS IN
HANDKNITTING

DESIGNS IN HANDKNITTING

There are a great many people who, over the years, have helped me to find my feet in handknitting, on the technical, the commercial and the personal side. My sincere gratitude is due in particular to Eva for being unflappable under pressure and didactic all the way along; to Jane for her dedication and tremendously hard work; to Dee and Daphne for each coping with hundreds of sweaters needed yesterday; to Jody for being in charge of the congratulations department; to Judy and Mike for their unfaltering support; to Mary for pushing me in the right direction; to my family for exercising patience and confidence; and to Winks for being a pillar of strength. My thanks are also due to the following people for the help they have given me, both past and present:

Andrew, Annie, Bassett, Bob, Caroline, Chris, Clarissa, Dana, Howard, Jeffrey, Joanne, John, Jeremy, June, Kate, Linda, Melvin, Peter, Rakhshinda, Susie, Tristan, Vicky, Victor, Wendy, Zoe

and of course to all the ladies who knitted up the designs in this book and all the others who have knitted for me over the years.

CREDITS

Photographer *Chris Edwick*
Photographer's assistants *Mark Fenn and Mark Douet*
Stylist *Jody Day*
Hair and make-up *Mark at Mark Nicholas*
Sketches *Kate Baker*
Outline diagrams *Brenda Armitt*
Designer *Karen Mack/Grid Graphics*

First published in Great Britain in 1987 by Sidgwick & Jackson Limited

ISBN 0-283-99403-7

Typeset by Rowland Phototypesetting Limited
Bury St Edmunds, Suffolk
Printed in Italy by Imago
for Sidgwick & Jackson Limited
1 Tavistock Chambers
Bloomsbury Way
London WC1A 2SG

FOREWORD

A fashion editor's life affords many pleasures. It is, as everyone knows, glamorous. You get to go to parties full of beautiful people in beautiful and expensive places, many of them deliciously far-flung. It is also, of course, gruelling, uncomfortable, exhausting and manically competitive. But when the toil pays off and you've got the story and the pictures and, best of all, got them before anyone else has, well, that's a pleasure in a class of its own. The headiest pleasure of all, however, is when the story you got first is in the nature of a discovery, when you proved your taste and judgement by being the first to spot a new and important talent.

I didn't exactly stumble across Christian de Falbe labouring in obscurity at his humble craft. He telephoned the *Guardian* and suggested, so politely but quite firmly, that it might be to my advantage to take a look at his work. I invited him to call. He arrived, on time, looking handsome, purposeful and absolutely confident. His yarns and his sweater designs were pretty impressive, too.

So I did the first story. And bought a sweater. I have bought several since and passed his name on endlessly to covetous friends, acquaintances and even the occasional bold stranger.

What makes a Christian de Falbe design so special? To begin with, he is a designer who never forces his materials to do what they were never meant to do. He understands the natural qualities of the yarn with which he is working and uses them as his starting point rather than some abstract idea of what sort of sweater would be fashionable right now.

Which is not to say that fashion has no part to play in his work. It does, but it is more a matter of the mood of the season than any high-fashion uniform. And it is this which gives the designs their classic, timeless quality. These sweaters do not date.

Another reason for this is the strength of what, in fashion writers' shorthand, is called the designer's signature or handwriting. Christian de Falbe revels in sensuousness of texture. The shapes of his garments are simple so that the tactile and visual qualities of the yarns can be exploited fully, can speak for themselves. Similarly, when he uses more than one colour the effects he achieves are either meltingly subtle or dramatically disciplined. There's no excess and no fuss. It is perfectly judged. Just like my decision to do that first story on Christian. At the time I regretted my two left hands and their unilateral refusal to knit. Looking at the pictures in this book, there's still plenty to regret.

Brenda Polan
The Guardian

5

I remember a jersey that I had as a little boy which was such a popular item of clothing that, inevitably it didn't last very long. In fact I immediately got glue all over the cuffs and subsequently spilt car-battery acid all down the front so that the next morning parts of it had simply disappeared. What a pity, because to me it really was the business. I thought it was smashing: it was grubby black with a very dashing racing-car across the tummy. The point of this story is that I myself had been allowed to select the colour scheme of this tremendous vehicle. Blue. Nothing has really changed since then, because the pleasure that can be derived from knitting, whether you are designing or just following a pattern, is that every jersey is a personal choice involving decisions of yarn, colour, stitch-pattern and shape. In dressmaking you are limited to your fabric and pattern; you cannot add racing-cars. I think it is this extra dimension – being able to design your own fabric, which first encouraged me to pick up a ball of wool instead of a yard of wool.

In that relatively short time since I first became seduced by the creative potential of handknitting, the manufacturers of knitting yarns have made huge steps in two directions: forwards and backwards. Whilst the technical refinements of modern spinning machinery are becoming increasingly sophisticated, the temptation to 'overdesign' a yarn is all the more available. Many of the multi-coloured and multi-fibred yarns on the market make a mockery of the art of creating your own material, stitch by stitch.

This book is all about designs which utilise the traditional techniques of hand-knitting, and yarns which are relatively simple in their construction; their beauty is in the fibre, the colour, the handle and the texture. Knitting for knitting's sake; designs for addicts and designs for potential addicts who hadn't realised there were any alternatives to brushed chunky acrylic.

It was a great compliment to be asked to compile this collection of designs, but the difficulty of deciding where to start and finish was onerous in the extreme. I like designing for women and men, in bright bold colours and in soft muted ones, for summer and for autumn, in textured stitches and in multi-colours, in cotton and in wool, for day and for evening . . . Should I start with a crocheted bikini and end with a tweed overcoat, or should the first ones be in cream and grey progressing through to acid yellow and black? Need I go on?

The only fair decision, it seemed, was none at all. I planned to amass a number of ideas and drawings and let them find their own niche in the jig-saw. This way, I thought, there would inevitably be designs which were naturally grouped together for reasons of colour, yarn, season, shape or whatever. It is thus that you find yourself at the beginning of a series of little mini-collections, or designs for a particular mood. Doubtless you have your personal preferences, just as I do from one day to another; and I have worked on the designs and patterns, whenever I felt in the mood to develop, say, those soft-coloured early-autumn designs for that September-y time of year. Equally I would very much hope that you too will have changes in preference, and that this may even encourage you to work on knitting up more than one jersey at a time, or at least produce your own personal variation of one of my designs. Before you even cast on one stitch, however, be sure to have a look at the words of guidance starting on page 8, regarding tension, abbreviations, etc. That way you can be sure of getting the right results, so at this point I should congratulate you on your first project, and hope there will be many more. Welcome aboard!

CONTENTS

HOW TO UNDERSTAND THE PATTERNS

At the beginning of each pattern you will find references to the page or pages where the design is shown. Doubtless sometimes you will be surprised by how different the same design can look when made up in a different colour, or colour combination, so I would strongly encourage you to look at the relevant pages before finally deciding which colour you are going to use. In some cases different versions (e.g. a longer length) are also shown in other parts of the book.

In many pattern books you will find a symbol at the beginning indicating the complexity of the pattern; I have purposely not included this as I think it can be deceptive. Some people find it complex working with more than one colour at a time, and yet can easily change stitch pattern. Some people prefer working from a graph. Some people can work with many colours, but only in stocking stitch. Therefore I have left it up to the reader to assess their individual ability by looking at the picture and reading through the pattern; where the pattern is easier than it appears, or there are hidden difficulties, I have pointed this out in the individual pattern introductions.

THE DIAGRAMS

The diagrams are a guide to help you check your measurements as you knit; they also give you a very good idea of exactly what you are going to end up with, and of course they facilitate any alterations to the pattern that you may be thinking of. Where only one figure is shown, this refers to all sizes. In order to keep the diagram clear, measurements are given only in inches, but if you need to know the dimensions in centimetres, this conversion table should help:

1 inch	=	2½cm	34 ins	=	86cm
2 ins	=	5cm	36 ins	=	91cm
4 ins	=	10cm	38 ins	=	97cm
8 ins	=	20cm	40 ins	=	102cm
16 ins	=	41cm	42 ins	=	107cm
32 ins	=	81cm	44 ins	=	112cm

SIZE

Actual size is the exact measurement around the bust or chest, so that when you measure across the garment it will show half the actual size.

To fit bust/chest is my advice on what size to make for yourself. Of course some people prefer more fitted or looser garments, which is why both figures are given. However, in handknitting, you should always allow 2 inches more than the actual bust/chest size. The 'to fit bust' measurement varies sometimes according to the design. Naturally the same individual would require a bigger 'actual size' on a sloppy tweed sweater than on a fitted one in lightweight wool.

Length from back neck – this dimension is the total length of the design. It is taken from the centre back (not including the neck ribbing) to the base of the welt. When a design has a shaped back neck of more than a few rows, the equivalent measurement is given from the same point.

Sleeve seam – this is the measurement along the underarm, not including any of the sleeve which may be sewn into the body sections.

INTERNATIONAL NEEDLE SIZES AND TERMS

Metric	British	American
3mm	11	2
3¼mm	10	3
3¾mm	9	4
4mm	8	5
4½mm	7	6
5mm	6	7
5½mm	5	8
6mm	4	9
6½mm	3	10
7mm	2	10
7½mm	1	11

English	American
Tension	Gauge
Cast off	Bind off
Moss stitch	Seed stitch
Stocking stitch	Stockinette stitch

MATERIALS

Yarn quantities required for each design are given in this table. For an explanation of yarns used, and yarn sources, refer to pages 172 and 176. If you are making alterations to the design you will need to recalculate the quantities; as a rough guide, a 50g ball will knit about 10cm in length on the front of a garment. It is also useful to know that a row of knitting will require about three times its length in yarn, i.e. 1 metre of yarn will work 33cm of knitting. Needle sizes are given, but of course this assumes your tension is the average; the garment will come out the wrong size if you knit tighter or looser than normal on the needle size given (see TENSION below).

TENSION

This is doubtless the most important requirement to obtain successful results, but also the area where so many people go wrong. I have heard it said again and again: 'Oh no, I never bother with a tension swatch.' Well, it's vital for all knitters to do one, no matter how experienced they may be. The method is as follows: cast on at least 30sts and work at least 40 rows in stocking stitch. From the central part of your square (avoiding the curly edges) mark out the stitches and rows prescribed. Then, with the swatch lying flat, check that the distance between your markers is exactly 10cm. If there are too many stitches, then your knitting is too tight, and you should change to a needle one size bigger and try again; too few stitches and you should change to a smaller needle, etc.

There are only two tensions used throughout this whole book, so take an extra moment – you've only got to do it twice!

ABBREVIATIONS

The following abbreviations are those most commonly used in all the patterns; where individual patterns have special abbreviations, these are explained at the beginning of the patterns; where cast-off stitches are given in the middle of a row, the last stitch of the cast off is always included in the following instruction.

k	knit
p	purl
st(s)	stitch(es)
inc	increase by knitting into front and back of next st
dec(s)	decrease(s), knit the next 2sts together
tog	together
beg	beginning
patt	pattern
rep	repeat
alt	alternate
foll	following
rem	remain(ing)
cont	continue
rev	reverse
cn	cable needle
yrn	yarn round needle
yf	yarn forward
yb	yarn back
s1	slip a stitch purlwise
psso	pass slipped st over
k2tog	knit next 2sts tog
p2tog	purl next 2sts tog
moss stitch	row 1:k1 p1, row 2:p1 k1 (on even number of sts), every row k1 p1 to last st, k1 (on odd number of sts)
M	main colour
C	contrast colour
*	repeat instructions between * and * number of times indicated
()	brackets refer to larger size; where only one figure is given this refers to all sizes figures in italics show the number of sts you should have on your needle; they are to check your work, not an instruction.

1 This exceedingly long coat, which could be anything from a wedding-dress to a snow-plough, is my introduction to this chapter of pure white designs. White because I feel it enhances the large variety of stitch patterns used throughout, although, of course, they would all work very well in any colour. I am really going to town here on the three-dimensional qualities which can be achieved in handknitting, and which are the sign of a truly hand-made jersey, stitch-by-stitch and row-by-row. I do try to work with stitches which complement one another and which agree with the shape and feeling of the whole design. The temptation to liberally sprinkle different patterns on any old silhouette must be avoided at all costs; this simply results in a sort of unco-ordinated patchwork of unrelated patterns. The instructions for this coat are found on page 57 in a cardigan of a more conventional length; if you want the coat, then ignore the armhole shaping and just carry on knitting.

CLARISSA

ONE OF MY FAVOURITE DESIGN IDEAS IS 'TONE-ON-TONE' WHERE THE CONTRAST OF DIFFERENT YARN TEXTURES COMPOSES THE PATTERN. WHEN THE LIGHT REFLECTS OFF THE SHINY DRAGONFLY YARN USED HERE YOU WILL SEE THE FLOWER DESIGN AGAINST A WOOL BACKGROUND.

Shown on page 15 in white Chandos and ivory Dragonfly.

See diagram at end of pattern

SIZE cm(in)
To fit bust:

81–86(32–34)	86–97(34–38)	97–107(38–42)

Actual size:

91(36)	99(39)	109(43)

Length from back neck:

62(24½)	63(25)	65(25½)

Sleeve seam:

44(17½)	46(18)	46(18)

MATERIALS
Chandos – 50g balls:

11	12	13

Dragonfly – 50g balls:

2	2	2

1 pair each of 3¼mm and 4mm needles

TENSION
22sts and 28 rows = 10cm square on 4mm needles over stocking stitch. See page 9.

ABBREVIATIONS
See page 9.

RIGHT SLEEVE
Using 3¼mm needles cast on 41sts and work 5cm in k1 p1 rib
Increase row: *inc rib 2* rep * to * to last 2sts inc k1 *55sts*
Change to 4mm needles and work in diagonal rib patt as follows:

Row 1: *k3 p1* 13 times k3.
Row 2: *k1 p3* 6 times k1 p5 *k1 p3* 6 times k1
Row 3: k1 *p1 k3* 13 times p1 k1
Row 4: p2 *k1 p3* 6 times k1 p1 k1 *p3 k1* 6 times p2
These 4 rows form patt repeat.
Cont in patt repeating from row 1 inc one st each end of next and every foll 6th row to 92(94:96)sts working extra sts into patt.
Cont without shaping until work measures 44(46:46)cm
NB The textured patt will cause the knitting to 'bounce up' slightly, so it is important to measure the work lying flat and with very gentle pressure downwards.

Shape sleevehead: cast off 4(5:5)sts at beg of next 2 rows. Dec each end of next 4 rows. Dec each end of next and every foll alt row to 30sts. Cast off.

LEFT SLEEVE
As for right sleeve, but in stocking st instead of diagonal rib patt. This sleeve will not 'bounce up' so it may be a few rows less to the armhole in order to match the other sleeve exactly.

BACK
Using 3¼mm needles, cast on 91(98:108)sts and work 5cm in k1 p1 rib.
Increase row: rib 4(3:8) *inc rib 8* 9(10:10) times inc rib 5(4:9) *101(109:119)sts*
Change to 4mm needles and work in diagonal rib patt as for right sleeve, but across right-hand side of back only (ie patt changes down centre back)
Row 1: k3(3:0) *p1 k3* 12(13:15) times k50(54:59)

Following page: Clarissa, in the foreground, relies on the different yarn textures to show up the flower design. The girl in the black and white hat is wearing Capulet, the pattern for that is on page 164.

170

160

150

140

130

120

110

100

90

80

70

60

50

40

30

20

10

SIZE 1

SIZE 2

SIZE 3

CLARISSA

Row 2: p51(55:60) *p3 k1* 12(13:14) times
p2(2:3)
Row 3: k1(1:2) *p1 k3* 13(14:15) times
k48(52:57)
Row 4: p49(53:58) *p3 k1* 13(14:15) times
p0(0:1)
These 4 rows form patt repeat. Cont in patt,
repeating from row 1, and foll graph for
armhole and shoulder shapings. Ignore front
neck shaping, and cast off all sts along last row
of shoulder shaping.

FRONT
Rib as for back.
Follow graph to work flower motif, noting that
the leaves and stem are all worked in Dragonfly,
and that squares with dots denote purl sts on
knit rows and knit sts on purl rows.
Do not carry any yarn across the back of the
motif, except on the stem.
Follow armhole and neck shapings from graph.

COLLAR
Join right shoulder seam. Using 4mm needles,
and with right side facing, pick up 27sts from
side neck and shaping, 19sts from centre front
neck, 27sts from side neck and 41sts from back
neck *114 sts*
Starting with a knit row, work 14cm in stocking
st. Change to 3¼mm needles and work 3 rows
in k1 p1 rib. Cast off in rib.

MAKING UP
Join left shoulder seam and collar seam. Join
sleeve seams and set in sleeves. Join side seams.
Fold collar over to outside and slip stitch down
on to line of neck shaping. Weave in any loose
ends.

CARE INSTRUCTIONS
See ball tag and page 172.

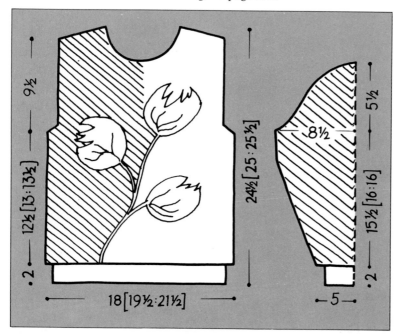

EDELWEISS

THIS SWEATER IS DIVIDED INTO DIAMOND SHAPES, EACH ONE USING A DIFFERENT STITCH PATTERN. THE FIRST PATTERN REPEAT WILL BE THE HARDEST, BUT THERE ARE NO COMPLICATED TECHNIQUES USED AND IT WILL BECOME EASIER AS YOU BEGIN TO MEMORIZE THE STITCHES.

Shown on page 18 in white Chandos.

See diagram at end of pattern

SIZE cm(in)
To fit bust:

81–86(32–34)	86–91(34–36)	91–97(36–38)
Actual size:		
94(37)	99(39)	104(41)
Length from back neck:		
69(27)	69(27)	69(27)
Sleeve seam:		
43(17)	44(17½)	45(18)

MATERIALS
Chandos – 50g balls:

12	13	14

1 pair each of 3¼mm and 4mm needles

Cable needle

TENSION
22sts and 28 rows = 10cm square on 4mm needles over stocking stitch. See page 9.

ABBREVIATIONS
See page 9.
tw2 = knit into front of second stitch then knit first stitch, take both sts off tog
mb = k1 p1 k1 p1 k1 into next st, turn, p5 turn, k5 then take 2nd, 3rd, 4th and 5th sts over first st
p3tog = purl next 3sts tog
c4f = place next 2sts on cn, leave at front of work, k2 then k2sts from cn
c4b = place next 2sts on cn, leave at back of work, k2 then k2sts from cn

BACK
Using 3¼mm needles cast on 105(111:117)sts and work 7cm in k1 p1 rib.
Increase row: rib 2(5:8) *inc rib 8* 11 times inc rib 3(6:9) 117(123:129)sts
Change to 4mm needles and work in patt as follows:
Row 1: 0(k2 p1:k5 p1) *k1 p1* 14 times k1 p29 k1 p6 *mb p7* twice mb p6 k1 *p1 k3* 7 times 0(p1 k2:p1 k5)
To clarify the 3 sizes, row 1 (above) is written out individually for all 3 sizes:
Size 1: *k1 p1* 14 times k1 p29 k1 p6 *mb p7* twice mb p6 k1 *p1 k3* 7 times
Size 2: k2 p1 *k1 p1* 14 times k1 p29 k1 p6 *mb p7* twice mb p6 k1 *p1 k3* 7 times p1 k2
Size 3: k5 p1 *k1 p1* 14 times k1 p29 k1 p6 *mb p7* twice mb p6 k1 *p1 k3* 7 times p1 k5
Row 2: 0(k1 p2:*p1 k1* twice p2) *k1 p3* 6 times k1 p1 k1 p3 k27 p3 k1 p25 k1 p3 *p1 k1* 13 times p1 0(p2 k1:p2 *k1 p1* twice)
Row 3: k2(5:8) *p1 k1* 12 times *k2 p1* twice k23 p1 k5 p25 k2 p1 k2 *p1 k3* 6 times p1 k1(k4:k7)
Row 4: p2(p1 k1 p3:*k1 p1* 3 times p2) *k1 p3* 5 times k1 p1 *k1 p3* twice k23 p2 k1 p1 k1 p2 k23 p2 k3 p2 *k1 p1* 11 times k1 p2(p3 k1 p1:p2 *k1 p1* 3 times)
Row 5: k3(6:9) *p1 k1* 10 times p1 k2 p5 k2 p1 k19 p1 k2 p2 k1 p2 k2 p6 mb p7 p6 *k4 p1* twice *k3 p1* 5 times k3(6:9)
Row 6: 0(k1:0) *p1 k1* 1(2:4) times p2 *k1 p3* 4 times k1 p1 *k1 p5* twice k19 p2 k3 p1 k3 p2 k1 p17 k1 p3 k5 p4 *k1 p1* 9 times p2 *k1 p1* 1(2:4) times 0(k1:0)
Row 7: k5(8:11) *k1 p1* 8 times k3 tw2 p5 tw2 k2 p17 k2 p4 k1 p4 k2 p17 k6 p1 k6 *p1 k3* 4 times p1 k5(8:11)

Row 8: 0(p1:0) *k1 p1* 1(2:4) times *k1 p3* 4 times k1 p1 k1 p2 *k1 p4* twice k1 p2 k15 p3 *k4 p1* twice p2 k1 p13 k1 p2 k1 p2 k5 p2 k1 p2 *k1 p1* 7 times k1 p3 *k1 p1* 1(3:4) times k1(0:k1)

Row 9: k7(10:13) *p1 k1* 6 times p1 k2 p2 tw2 p5 tw2 p2 k2 p1 k11 p1 k2 p1 *k1 p4* twice k1 p1 k2 p6 mb p6 k2 p2 c4f p1 c4b p2 k2 *p1 k3* 4 times k4(7:10)

Row 10: 0(k1:0) *p1 k1* 3(4:6) times p2 *k1 p3* twice k1 p1 k1 p2 k3 p4 k1 p4 k3 p2 k11 p2 k2 *p1 k4* twice p1 k2 p2 k11 p2 k3 p2 k5 p2 k3 p3 *k1 p1* 5 times p2 *k1 p1* 3(4:6) times 0(k1:0)

Row 11: k10(13:16) *p1 k1* 3 times p1 k3 p4 tw2 p5 tw2 p4 k2 p1 k7 p1 k2 p3 *k1 p4* twice k1 p3 k2 p9 k2 p4 k4 p1 k4 p4 k2 *p1 k3* twice p1 k9(12:15)

Row 12: 0(p1:0) *k1 p1* 4(5:7) times p2 k1 p3 k1 p1 k1 p2 k5 p4 k1 p4 k5 p2 k7 p2 *k4 p1* 3 times k4 p2 k1 p5 k1 p2 *k5 p2* twice k5 p2 *k1 p1* 3 times k1 p3 *k1 p1* 3(5:6) times k1(0:k1)

Row 13: k11(14:17) *p1 k1* twice p1 k2 p6 tw2 p5 tw2 p6 k2 p5 k3 *p4 k1* 4 times k2 p5 k2 p6 c4f p1 c4b p6 k2 *p1 k3* twice k8(11:14)

Row 14: 0(k1:0) *p1 k1* 5(6:8) times p2 k1 p1 k1 p2 k7 p4 k1 p4 k7 p2 k3 p2 k1 *p1 k4* 4 times *p1 k1 p2 k1* twice k6 p2 k5 p2 k7 p3 k1 p3 *k1 p1* 5(6:8) times 0(k1:0)

Row 15: k16(19:22) p8 tw2 p5 tw2 p8 k2 p1 k2 p2 *k1 p4* 4 times k1 p2 k2 p1 k2 p8 k4 p1 k4 p8 k2 p1 k13(16:19)

Row 16: 0(p1:0) *k1 p1* 6(7:9) times p3 k9 p4 k1 p4 k9 p3 k3 *p1 k4* 4 times p1 k3 p3 k9 p2 k5 p2 k9 p4 *k1 p1* 5(7:8) times k1(0:k1)

Row 17: k14(17:20) p10 tw2 p5 tw2 p10 k1 *p4 k1* 6 times p10 c4f k1 c4b p10 k14(17:20)

Row 18: 0(k1:0) *p1 k1* 6(7:9) times p3 k9 p4 k1 p4 k9 p3 k3 *p1 k4* 4 times p1 k3 p3 k9 p2 k5 p2 k9 p3 *k1 p1* 6(7:9) times 0(k1:0)

Row 19: as row 15

Row 20: k1(0:k1) *p1 k1* 4(6:7) times p3 k1 p1 k1 p2 k7 p4 k1 p4 k7 p2 k3 p2 k1 *p1 k4* 4 times p1 k1 p2 k1 p1 k1 p2 k7 p2 k5 p2 k7 p2 k1 p1 k1 p3 *k1 p1* 4(6:7) times k1(0:k1)

Row 21: as row 13

Row 22: 0(k1:0) *p1 k1* 4(5:7) times p2 k1 p1 k1 p3 k1 p2 k5 p4 k1 p4 k5 p2 k7 p2 *k4 p1* 3 times k4 p2 k1 p5 k1 p2 *k5 p2* twice k5 p3 *k1 p1* twice k1 p3 *k1 p1* 4(5:7) times 0(k1:0)

Row 23: as row 11

Row 24: k1(0:1) *p1 k1* 2(4:5) times p3 k1 p1 *k1 p3* twice k1 p2 k3 p4 k1 p4 k3 p2 k11 p2 k2 *p1 k4* twice p1 k2 p2 k11 p2 k3 p2 k5 p2 k3 p2 *k1 p1* 5 times k1 p3 *k1 p1* 2(4:5) times k1(0:k1)

Row 25: as row 9

Row 26: 0(k1:0) *p1 k1* 2(3:5) times p2 k1 p1 *k1 p3* 3 times k1 p2 *k1 p4* twice k1 p2 k15

p3 k4 p1 k4 p3 k1 p13 k1 p2 k1 p2 k5 p2 k1 p3 *k1 p1* 7 times p2 *k1 p1* 2(3:5) times 0(k1:0)

Row 27: as row 7

Row 28: 0(p1:0) *k1 p1* 1(2:4) times p2 k1 p1 *k1 p3* 4 times *k1 p5* twice k19 p2 k3 p1 k3 p2 k1 p17 k1 p3 k5 p3 *k1 p1* 9 times k1 p2 *k1 p1* 1(2:4) times 0(p1:0)

Row 29: as row 5

Row 30: 0(k1 p1 k1:*p1 k1* 3 times) p2 k1 p1 *k1 p3* 7 times k23 p2 k1 p1 k1 p2 k23 p2 k3 p3 *k1 p1* 10 times k1 p3 0(k1 p1 k1:*k1 p1* 3 times)

Row 31: as row 3

Row 32: 0(p1:0) *k1 p1* 1(2:4) times *k1 p3* 7 times k27 p3 k1 p25 k1 p3 *k1 p1* 13 times k1 0(p1 k1 p1:*p1 k1* 3 times)

These 32 rows form patt rep. Cont in patt until work measures 46cm.

Shape armhole: cast off 5(6:7)sts beg next 2 rows. Dec armhole edge on next 4 rows. Dec armhole edge on next 5(6:7) alt rows *89(91:93)sts*

Cont without shaping until work measures 68cm

Shape shoulders and neck: cast off 7sts, work 25(26:27), cast off 25, work to end.

On 32(33:34)sts:

Row 1: cast off 7sts work to end
Row 2: cast off 2sts work to end
Rows 3–4: as rows 1–2
Row 5: as row 1
Row 6: dec, work to end
Row 7: cast off

Rejoin yarn to neck edge of rem sts and work other side to match.

FRONT

As for back until work is 18 rows less than to back shoulder shaping

Shape neck: work 39(40:41)sts, cast off 11, work to end

On 39(40:41)sts:

Row 1: patt
Row 2: cast off 3sts, patt to end
Rows 3–4: as rows 1–2
Row 5: as row 1
Row 6: cast off 2sts, patt to end
Row 7: as row 1
Row 8: dec, patt to end
Rows 9–14: as rows 7–8 3 times

Work 4 rows

Cast off 7sts beg next and foll 2 alt rows, work 1 row, cast off.

Rejoin yarn to neck edge of rem sts and work to match, starting on row 2

SLEEVES

Using 3¼mm needles cast on 51 sts and work 7cm in k1 p1 rib

Increase row: rib 2 *inc rib 4* 9 times inc rib 3 *61sts*

Following page:
This design,
Edelweiss, shows off
the possibilities of
different stitch
textures to their best
advantage.

EDELWEISS

Change to 4mm needles and patt as follows:
Row 1: knit
Row 2: *k1 p1* 14 times k1 p3 k1 *p1 k1* 14 times
Row 3: knit
Row 4: *p1 k1* 13 times p3 k1 p1 k1 p3 *k1 p1* 13 times
Row 5: inc, k27 p2 k1 p2 k27, inc *63sts*
Row 6: *p1 k1* 13 times p2 k3 p1 k3 p2 *k1 p1* 13 times
Row 7: k27 p4 k1 p4 k27
Row 8: *k1 p1* 12 times p3 k4 p1 k4 p3 *p1 k1* 12 times
Row 9: k25 p1 *k1 p4* twice k1 p1 k25
Row 10: *p1 k1* 11 times p2 k2 *p1 k4* twice p1 k2 p2 *k1 p1* 11 times
Row 11: inc, k22 p3 *k1 p4* twice k1 p3 k22, inc *65sts*
Row 12: *p1 k1* 10 times p3 *k4 p1* 4 times p2 *k1 p1* 10 times
Row 13: k23 *p4 k1* 4 times k22
Row 14: *k1 p1* 10 times p1 k1 *p1 k4* 4 times p1 k1 p1 *p1 k1* 10 times
Row 15: k20 p2 *k1 p4* 4 times k1 p2 k20
Row 16: *p1 k1* 8 times p3 k3 *p1 k4* 4 times p1 k3 p3 *k1 p1* 8 times

Row 17: inc, k17 *p4 k1* 6 times k16, inc *67sts*
Row 18: *p1 k1* 9 times p2 k3 *p1 k4* 4 times p1 k3 p2 *k1 p1* 9 times
Row 19: k21 p2 *k1 p4* 4 times k1p2 k21
Row 20: *k1 p1* 10 times p2 k1 *p1 k4* 4 times p1 k1 p2 *k1 p1* 10 times
Row 21: k24 *p4 k1* 4 times k23
Row 22: *p1 k1* 11 times p2 *k4 p1* 4 times p1 *k1 p1* 11 times
Row 23: inc, k24 p3 *k1 p4* twice k1 p3 k24, inc *69sts*
Row 24: *p1 k1* 12 times p3 k2 *p1 k4* twice p1 k2 p3 *k1 p1* 12 times
Row 25: k28 p1 *k1 p4* twice k1 p1 k28
Row 26: *p1 k1* 14 times p2 k4 p1 k4 p2 *p1 k1* 14 times
Row 27: k30 p4 k1 p4 k30
Row 28: *p1 k1* 14 times p3 k3 p1 k3 p3 *k1 p1* 14 times
Row 29: inc, k31 p2 k1 p2 k31, inc *71sts*
Row 30: *p1 k1* 16 times p2 k1 p1 k1 p2 *k1 p1* 16 times
Row 31: knit
Row 32: *k1 p1* 17 times p3 *p1 k1* 17 times
These 32 rows form patt. Cont in patt inc 1st each end of 3rd and every foll 6th row to 89sts working extra sts into edge patt. Cont without shaping until work measures 43(44:45)cm
Shape sleevehead: cast off 5(3:3)sts beg next 2(4:4) rows. Dec each end next 4 rows. Dec each end next and foll alt rows until 43sts remain. Dec each end next 4 rows. Cast off 3sts beg next 6 rows.
Cast off.

NECKBAND
Join right shoulder seam.
Using 3¼mm needles and with right side facing, pick up knitwise 26sts down left front neck, 11sts centre front, 26sts up right front neck, 39sts across back neck *102sts*
Work 5cm in k1 p1 rib. Cast off loosely in rib.

MAKING UP
Join left shoulder seam. Join side and sleeve seams. Set in sleeves and stitch into position. Fold neckband over to inside and slipstitch into position. Weave in any loose ends.

CARE INSTRUCTIONS
See ball tag and page 172.

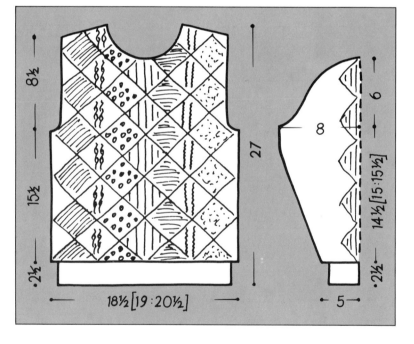

COLOMBE

I N THIS CARDIGAN, WITH A SIMPLE CABLE DESIGN, THE YARN IS USED DOUBLE SO IT'S WORKED ON BIG NEEDLES AND IS CHUNKY AND WARM; THIS MAY BE A GOOD ONE TO START ON FOR SOMEBODY WHO'S JUST LEARNING TO DO CABLES.

Shown on page 22 in white Chandos.

See diagram at end of pattern

SIZE cm(in)
To fit bust:

81–91(32–36)	97–101(38–40)

Actual size:

97(38)	107(42)

Length from back neck:

66(26)	69(27)

Sleeve seam:

43(17)	46(18)

MATERIALS
Chandos – 50g balls:

18	20

1 pair each of 5mm and 6mm needles

Cable needle. 10 buttons

TENSION
15sts and 20 rows = 10cm square on 6mm needles over stocking stitch with yarn used DOUBLE (ie 2 ends together). See page 9.

ABBREVIATIONS
See page 9.
c3f = place next 2sts on cn, leave at front of work, k1, then k2 from cn
c3b = place next st on cn, leave at back of work, k2, then k1 from cn
c4f = place next 2sts on cn, leave at front of work, k2, then k2 from cn
tw3b = place next st on cn, leave at back of work, k2, then p1 from cn
tw3f = place next 2sts on cn, leave at front of work, p1, then k2 from cn

SPECIAL NOTE
Chandos is used DOUBLE (ie 2 ends together) throughout.

BACK
Using 5mm needles and yarn DOUBLE (ie 2 ends together), cast on 75(83)sts and work 9cm in k1 p1 rib.
Increase row: rib 1(5) *inc rib 11* 6 times inc rib 1(5) *82(90)sts*
Change to 6mm needles and work in patt as follows:
Row 1: knit
Row 2: purl
Row 3: k3(7) *p4 k20* 3 times, p4 k3(7)
Row 4: p3(7) *k4 p20* 3 times, k4 p3(7)
Rows 5–6: as rows 3–4
Row 7: k1(5) *c3f p2 c3b k16* 3 times, c3f p2 c3b k1(5)
Row 8: p4(8) *k2 p22* 3 times, k2 p4(8)
Row 9: k2(6) *c3f c3b k18* 3 times, c3f c3b, k2(6)
Row 10: purl
Row 11: k3(7) *c4f k20* 3 times, c4f k3(7)
Row 12: purl
Row 13: k2(6), *tw3b tw3f k18* 3 times, tw3b tw3f k2(6)
Row 14: as row 8
Row 15: k1(5) *tw3b p2 tw3f k16* 3 times, tw3b p2 tw3f k1(5)
Row 16: as row 6
Rows 17–18: as rows 3–4.
Row 19: as row 3
Row 20: purl
Rows 21–22: as rows 1–2
Row 23: k15(19), *p4 k20* twice, p4 k15(19)
Row 24: p15(19), *k4, p20* twice, k4 p15(19)
Rows 25–26: as rows 23–24
Rows 23–26: set new positions for 'crossovers'.
Keeping 'crossovers' correct, work rows 27–39.

*Following page:
The girl's cardigan, Colombe, is worked in a very simple cable pattern using the yarn double; the little fairisle sweater, Gloucester, is also shown in adult sizes on page 79.*

Row 40: purl
These 40 rows form patt repeat. Cont in patt until work measures 62½(65)cm.**
Shape shoulders: cast off 4(5)sts at beg of next 8 rows. Cast off 10sts at beg of next 2 rows. Cast off.

LEFT FRONT

Using 5mm needles and yarn DOUBLE (ie 2 ends together) cast on 35(39)sts and work 9cm in k1 p1 rib.
Increase row: rib 2(4) *inc rib 9* 3 times inc rib 2(4) *39(43)sts*
Change to 6mm needles and work in patt as follows:
Row 1: knit
Row 2: purl
Row 3: k3(7) p4 k20 p4 k8
Row 4: p8 k4 p20 k4 p3(7)
This sets patt as on back. Cont in patt until work measures 4 rows less than ** on back.
Shape neck and shoulders:
Row 1: patt
Row 2: cast off 6sts, patt to end
Row 3: patt to last 2sts, dec
Row 4: dec, patt to end
Row 5: cast off 4(5)sts, patt to last 2sts, dec
Rows 6–9: as rows 4–5 twice
Row 10: patt
Row 11: cast off 4(5)sts, patt to end

Row 12: patt
Row 13: cast off rem sts

RIGHT FRONT

Rib as for left front.
Change to 6mm needles and patt in reverse (row 3: k8, p4, k20, p4, k3(7)sts) until work measures 4 rows less than ** on back.
Shape neck and shoulders: Work rows 2–13 as for left front.

SLEEVES

Using 5mm needles and yarn DOUBLE (ie 2 ends together) cast on 35sts and work 6cm in k1 p1 rib.
Increase row: rib 1 *inc rib 3* 8 times inc rib 1 *44sts*
Change to 6mm needles and patt (row 3: k20 p4 k20) inc each end of next row (row 4) and every foll 3rd row to 80sts, working extra sts into patt. Cont until work measures 43(46)cm.
Shape sleevehead: cast off 6sts at beg of next 10 rows. Cast off.

BUTTON BAND

Using 5mm needles and yarn DOUBLE (ie 2 ends together), pick up 103(107)sts along left front and work 5 rows in k1 p1 rib. Cast off in rib.

BUTTONHOLE BAND

Using 5mm needles and yarn DOUBLE, and right side facing, pick up 103(107)sts along right front and work 2 rows in k1 p1 rib.
Row 3 (wrong side facing): rib 8 *dec yrn rib 10* 6 times *dec yrn rib 7(9)* twice dec yrn rib 3.
Work 2 more rows in rib. Cast off in rib.

NECKBAND

Join shoulder seams. Using 5mm needles and yarn DOUBLE, pick up 4sts across buttonhole band, 17sts from right front neck, 28sts across back neck, 17sts from left front neck and 4sts across button band. *70sts.* Work 5 rows in k1 p1 rib, making further buttonhole in row 3. Cast off in rib.

MAKING UP

Working from shoulder seam downwards, ease sleeves into position and stitch. Join side and sleeve seams. Weave in any loose ends. Sew on buttons.

CARE INSTRUCTIONS

See ball tag and page 172.

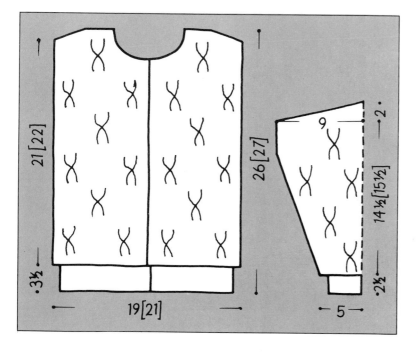

TESS

NONE OF THE INDIVIDUAL STITCH PATTERNS USED IN THIS CARDIGAN SHOULD GIVE YOU ANY PROBLEMS, AND THE SHAPE ITSELF IS VERY SIMPLE. THIS PATTERN IS DESIGNED WITH THE INTERMEDIATE KNITTER IN MIND, AND IF YOU CAN DO A CABLE, YOU WILL FIND THIS ONE SURPRISINGLY EASY.

Shown on page 26 in white Chandos.

See diagram at end of pattern

SIZE cm(in)
To fit bust:

79–84(31–33)	89–94(35–37)	96–102(38–40)
107–112(42–44)		

Actual size:

89(35)	99(39)	107(42)
116(45)		

Length from back neck:

66(26)	66(26)	66(26)
66(26)		

Sleeve seam:

43(17)	44(17½)	44(17½)
45(18)		

MATERIALS
Chandos – 50g balls:

12	13	14
14		

1 pair each of 3¼mm and 4mm needles

Cable needle. 8 buttons

TENSION
22sts and 28 rows = 10cm square on 4mm needles over stocking stitch. See page 9.

ABBREVIATIONS
See page 9.
t2r = knit into the front of the second st, then purl the first st, slipping both sts off needle tog.
t2l = purl into the back of the second st, then knit first st, slipping both sts off needle tog

tw2 = knit into the front of the second st, then knit the first st, slipping both sts off needle tog
c6 = place next 3sts on cn, leave at back of work k3 k3 from cn
mb = k1 p1 k1 p1 into next st, turn p4 turn, k4tog

BACK
Using 3¼mm needles, cast on 97(107:115:125)sts and work 19 rows in k1 p1 rib.
Row 20: rib 8(13:7:12), *inc rib 9* 8(8:10:10) times, inc rib 8(13:7:12) *106(116:126:136)sts*
Change to 4mm needles and work in patt as follows:
Row 1: † k0(5:0:5) *p5 k5* 2(2:3:3) times p3 k6 p4 t2r p1 k1 p6 k6 † p3 tw2 p3 # k6 p6 k1 p1 t2l p4 k6 p3 *k5 p5* 2(2:3:3) times k0(5:0:5)#.
Rows 2 and 4: knit the k sts and purl the p sts as they appear
Row 3: † k0(5:0:5) *p5 k5* 2(2:3:3) times p3 c6 p3 t2r p2 k1 p6 c6 † p3 tw2 p3 # c6 p6 k1 p2 t2l p3 c6 p3 *k5 p5* 2(2:3:3) times k0(5:0:5)#.
Row 5: † k0(5:0:5) *p5 k5* 2(2:3:3) times p3 k6 p3 mb p3 t2l p5 k6† p3 tw2 p3 # k6 p5 t2r p3 mb p3 k6 p3 *k5 p5* 2(2:3:3) times k0(5:0:5)#.
Row 6: # p20(25:30:35) k3 p6 k8 p1 k5 p6 # k3 p2 k3 † p6 k5 p1 k8 p6 k3 p20(25:30:35)†.
Row 7: † p0(5:0:5) *k5 p5* 1(1:2:2) times k5 p8 k6 p6 k1 p1 t2l p4 k6 † p3 tw2 p3 # k6 p4 t2r p1 k1 p6 k6 p8 k5 *p5 k5* 1(1:2:2) times p0(5:0:5)#.
Row 8: as row 2
Row 9: † p0(5:0:5) *k5 p5* 1(1:2:2) times k5 p8 c6 p6 k1 p2 t2l p3 c6 † p3 tw2 p3 # c6 p3 t2r p2 k1 p6 c6 p8 k5 *p5 k5* 1(1:2:2) times p0(5:0:5)#.

The cardigan on the left, Tess, is a simple drop-shouldered silhouette with fairly easy stitch textures. Barocco on the right, is more complex and is shown again on page 65.

Row 10: as row 2

Row 11: † p0(5:0:5) *k5 p5* 1(1:2:2) times k5 p8 k6 p5 t2r p3 mb p3 k6 † p3 tw2 p3 # k6 p3 mb p3 t2l p5 k6 p8 k5 *p5 k5* 1(1:2:2) times p0(5:0:5)#.

Row 12: # p20(25:30:35) k3 p6 k5 p1 k8 p6 # k3 p2 k3 † p6 k8 p1 k5 p6 k3 p20(25:30:35)†. These 12 rows form patt rep. Cont in patt, inc each end of next and every foll 12th row to 116(126:136:146)sts, working extra sts into edge patt. Cont without shaping until work measures 66cm. Cast off.

LEFT FRONT

Using 3¼mm needles, cast on 46(51:56:61)sts and work 19 rows in k1 p1 rib.

Row 20: rib 3(5:8:10) *inc rib 9* 4 times inc rib 2(5:7:10) *51(56:61:66)sts*

Change to 4mm needles and work 12 rows in patt as for half back, working from † to † and ending right side rows p2, and starting wrong side rows k2. Cont in patt, inc at beg of next and every foll 12th row to 56(61:66:71)sts working extra sts into edge patt. Cont without shaping until work measures 57cm, ending on a wrong side row.

Shape neck: work one row. Wrong side facing: cast off 6(8:9:10)sts at beg of next row, patt to end. Dec neck edge on next and foll alt rows to 38(43:47:51)sts. Cont until work measures 66cm. Cast off.

RIGHT FRONT

Rib and inc row as for left front.

Change to 4mm needles and patt as for half back, working from # to # and starting right side rows p2, ending wrong side rows k2, and reversing all shapings.

SLEEVES

Using 3¼mm needles, cast on 49sts and work 23(23:19:19) rows in k1 p1 rib.

Increase row: *inc rib 3* to last st inc *62sts*

Change to 4mm needles and patt as follows:

Row 1: k5 p5 k5 p3 k6 p6 k1 p1 t2l p4 k6 p3 k5 p5 k5

Row 2: knit the k sts and purl the p sts as they appear

Row 3: k5 p5 k5 p3 c6 p6 k1 p2 t2l p3 c6 p3 k5 p5 k5

Row 4: as row 2

Row 5: inc k4 p5 k5 p3 k6 p5 t2r p3 mb p3 k6 p3 k5 p5 k4 inc

Row 6: p16 k3 p6 k8 p1 k5 p6 k3 p16

Row 7: k1 p5 k5 p8 k6 p4 t2r p1 k1 p6 k6 p8 k5 p5 k1

Row 8: as row 2

Row 9: inc p5 k5 p8 c6 p3 t2r p2 k1 p6 c6 p8 k5 p5 inc

Row 10: as row 2

Row 11: k2 p5 k5 p8 k6 p3 mb p3 t2l p5 k6 p8 k5 p5 k2

Row 12: p17 k3 p6 k5 p1 k8 p6 k3 p17 These 12 rows form patt rep. Cont in patt, inc at each end of rows 1, 5 and 9 to 104(108:110:114)sts, working extra sts into basket st (rows 6 and 12, purl, etc). Cont without shaping until work measures 43(44:44:46)cm.

Shape sleevehead: cast off 6 sts at beg of next 16 rows. Work 1 row. Cast off.

BUTTON BAND

Using 3¼mm needles and right side facing, pick up 157sts along left front. Work 5 rows in k1 p1 rib. Cast off in rib.

BUTTONHOLE BAND

Using 3¼mm needles and right side facing, pick up 157sts along right front. Work 2 rows in k1 p1 rib.

Row 3: *rib 20, yrn dec* 7 times, rib 3.

Rows 4–5: rib. Cast off in rib.

NECKBAND

Join shoulder seams. Using 3¼mm needles, pick up 5sts across buttonhole band, 22(24:25:26)sts from right front neck, 40(40:42:44)sts from back neck, 22(24:25:26)sts from left front neck, and 5sts across button band 94(98:102:106)sts Work 2 rows in k1 p1 rib.

Row 3: rib to last 3 sts, yrn dec rib 1. Work 2 more rows in rib. Cast off in rib.

MAKING UP

Place centre of sleeveheads to shoulder seams. Sew sleeveheads evenly along side seams. Join side and sleeve seams. Sew on buttons. Weave in any loose ends.

CARE INSTRUCTIONS

See ball tag and page 172.

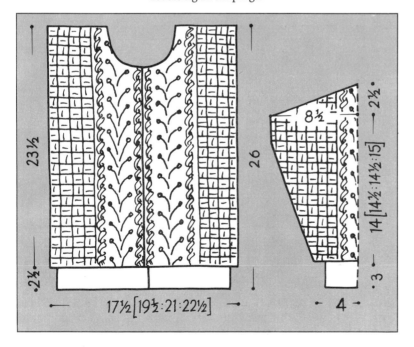

NEVIS

THIS DESIGN IS BASED ON THE IDEA OF A SORT OF EXPLODING CABLE, WHERE THE COMPONENT STITCHES SPREAD OUT TO FORM A BALLOON AND THEN TAPER BACK IN TO THE CABLE. IN THE PHOTOGRAPH IT IS WORN BACK TO FRONT, BUT THE BACK IS IN THE SAME DIAMOND PATTERN AS THE SLEEVES.

Shown on page 31 in white Chandos.
Please note that the back of the design is in the same stitch pattern as the sleeves.

See diagram at end of pattern

SIZE cm(in)
To fit bust:

81–86(32–34)	91–96(36–38)	97–107(38–42)

Actual size:

89(35)	99(39)	109(43)

Length from back neck:

61(24)	61(24)	61(24)

Sleeve seam:

43(17)	45(17½)	46(18)

MATERIALS
Chandos – 50g balls:

12	13	14

1 pair each of 3¼mm and 4mm needles

Cable needle

TENSION
22sts and 28 rows = 10cm square on 4mm needles over stocking stitch. See page 9.

ABBREVIATIONS
See page 9.
tw2f = k into front of second st, then k first st, slipping both sts off needle tog
tw2b = k into back of second st, then k first st, etc
t2r = k into front of second st, then p first st, etc
t2l = p into back of second st, then k first st, etc
c7 = place next 3sts on cn, leave at front of work, k4, then k3 from cn
cr6b = place next 3sts on cn, leave at back of work, *k1 from left-hand needle, then p1 from cn* 3 times
cr6f = place next 3sts on cn, leave at front of work, *p1 from left-hand needle, then k1 from cn* 3 times
cr3b = place next 2sts on cn, leave at back of work, k1, then p2 from cn
cr3f = place next st on cn, leave at front of work, p2, then k1 from cn
tw13 = *place next st on cn, leave at front, p1* 3 times, k3 from cn, k1, *place next st on cn, leave at back, k1* 3 times, p3 from cn.

BACK
Using 3¼mm needles, cast on 104(112:120)sts and work 7cm in k1 p1 rib.
Increase row: rib 8(4:0) *inc rib 5* to end 120(130:140)sts
Change to 4mm needles and patt as follows:
Row 1: p4 *tw2f p8* to last 6sts tw2f p4
Row 2 and alternate rows: knit the k sts and purl the p sts as they appear
Row 3: p3 *t2r t2l p6* to last 7sts t2r t2l p3
Row 5: p2 *t2r p2 t2l p4* to last 8sts t2r p2 t2l p2
Row 7: p1 *t2r p4 t2l p2* to last 9sts t2r p4 t2l p1
Row 9: *t2r p6 t2l* to end of row
Row 11: k1 *p8 tw2f* to last 9sts p8 k1
Row 13: *t2l p6 t2r* to end of row
Row 15: p1 *t2l p4 t2r p2* to last 9sts t2l p4 t2r p1
Row 17: p2 *t2l p2 t2r p4* to last 8sts t2l p2 t2r p2
Row 19: p3 *t2l t2r p6* to last 7sts t2l t2r p3
Row 20: as row 2

Following page: Nevis, on the left, has an intricate stitch design on a classic sweater shape. By contrast Beauchamp, on the right, is an original sleeveless silhouette with no more than a simple cable detail on the shoulder panels; it is also shown as a cardigan on page 75 and the pattern is on page 76.

These 20 rows form patt repeat. Cont in patt until work measures 37cm. Inc each end of next and every foll 8th row to 132(142:152)sts. Cont without shaping until work measures 60cm ending on a wrong side row.***

Shape shoulders and neck: cast off 6(7:8)sts at beg of next 6 rows.

Row 7: cast off 6(7:8)sts patt 32(33:34) cast off 20sts patt 38(40:42)

On 38(40:42)sts:

Row 8: cast off 6(7:8)sts, patt to end

Row 9: cast off 7sts, patt to end

Rows 10–11: as rows 8–9

Row 12: cast off

Rejoin yarn to rem sts at neck edge, and work rows 9–12 on other side to match.

SLEEVES

Using 3¼mm needles cast on 49sts and work 7cm in k1 p1 rib.

Increase row: rib 4 *inc rib 3* 11 times rib 1 *60sts*

Change to 4mm needles and patt as for back, inc at each end of 3rd and every foll 4th row, working extra sts into patt. Cont inc until work measures 43(45:46)cm.

Shape sleevehead: cast off 8sts at beg of next 8 rows. Cast off.

FRONT

Rib and inc row as for back.

Change to 4mm needles and patt as follows:

Row 1: p1 *k1 p4* 2(3:4) times k1 p8 k1 p12 k7 p9 *k1 p2* 8 times p7 k7 p12 k1 p8 k1 *p4 k1* 2(3:4) times p1

Row 2 and alt rows: knit the k sts and purl the p sts as they appear

Row 3: p1 *k1 p4* 2(3:4) times t2l p6 t2r p12 k7 p9 *k1 p2* 3 times t2l t2r *p2 k1* 3 times p9 k7 p12 t2l p6 t2r *p4 k1* 2(3:4) times p1

Row 5: p1 *k1 p4* 2(3:4) times p1 t2l p4 t2r p13 c7 p9 *k1 p2* twice t2l p2 tw2b p2 t2r *p2 k1* twice p9 c7 p13 t2l p4 t2r p1 *p4 k1* 2(3:4) times p1

Row 7: p1 *k1 p4* 2(3:4) times p2 t2l p2 t2r p14 k7 p9 k1 *p2 t2l* twice t2r t2l *t2r p2* twice k1 p9 k7 p14 t2l p2 t2r p2 *p4 k1* 2(3:4) times p1

Row 9: p1 *k1 p4* 2(3:4) times p3 t2l t2r p12 cr6b k1 cr6f p6 *t2l p2* twice *tw2f p2* twice t2r p2 t2r p6 cr6b k1 cr6f p12 t2l t2r p3 *p4 k1* 2(3:4) times p1

The p1 *k1 p4* rep at the beginning, and the *p4 k1* rep, p1 at the end of each row, are now the same for all rows following. Hence, the instructions are given only for the patterning between these repeats.

Row 11: p4 tw2f p11 [cr3b *p1 k1* 5 times p1 cr3f] p5 t2l p2 t2l *t2r t2l* twice t2r p2 t2r p5 rep [ ] again p11 tw2f p4

Row 13: p3 t2r t2l p8 [cr3b p1 cr3b t2r p1 k1 p1 t2l cr3f p1 cr3f] p4 t2l p2 *tw2b p2* 3 times t2r p4 rep [ ] again p8 t2r t2l p3

Row 15: p2 t2r p2 t2l p6 [*t2r p2* twice *k1 p2* 3 times t2l p2 t2l] p4 *t2l t2r* 4 times p4 rep [ ] again p6 t2r p2 t2l p2

Row 17: p1 t2r p4 t2l p4 [*t2r p2* 3 times k1 *p2 t2l* 3 times] p4 *tw2f p2* 4 times p2 rep [] again p4 t2r p4 t2l p1

Row 19: t2r p6 t2l *p3 k1* 7 times p3 *t2r t2l* 4 times *p3 k1* 7 times p3 t2r p6 t2l

Row 21: k1 p8 *k1 p3* 8 times k1 p2 *tw2b p2* 3 times *k1 p3* 8 times k1 p8 k1

Row 23: t2l p6 t2r *p3 k1* 7 times p3 *t2l t2r* 4 times *p3 k1* 7 times p3 t2l p6 t2r

Row 25: p1 t2l p4 t2r [p4 *t2l p2* 3 times k1 *p2 t2r* 3 times p4] *tw2f p2* 3 times tw2f rep [] again t2l p4 t2r p1

Row 27: p2 t2l p2 t2r p6 [*t2l p2* twice *k1 p2* twice k1 *p2 t2r* twice] p4 *t2r t2l* 4 times p4 rep [] again p6 t2l p2 t2r p2

Row 29: p3 t2l t2r p8 [cr3f p1 cr3f t2l p1 k1 p1 t2r cr3b p1 cr3b] p4 t2r p2 *tw2b p2* 3 times t2l p4 rep [] again p8 t2l t2r p3

Row 31: p4 tw2f p11 [cr3f *p1 k1* 5 times p1 cr3b] p5 t2r p2 *t2r t2l* 3 times p2 t2l p5 rep [] again p11 tw2f p4

Row 33: p3 t2r t2l p12 tw13 p6 *t2r p2* twice *tw2f p2* twice t2l p2 t2l p6 tw13 p12 t2r t2l p3

Row 35: p2 t2r p2 t2l p14 k7 p9 k1 p2 t2r p2 *t2r t2l* twice p2 t2l p2 k1 p9 k7 p14 t2r p2 t2l p2

Row 37: p1 t2r p4 t2l p13 c7 p9 *k1 p2* twice t2r p2 tw2b p2 t2l *p2 k1* twice p9 c7 p13 t2r p4 t2l p1

Row 39: t2r p6 t2l p12 k7 p9 *k1 p2* 3 times t2r t2l *p2 k1* 3 times p9 k7 p12 t2r p6 t2l

Row 40: as row 2

These 40 rows form patt rep. Cont in patt until work measures 37cm. Inc at each end of next and every foll 8th row to 132(142:152)sts working extra sts into *k1 p4* patt. Cont to 12 rows less than back at ***.

Shape neck:

Row 1: patt 55(60:65) cast off 22sts patt 55(60:65)

On 55(60:65)sts:

Row 2: patt

Row 3: cast off 3sts patt to end

Rows 4–9: as rows 2–3 3 times

Rows 10–11: dec at neck edge

Row 12: patt

Shape shoulders: work 1 row. Cast off 6(7:8)sts at beg of next 5 alt rows. Work 1 row and cast off.

Rejoin yarn to rem sts at neck edge and work rows 3 to end on other side to match.

NECKBAND

Join right shoulder seam. Using 3¼mm needles pick up 20sts along front side neck, 20sts across centre front neck, 20sts along side front neck, and 50sts across back neck *110sts*

Work 5 rows in k1 p1 rib.

Cast off loosely.

MAKING UP

Join left shoulder and neckband seam. Working from shoulder seam downwards, ease sleeves into position. Join side and sleeve seams. Weave in any loose ends.

CARE INSTRUCTIONS

See ball tag and page 172.

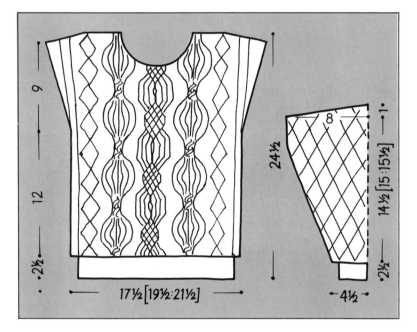

9

12

2½

24½

14½ [15:15½]

2½

17½ [19½:21½]

8

1

4½

ELOUISE

As you can see, the gradation of cables tapering into the waist is a very figure-flattering line. This shape is accentuated by the ribbing which gently hugs the waist and wrists.

Shown on page 34 in white Chandos.

See diagram at end of pattern

SIZE cm(in)
To fit bust:

81–86(32–34)	91–96(36–38)	97–102(38–40)

Actual size:

87(34)	97(38)	107(42)

Length from back neck:

58(23)	61(24)	64(25)

Sleeve seam:

43(17)	45(17½)	46(18)

MATERIALS
Chandos – 50g balls:

11	12	13

1 pair each of 3¼mm and 4mm needles

Cable needle

TENSION
22sts and 28 rows = 10cm square on 4mm needles over stocking stitch. See page 9.

ABBREVIATIONS
See page 9.
cr4b = place next st on cn, leave at back of work, k3, then p1 from cn
cr4f = place next 3sts on cn, leave at front of work, p1, then k3 from cn
c6b = place next 3sts on cn, leave at back of work, k3, then k3 from cn
c6f = place next 3sts on cn, leave at front of work, k3, then k3 from cn

BACK
Using 3¼mm needles cast on 124(138:152)sts and work as follows:
Row 1: p3 *k3 p4* 8(9:10) times k6 *p4 k3*
8(9:10) times p3
Row 2: k3 *p3 k4* 8(9:10) times p6 *k4 p3*
8(9:10) times k3
Rep rows 1–2 until work measures 10cm ending with row 2.
Change to 4mm needles and work as follows:
Rows 1–2: as above
Row 3: p3 [*k3 p4* 7(8:9) times] k3 p3 cr4b cr4f p3 rep [ ] again k3 p3
Row 4 and alt rows: knit the k sts and purl the p sts as they appear
Row 5: p3 [*k3 p4* 7(8:9) times] k3 p2 cr4b p2 cr4f p2 rep [ ] again k3 p3
Row 7: p3 [*k3 p4* 7(8:9) times] k3 p1 cr4b p4 cr4f p1 rep [ ] again k3 p3
Row 9: p3 [*k3 p4* 7(8:9) times] k3 cr4b p6 cr4f rep [ ] again k3 p3
Row 11: p3 *k3 p4* 7(8:9) times c6b p8 c6f *p4 k3* 7(8:9) times p3
Row 13: p3 *k3 p4* 7(8:9) times k6 p8 k6 *p4 k3* 7(8:9) times p3
Rows 15 and 17: as row 13
Row 19: as row 11
Row 21: p3 [*k3 p4* 6(7:8) times] k3 p3 cr4b cr4f p6 cr4b cr4f p3 rep [ ] again k3 p3
Row 23: p3 [*k3 p4* 6(7:8) times] k3 p2 cr4b p2 cr4f p4 cr4b p2 cr4f p2 rep [ ] again k3 p3
Row 25: p3 [*k3 p4* 6(7:8) times] k3 p1 # cr4b p4 cr4f # p2 rep # # again p1 rep [ ] again k3 p3
Row 27: p3 [*k3 p4* 6(7:8) times] k3 *cr4b p6 cr4f* twice rep [ ] again k3 p3
Row 29: p3 *k3 p4* 6(7:8) times *c6b p8* twice c6f *p4 k3* 6(7:8) times p3
Row 31: p3 *k3 p4* 6(7:8) times *k6 p8* twice k6 *p4 k3* 6(7:8) times p3
Rows 33 and 35: as row 31
Row 37: as row 29
Row 39: p3 [*k3 p4* 5(6:7) times] k3 p3 *cr4b cr4f p6* twice cr4b cr4f p3 rep [ ] again k3 p3
Row 41: p3 [*k3 p4* 5(6:7) times] k3 p2 *cr4b p2 cr4f p4* twice cr4b p2 cr4f p2 rep [ ] again

*Following page:
There is no separate ribbing on this design, Elouise, because the cable pattern forms its own rib as it goes towards the wrists and hips.*

k3 p3

Row 43: p3 [*k3 p4* 5(6:7) times] k3 p1 *cr4b p4 cr4f p2* twice cr4b p4 cr4f p1 rep [ ] again k3 p3

Row 45: p3 [*k3 p4* 5(6:7) times] k3 *cr4b p6 cr4f* 3 times rep [ ] again k3 p3

Row 47: p3 *k3 p4* 5(6:7) times *c6b p8* twice c6f p8 c6f *p4 k3* 5(6:7) times p3

Row 49: p3 *k3 p4* 5(6:7) times *k6 p8* 3 times k6 *p4 k3* 5(6:7) times p3

Rows 51 and 53: as row 49

Row 55: as row 47

Cont moving the centre cables in this way, until work measures 38(39:40)cm.

Shape armholes: cast off 6sts at beg of next 2 rows. Dec each end of next 4 rows. Dec each end of next and foll alt rows to 94(108:122)sts. Cont in patt until work measures 58(61:64)cm.

Shape neck: patt 32(37:42) cast off 30(34:38) patt 32(37:42).

On 32(37:42)sts:

Row 1: patt

Row 2: cast off 5sts patt to end

Rows 3–4: as rows 1–2

Row 5: cast off

Rejoin yarn to rem sts at neck edge and work rows 2–5.

FRONT

As back until work measures 49(52:54)cm.

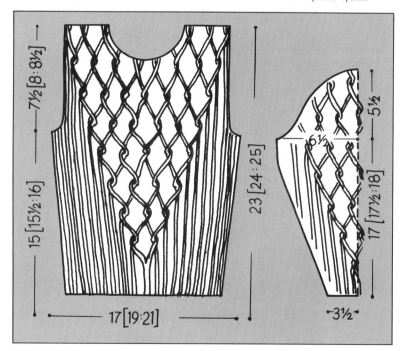

Shape neck: patt 34(40:46) cast off 26(28:30) patt 34(40:46).

On 34(40:46)sts: dec neck edge on next 6(8:8) rows. Dec neck edge on next and foll alt rows to 22(27:32)sts. Work to match back length. Cast off.

Rejoin yarn to rem sts and work to match.

SLEEVES

Using 3¼mm needles cast on 46sts and work as follows:

Row 1: p2 *k3 p3* 3 times k6 *p3 k3* 3 times p2

Row 2: k2 *p3 k3* 3 times p6 *k3 p3* 3 times k2

Rows 3–18: as rows 1–2

Row 19: as row 1

Row 20: inc k1 *p3 k1 inc k1* 3 times p6 *k1 inc k1 p3* 3 times k1 inc *54sts*

Change to 4mm needles work in patt as follows:

Row 1: p3* k3 p4* 3 times k6* p4 k3* 3 times p3

Row 2 and alt rows: knit the k sts and purl the p sts as they appear

Row 3: inc p2 *k3 p4* twice k3 p3 cr4b cr4f p3* k3 p4* twice p2 inc

These 3 rows establish the position of the patt. Cont in patt, moving the cables as on the back, AT THE SAME TIME, inc each end of every 4th row to 98(102:104)sts, working extra sts into p4, k3 rib then into cables. Cont until sleeve measures 43(45:46)cm.

Shape sleevehead: cast off 3sts at beg of next 2 rows. Cast off 2sts at beg of next 4 rows. Dec each end of next and foll alt rows to 64sts. Dec each end of next 6 rows. Cast off 6sts at beg of next 4 rows.

Cast off.

NECKBAND

Join right shoulder seam. Using 3¼mm needles pick up 22(22:24)sts from side front neck 22(24:26)sts from centre front neck 22(22:24)sts from side front neck and 46(50:52)sts from back neck *112(118:126)sts* Work 5cm in k1 p1 rib. Cast off loosely in rib.

MAKING UP

Join left shoulder seam and neckband. Fold neckband in half to inside and slipstitch into position. Join side and sleeve seams. Set in sleeves and stitch into position. Weave in any loose ends.

CARE INSTRUCTIONS

See ball tag and page 172.

MONTAGUE

I T WAS POSSIBLE TO ACHIEVE A VERY UNUSUAL EFFECT TO THE CABLE ON THIS DESIGN BY WORKING THE BACKGROUND IN STOCKING STITCH ON ONE SIDE AND REVERSE ON THE OTHER. THIS FORMS A SORT OF RIDGE WHICH HIGHLIGHTS THE CABLE. THE CHILD'S SWEATER IS SCALED DOWN, NOT JUST IN SIZE BUT ALSO IN THE PATTERN REPEAT ITSELF.

Shown on page 38 in white Chandos. Also shown in a child's version.

See diagram at end of pattern

SIZE cm(in) ADULT'S VERSION
To fit bust:

86-91(34-36)	91-96 (36-38)	102-107(40-42)

Actual size:

94(37)	102(40)	109(43)

Length from back neck:

66(26)	67(26½)	68(27)

Sleeve seam:

42(16½)	43(17)	44(17½)

MATERIALS
Chandos – 50g balls:

12	13	14

1 pair each of 3¼mm and 4mm needles

Cable needle

TENSION
22sts and 28 rows = 10cm square on 4mm needles over stocking stitch. See page 9.

ABBREVIATIONS
See page 9.
c12b = place next 6sts on cn leave at back of work k6 then k6 from cn.

BACK
Using 3¼mm needles cast on 99(105:113)sts and work 7cm in k1 p1 rib.
Increase row: rib 9(2:6) *inc rib 9* 8(10:10) times inc rib 9(2:6) *108(116:124)sts*
Change to 4mm needles and stocking st and cont until work measures 42(43:44)cm.
Inc each end of next row and every foll 8th row to 120(128:136)sts. Cont without shaping until work measures 66(67:68)cm.
Shape neck: k47(50:53) cast off 26(28:30) k47(50:53).
On 47(50:53)sts: cast off 3sts at neck edge on next 2 alt rows. Cast off. Work rem sts to match.

FRONT
Using 3¼mm needles cast on 99(107:115)sts and work 7cm in k1 p1 rib.
Increase row: rib 2(6:10) *inc rib 8* 5 times inc in next 5sts *rib 8 inc* 5 times rib 2(6:10) *114(122:130)sts*
Change to 4mm needles and patt as follows:
Row 1: p3(7:11) *k1 p11* 4 times k63(67:71)
Row 2: p63(67:71) *k11 p1* 4 times k3(7:11)
Rows 3–6: as rows 1–2 twice
Row 7: as row 1
Row 8: k51(55:59) p12 *k11 p1* 4 times k3(7:11)
Row 9: p3(7:11) *k1 p11* 4 times c12b k51(55:59)
Row 10: as row 2
Rows 11–14: as rows 1–2 twice
These 14 rows form patt rep. Cont in patt until work measures 42(43:44)cm. Inc each end of next and every foll 8th row to 126(134:142)sts working extra sts into patt. Cont until work measures 58(59:60)cm.
Shape neck: patt 50(53:56) cast off 26(28:30) patt 50(53:56).
On 50(53:56)sts: dec neck edge on next 4 rows. Dec neck edge on alt rows to 41(44:47)sts. Cont

Following page: It was an irresistible temptation to do this design in two versions, and here they are. Yours could be in a pair of bright contrasting colours.

MONTAGUE

to match back length at shoulder. Cast off.
Work rem sts to match.

SLEEVES
Using 3¼mm needles cast on 47sts and work
7cm in k1 p1 rib.
Increase row: *rib 2 inc* 15 times rib 2. *62sts*
Change to 4mm needles and patt as follows:
Row 1: p1 *k1 p11* twice k37
This sets patt as for front. Cont in patt inc each
end of every 4th row to 106sts. Cont until work
measures 42(43:44)cm.
Shape sleevehead: cast off 7sts at beg of next 10
rows. Cast off.

COLLAR
Using 4mm needles, cast on 125sts and work
7cm in k1 p1 rib. Change to 3¼mm needles and
work a further 6 rows. Cast off.

MAKING UP
Join shoulder, side and sleeve seams. Set in
sleeves. Pin cast off edge of collar to neck,
overlapping by 2cm at centre front neck. Stitch
into position. Weave in any loose ends.

CARE INSTRUCTIONS
See ball tag and page 172.

See diagram at end of pattern

SIZE cm(in) CHILD'S VERSION
To fit chest:

56–61(22–24)	66–71(26–28)	76–81(30–32)

Actual size:

64(25)	74(29)	84(33)

Length from back neck:

41(16)	46(18)	60(23½)

Sleeve seam:

31(12)	38(15)	43(17)

MATERIALS
Chandos – 50g balls:

6	7	9

1 pair each of 3¼mm and 4mm needles

Cable needle

TENSION
As adult's version.

ABBREVIATIONS
See page 9.
c8b = place next 4sts on cn, leave at back of
work, k4, then k4 from cn.

BACK
Using 3¼mm needles cast on 74(84:94)sts and
work 10 rows in k1 p1 rib.
Change to 4mm needles and stocking st and
cont until work measures 41(46:60)cm.
Shape neck: k25(29:33) cast off 24(26:28)

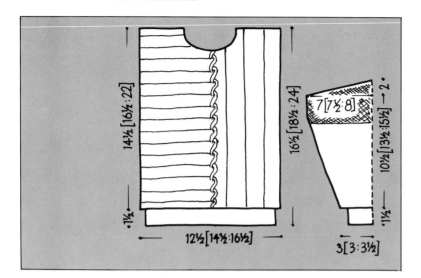

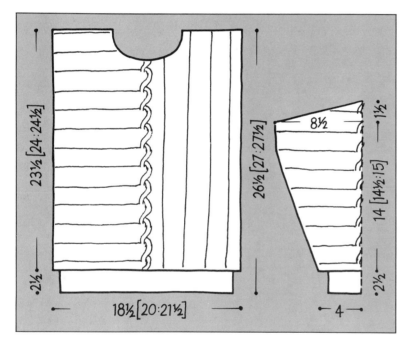

k25(29:33).
On 25(29:33)sts:
Row 1: purl
Row 2: cast off 2(2:3)sts work to end
Rows 3–4: as rows 1–2
Row 5: purl
Row 6: cast off
Rejoin yarn to rem sts and work to match.

FRONT

Using 3¼mm needles cast on 74(84:94)sts and
work 9 rows in k1 p1 rib.
Increase row: rib 35(40:45) inc in next 4sts rib
35(40:45) *78(88:98)sts*
Change to 4mm needles and patt as follows:
Row 1: p5(0:5) *k1 p9* 3(4:4) times
k43(48:53)
Row 2: p43(48:53) *k9 p1* 3(4:4) times
k5(0:5)
Rows 3–4: as rows 1–2
Row 5: p5(0:5) *k1 p9* 3(4:4) times c8b
k35(40:45)
Row 6: k35(40:45) p8 *k9 p1* 3(4:4) times
k5(0:5)
Rows 7–8: as rows 1–2
These 8 rows form patt rep. Cont in patt until
work measures 36(41:53)cm.
Shape neck: patt 33(37:40) cast off 12(14:18)
patt 33(37:40).
On 33(37:40)sts:
Row 1: patt
Row 2: cast off 2(3:4)sts patt to end
Rows 3–6: patt dec at neck edge every row
Cont dec at neck edge on next and foll alt rows
until 21(25:27)sts rem. Cont to match back
length at shoulder. Cast off.
Rejoin yarn to rem sts and work to match.

SLEEVES

Using 3¼mm needles cast on 36(38:44)sts and
work 9 rows in k1 p1 rib.
Increase row: rib 0(2:0) *inc rib 3* to end
45(47:55)sts
Change to 4mm needles and cont in stocking st
inc each end of every 4th row to 71(81:91)sts.
Cont until work measures 25(33:38)cm. Change
to moss st and cont until work measures
31(38:43)cm.
Shape sleevehead: cast off 4(4:5)sts at beg of
next 14 rows. Cast off.

COLLAR

Using 4mm needles cast on 111(115:121)sts and
work 5(6:7)cm in k1 p1 rib. Change to 3¼mm
needles and work a further 6 rows.
Cast off in rib.

MAKING UP

Join shoulder seams. Working from shoulder
seam downwards ease sleeves into position and
stitch. Join side and sleeve seams. Collar as for
adult's version. Weave in any loose ends.

CARE INSTRUCTIONS

See ball tag and page 172.

SOPHIE

ERE IS THE FIRST, AND EASIEST, OF SEVERAL 'ENTRELAC' SWEATERS IN THE BOOK. THE TONE-ON-TONE SQUARES ARE IN PLAIN STOCKING STITCH, AND THE TECHNIQUE SIMPLY INVOLVES PICKING UP STITCHES ALONG THE SIDE OF THE LAST SQUARE YOU HAVE KNITTED; SIMPLE BUT EFFECTIVE!

Shown on page 42 in white Chandos and ivory Dragonfly.

See diagram at end of pattern

SIZE cm(in)
One size only to fit bust:

	81–107(32–42)
Actual size:	
	112(44)
Length from back neck:	
	69(27)
Sleeve seam:	
	43(17)

MATERIALS
Chandos and Dragonfly – 50g balls:

A Dragon (ivory):	
	6
B Chandos (white):	
	10

1 pair each of 3¼mm and 4mm needles. Cable needle.

TENSION
22sts and 28 rows = 10cm square on 4mm needles over stocking stitch. See page 9.

SPECIAL NOTE
The success of this garment depends upon careful knitting. The following may help with this. Each edge st must be worked – not slipped at beg of row and knitted on return. Picking up along edges of squares must be even.

ABBREVIATIONS
See page 9.
k2togb/p2togb = knit/purl next 2sts together through back of sts
c6f = place next 3sts on cn leave at front of work k3 k3 from cn;
c6b = place next 3sts on cn leave at back k3 k3 from cn

FRONT
Using 3¼mm needles and B cast on 97sts and work 7cm in k1 p1 rib.
Next row: change to 4mm needles and p47 p2tog p48 *96sts*
Start entrelac knitting as follows:
Section 1
Base Triangles (using B)
Row 1: k1 s1 turn
Row 2: p2 turn
Row 3: k3 s1 turn
Row 4: p4 turn
Row 5: k5 turn
Row 6: p5 turn
Row 7: k6 s1 turn
Row 8: p7 turn
Row 9: k8 turn
Row 10: p8 turn
Row 11: k9 s1 turn
Row 12: p10 turn
Row 13: k11 turn
Row 14: p11 turn
Row 15: k12 s1 turn
Row 16: p13 turn
Row 17: k14 turn
Row 18: p14 turn
Row 19: k15 s1 turn
Row 20: p16 turn
Row 21: k17 turn
Row 22: p17 turn

Following page: The entrelac technique, used in Sophie, is much easier than it first appears, and is highlighted by the contrasting yarn textures.

Row 23: k18 s1 turn
Row 24: p19 turn
Row 25: k20 turn
Row 26: p20 turn
Row 27: k21 s1 turn
Row 28: p22 turn
Row 29: k23 turn
Row 30: p23 turn
Row 31: k25 s1 turn
Repeat rows 2–31 twice more then 2–30 again
Next row: k24 turn
Section 2
Side Triangle 2a (wrong side facing and using A)
Row 1: p1 s1 turn
Row 2: k2 turn
Row 3: inc p2tog s1 turn
Row 4: k2tog k1 inc turn
Row 5: inc p2 p2tog turn
Row 6: k5 turn
Row 7: inc p3 p2tog s1 turn
Row 8: k2tog k4 inc turn
Row 9: inc p5 p2tog turn
Row 10: k8 turn
Row 11: inc p6 p2tog s1 turn
Row 12: k2tog k7 inc turn
Row 13: inc p8 p2tog turn
Row 14: k11 turn
Row 15: inc p9 p2tog s1 turn
Row 16: k2tog k10 inc turn
Row 17: inc p11 p2tog turn
Row 18: k14 turn
Row 19: inc p12 p2tog s1 turn
Row 20: k2tog k13 inc turn
Row 21: inc p14 p2tog turn
Row 22: k17 turn
Row 23: inc p15 p2tog s1 turn
Row 24: k2tog k16 inc turn
Row 25: inc p17 p2tog turn
Row 26: k20 turn
Row 27: inc p18 p2tog s1 turn
Row 28: k2tog k19 inc turn
Row 29: inc p20 p2tog turn
Row 30: k23 turn
Row 31: p24 pick up 24sts along base triangle s1 from next base triangle turn
Diamond 2b (using A)
Row 1: k2tog k23 turn
Row 2: p23 p2tog s1 turn
Row 3: k2tog k23 turn
Row 4: p23 p2tog turn
Row 5: k24 turn
Rows 6–29: as 2–5 6 times
Rows 30–31: as rows 2–3
Row 32: p24 pick up 24 along base triangle s1 from next base triangle turn #
Rep # to # twice more omitting the s1 on the final repeat.
Edge Triangle 2c (using A)
Row 1: k24 turn
Row 2: p22 p2tog turn
Row 3: k2tog k21 turn
Row 4: p20 p2tog turn
Row 5: k21 turn
Row 6: p19 p2tog turn
Row 7: k2tog k18 turn

Row 8: p17 p2tog turn
Row 9: k18 turn
Row 10: p16 p2tog turn
Row 11: k2tog k15 turn
Row 12: p14 p2tog turn
Row 13: k15 turn
Row 14: p13 p2tog turn
Row 15: k2tog k12 turn
Row 16: p11 p2tog turn
Row 17: k12 turn
Row 18: p10 p2tog turn
Row 19: k2tog k9 turn
Row 20: p8 p2tog turn
Row 21: k9 turn
Row 22: p7 p2tog turn
Row 23: k2tog k6 turn
Row 24: p5 p2tog turn
Row 25: k6 turn
Row 26: p4 p2tog turn
Row 27: k2tog k3 turn
Row 28: p2 p2tog turn
Row 29: k2tog k1 turn
Row 30: p2tog turn
Section 3
Diamonds (right side facing and using B)
k1 from side triangle pick up 23sts along side triangle s1 from diamond turn. †
Row 1: p2togb p23 turn
Row 2: k23 k2togb s1 turn
Row 3: p2togb p23 turn
Row 4: k23 k2togb turn
Row 5: p24 turn
Rows 6–29: as rows 2–5 6 times
Rows 30–31: as rows 2–3
Row 32: k24 pick up 24sts along diamond s1 from next diamond turn †
Rep † to † 3 more times ending last repeat k24
Work section 2 then section 3 twice more.
Section 4
Top triangles
Complete as for 2a up to row 16.
Follow patt as set but noting casting off instructions below. These are to be done at the beginning of the row specified.
Row 17: cast off 2
Row 19: cast off 1
Row 21: cast off 2
Row 23: cast off 1
Row 25: cast off 2
Row 27: cast off 1
Row 29: cast off 2
Top Triangle 4b complete as for 2b but note following casting off instructions.
Row 2: cast off 2
Row 4: cast off 1
Row 6: cast off 2
Row 8: cast off 1
Continue casting off as set.
Rep 4b twice.
Top Triangle 4c complete as for 2c but note following casting off instructions.
Row 2: cast off 2
Row 4: cast off 1
Row 6: cast off 2
Row 8: cast off 1
Continue casting off as set.

YOKE

Using 4mm needles and B pick up
14 + 29 + 29 + 28 + 14 *114sts* across top of
triangles. Work in patt as folls:
Every row: *k2 p2* rep * to * to last 2sts k2.
Working in patt cont without shaping until
work measures 61cm.
Shape neck: patt 48 cast off 18sts patt 48. On
48sts dec at neck edge on next 8 rows then on alt
rows to 34sts. Cont without shaping until work
measures 69cm ending at armhole edge.
Shape shoulders: cast off 5sts beg next and foll
alt row and 8sts beg foll 2 alt rows. Work 1 row.
Cast off.
Rejoin yarn at neck edge to rem sts and work to
match.

BACK

As front and pick up 114sts across top triangles
cont without shaping until work measures 69cm
ending on a wrong side row.
Shape shoulders and neck:
Rows 1–4: cast off 5sts patt to end
Row 5: cast off 8sts patt 26 cast off 26sts patt
34
On 34sts
Row 6: cast off 8sts patt to end
Row 7: cast off 5sts
Rows 8–9: as rows 6–7
Row 10: cast off
Rejoin yarn to rem sts at neck edge and work
rows 7–10 inclusive.

SLEEVES

Using 3¼mm needles and B cast on 49sts and
work 7cm in k1 p1 rib.
Increase row: rib 1 *inc rib 2* to end *65sts*
Change to 4mm needles and patt as follows:
Row 1: inc *p2 k9 p2 k12* twice p2 k9 p2 inc
Row 2 and alt rows: knit the k sts and purl the p
sts as they appear
Row 3: inc k1 *p2 c6b k3 p2 k12* twice p2 c6b
k3 p2 k1 inc
Row 5: k3 *p2 k9 p2 k12* twice p2 k9 p2 k3
Row 7: inc k2 *p2 k3 c6f p2 k12* twice p2 k3
c6f p2 k2 inc
Row 8: as row 2
These 8 rows form cable patt rep. Cont in patt

inc each end of every 3rd and 7th row to 107sts,
then on alt rows to 121sts, working extra sts in
stocking stitch. Cont without shaping until
work measures 44cm.
Shape sleevehead: cast off 8sts beg next 10 rows.
Cast off.

NECKBAND

Join right shoulder seam. Using 3¼mm needles
and B pick up 26sts from side front neck, 18sts
from centre front neck, 26sts from side front
neck, and 50sts from back neck. *120sts.* Work
5cm in k1 p1 rib. Cast off loosely.

MAKING UP

Join left shoulder seam and neckband. Fold
neckband in half to inside and slipstitch into
position. Starting from shoulder, set sleeves into
body. Join side and sleeve seams. Weave in any
loose ends.

CARE INSTRUCTIONS

See ball bands and page 172

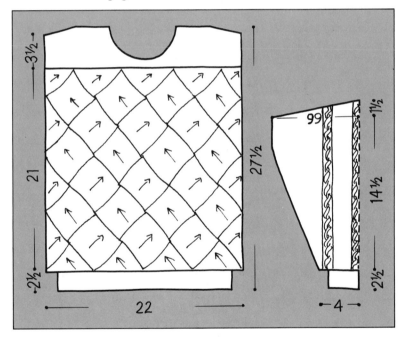

ROSE

THE GENEROUS PLEATED SLEEVE, SMALL CROSSOVER COLLAR AND SLIGHTLY TAPERED BODY ARE REALLY A MAGIC FORMULA FOR A CLASSICALLY FEMININE SILHOUETTE. ADD THE INTRICATE INTERWEAVING STEMS AND FLOWER BUDS, AND WE REACH A POINT WHERE 'PRISSY' BECOMES SEXY.

Shown on opposite page in white Chandos.

See diagram at end of pattern

SIZE cm(in)
To fit bust:

81–86(32–34)	89–94(35–37)	97–102(38–40)
Actual size:		
91(36)	99(39)	107(42)
Length from back neck:		
59(23)	59(23)	59(23)
Sleeve seam:		
42(16½)	43(17)	44(17½)

MATERIALS
Chandos – 50g balls:

11	12	13

1 pair each of 3¼mm and 4mm needles

Cable needle

TENSION
22sts and 28 rows = 10cm square on 4mm needles over stocking stitch. See page 9.

ABBREVIATIONS
See page 9.
patt 9 = place next 3sts on cn, leave at back, s1 undoing extra loop, k1 from cn, psso, k2 from cn, s1 undoing loop, place next st on cn undoing extra loop, leave at front, k2, s1 from cn, k1, psso
c2b = place next st on cn, leave at back, k1, k1 from cn
c2f = place next st on cn, leave at front, k1, k1 from cn
mb = k1 yrn k1 into next st, turn p3, turn k3, pass 2nd and 3rd st over 1st
t4ba = place next 2sts on cn, leave at back, p2, k2 from cn
t4fa = place next 2sts on cn, leave at front, k2, p2 from cn
t3f = place next st on cn, leave at front, p2, k1 from cn
t3b = place next 2sts on cn, leave at back, k1, p2 from cn
t2b = place next st on cn, leave at back, k1, p1 from cn
t2f = place next st on cn, leave at front, p1, k1 from cn
t4by = place next 2sts on cn, leave at back, k2, p2 from cn
t4fy = place next 2sts on cn, leave at front, p2, k2 from cn
tw3 = place next st on cn, leave at front, p1 k1, k1 from cn
c3f = place next st on cn, leave at front, k2, k1 from cn
c3b = place next 2sts on cn, leave at back, k1, k2 from cn
x3ba = place next 2sts on cn, leave at back, k1, k1 p1 from cn
x3fa = place next st on cn, leave at front, p1 k1, k1 from cn
x3by = place next 2sts on cn, leave at back, k1, p1 k1 from cn
x3fy = place next st on cn, leave at front, k1 p1, k1 from cn
NB Extra sts are not included in shaping instructions.

BACK
Using 3¼mm needles cast on 95(103:111)sts and work 20 rows in k1 p1 rib.
Change to 4mm needles and patt as follows:
Rows 1–4 stocking st

Row 5: k7(11:15) *k1-yrn-k1 into next st k19* 4 times k1-yrn-k1 into next st k7(11:15)
Row 6: p7(11:15) *p3 winding yarn round needle twice for each st p19* 4 times p3 winding yarn round needle twice for each st p7(11:15)
Row 7: k4(8:12) *patt 9 k13* 4 times patt 9 k4(8:12)
Row 8: p7(11:15) *s1 p19* 4 times s1 p7(11:15)
Rows 9–16: stocking st
Inc each end row 9 on 2nd and 3rd sizes only
Inc each end row 15 on all three sizes
Row 17: k18(3:7) *k1-yrn-k1 into next st k19* 3(5:5) times k1-yrn-k1 into next st k18(3:7)
Row 18: p18(3:7) *p3 winding yarn round needle twice for each st p19* 3(5:5) times p3 winding yarn round needle twice for each st p18(3:7)
Row 19: k15(0:4) *patt 9 k13* 3(5:5) times patt 9 k15(0:4)
Row 20: p18(3:7) *s1 p19* 3(5:5) times s1 p18(3:7)
Rows 21–24: stocking st
These 24 rows form patt rep, cont in patt inc each end of next and every foll 12th row to 105(113:121)sts.
Cont until work measures 35cm.
Shape armhole: cast off 4(6:7)sts beg next 2 rows. Dec each end alt rows to 85(87:91)sts. Cont to 59cm. Cast off.

SLEEVES

Using 3¼mm needles cast on 49sts and work 23(23:19) rows in k1 p1 rib.
Increase row: *inc rib 3* to last st inc *62sts*
Change to 4mm needles and patt as follows:
Row 1: k18 p12 c2b p2 mb p9 k18
Row 2: p18 k12 p2 k12 p18
Row 3: k16 t4ba p9 c2b t3f p8 t4fa k16
Row 4: p16 k2 p2 k8 p1 k2 p2 k9 p2 k2 p16
Row 5: inc * k7 k1-yrn-k1 into next st k7* p2 k2 p8 t2b c2f p1 t3f p6 k2 p2 rep * to * again inc
Row 6: p9 *p3 wrapping yarn twice round needle for each st* p7 k2 p2 k6 p1 k3 p2 k1 p1 k8 p2 k2 p7 rep * to * again p9
Row 7: k6 patt 9 k4 p2 k2 p6 t3b c2b t2f p2 t3f p4 k2 p2 k4 patt 9 k6
Row 8: p9 s1 p7 k2 p2 *k4 p1* twice k1 p2 k2 p1 k6 p2 k2 p7 s1 p9
Row 9: inc k16 t4by p4 t3b p1 t2b k1 p1 t3f p2 mb p4 t4fy k16 inc
Row 10: p20 k9 p1 k3 p1 k1 p1 k3 p1 k6 p20
Row 11: k20 p6 mb p2 t2b p1 k1 p3 mb p9 k20
Row 12: p20 k13 p1 k2 p1 k9 p20
Row 13: inc k19 p9 mb p1 c2b p13 k19 inc
Row 14: p21 k13 p2 k11 p21
Row 15: k19 t4ba p8 t2b x3fa p9 t4fa k19
Row 16: p19 k2 p2 k9 p2 k2 p1 k8 p2 k2 p19
Row 17: inc k18 p2 k2 p6 t3b p1 c2b t2f p8 k2 p2 k18 inc
Row 18: p20 k2 p2 k8 p1 k1 p2 k3 p1 k6 p2 k2 p20
Row 19: k20 p2 k2 p4 t3b p2 t2b c2f t3f p6 k2 p2 k20
Row 20: p20 k2 p2 k6 p1 k2 p2 k1 p1 k4 p1 k4 p2 k2 p20
Row 21: inc k19 t4by p4 mb p2 t3b p1 k1 t2f p1 t3f p4 t4fy k19 inc
Row 22: p23 k6 p1 k3 p1 k1 p1 k3 p1 k9 p23
Row 23: k23 p9 mb p3 k1 p1 t2f p2 mb p6 k23
Row 24: p23 k9 p1 k2 p1 k13 p23
These 24 rows form patt rep. Cont in patt, inc each end next and every foll 4th row to 104(108:110)sts working extra sts into 'flower patt' as on back. Cont until work measures 42(43:44)cm
Shape sleevehead: cast off 4(6:7)sts beg next 2 rows. Dec each end next 8 alt rows. Work 3 rows. Dec each end next and every foll 4th row 7 times. Work 3 rows. Dec each end next and every foll alt row 4 times (ie 8 decs then 5 decs). Cast off.

FRONT

Using 3¼mm needles cast on 95(103:111)sts and work 19 rows k1 p1 rib.
Increase row: rib 7(11:15) * inc rib 9* 8 times inc rib 7(11:15) *104(112:120)sts*
Change to 4mm needles and patt:
Row 1: k14(18:22) * p6 k1-yrn-k1 into next st p6* t2b p1 t3f t4by p14 c2b p2 mb p11 t4fy t3b p1 t2f rep * to * again k14(18:22)
Row 2: p14(18:22) k6 p3 k6 p1 k4 p3 k16 p2 k16 p3 k4 p1 k6 p3 k6 p14(18:22)
Row 3: k12(16:20) t4ba p4 *k1 yrn* twice k1 p5 t2b p4 c3f p15 c2b t3f p14 c3b p4 t2f p5 *k1 yrn* twice k1 p4 t4fa k12(16:20)
Row 4: p12(16:20) k2 p2 k4 p5 k5 p1 k5 p3 k14 p1 k2 p2 k15 p3 k5 p1 k5 p5 k4 p2 k2 p12(16:20)
Row 5: k4(8:12) k1-yrn-k1 into next st k7 p2 k2 p4 s1 k1 psso k1 k2tog p5 mb p3 t4by t3f p12 t2b c2f p1 t3f p10 t3b t4fy p3 mb p5 s1 k1 psso k1 k2tog p4 k2 p2 k7 k1-yrn-k1 into next st k4(8:12)
Row 6: p4(8:12) *p3 wrapping yarn twice round needle for each st* p7 k2 p2 k4 p3 k9 p2 k4 p1 k10 p1 k3 p2 k1 p1 k12 p1 k4 p2 k9 p3 k4 p2 k2 p7 rep * to * again p4(8:12)
Row 7: k1(5:9) patt 9 k4 p2 k2 p4 s1 k2tog psso p7 x3ba k1 p4 t3f p8 t3b c2b t2f p2 t3f p6 t3b p4 k1 x3fa p7 s1 k2tog psso p4 k2 p2 k4 patt 9 k1(5:9)
Row 8: p4(8:12) s1 p7 k2 p2 k12 p2 k1 p1 *k6 p1* twice k4 p1 k1 p2 k2 p1 k8 p1 k6 p1 k1 p2 k12 p2 k2 p7 s1 p4(8:12)
Row 9: k12(16:20) t4by p10 t4by p1 t2f p5 t3f p4 t3b p1 t2b k1 p1 t3f p2 mb p4 t3b p5 t2b p1 t4fy p10 t4fy k12(16:20)
Row 10: p14(18:22) k12 p2 k4 p1 *k7 p1* twice k3 p1 k1 p1 k3 p1 k4 p1 k7 p1 k4 p2 k12 p14(18:22)
Row 11: k14(18:22) p10 t4by p2 x3by p7 k1 p4 mb p2 t2b p1 k1 p3 mb p7 k1 p7 x3fy p2 t4fy p10 k14(18:22)
Row 12: p14(18:22) k10 p2 k4 p1 k1 p1 k7 p1 k11 p1 k2 p1 *k7 p1* twice k1 p1 k4 p2 k10 p14(18:22)
Row 13: inc k13(17:21) p10 t4fy t3b p1 t2f p6 *k1-yrn-k1 into next st* p7 mb p1 c2b p11 rep

* to * again p6 t2b p1 t3f t4by p10 k13(17:21) inc

Row 14: p15(19:23) k12 p3 k4 p1 k6 p3 k11 p2 k9 p3 k6 p1 k4 p3 k12 p15(19:23)

Row 15: k13(17:21) t4ba p10 c3b p4 t2f p5 *k1 yrn* twice k1 p8 t2b x3fa p9 *k1 yrn* twice k1 p5 t2b p4 c3f p10 t4fa k13(17:21)

Row 16: p13(17:21) k2 p2 k10 p3 k5 p1 k5 p5 k9 p2 k2 p1 k8 p5 k5 p1 k5 p3 k10 p2 k2 p13(17:21)

Row 17: k13(17:21) p2 k2 p8 t3b t4fy p3 mb p5 *s1 k1 psso k1 k2tog* p6 t3b p1 c2b t2f p8 rep* to * again p5 mb p3 t4by t3f p8 k2 p2 k13(17:21)

Row 18: p13(17:21) k2 p2 k8 p1 k4 p2 k9 p3 k8 p1 k1 p2 k3 p1 k6 p3 k9 p2 k4 p1 k8 p2 k2 p13(17:21)

Row 19: k13(17:21) p2 k2 p6 t3b p4 k1 x3fa p7 s1 k2tog psso p4 t3b p2 t2b c2f t3f p6 s1 k2tog psso p7 x3ba k1 p4 t3f p6 k2 p2 k13(17:21)

Row 20: p13(17:21) k2 p2 * k6 p1* twice k1 p2 k14 p1 k2 p2 k1 p1 k4 p1 k12 p2 k1 *p1 k6* twice p2 k2 p13(17:21)

Row 21: k13(17:21) t4by p4 t3b p5 t2b p1 t4fy p10 mb p2 t3b p1 k1 t2f p1 t3f p10 t4by p1 t2f p5 t3f p4 t4fy k13(17:21)

Row 22: p15(19:23) k6 p1 k7 p1 k4 p2 k10 p1 k3 p1 k1 p1 k3 p1 k13 p2 k4 p1 k7 p1 k6 p15(19:23)

Row 23: k15(19:23) p6 k1 p7 x3fy p2 t4fy p11 mb p3 k1 p1 t2f p2 mb p8 t4by p2 x3by p7 k1 p6 k15(19:23)

Row 24: p15(19:23) k6 p1 k7 p1 k1 p1 k4 p2 k11 p1 k2 p1 k15 p2 k4 p1 k1 p1 k7 p1 k6 p15(19:23)

These 24 rows form patt rep. Cont in patt inc each end of next and every foll 12th row 3 more times (5 incs in all) *114(122:130)sts*
Cont until work measures 35cm.
Shape armhole: cast off 4(6:7)sts beg next 2 rows. Dec each end of next and every foll 5(6:7) alt rows to 94(96:100)sts. Cont without shaping until work measures 49cm.
Shape neck: patt 37(38:40)sts cast off 20sts patt

37(38:40)sts. Dec at neck edge on next and foll alt rows to 27(28:29)sts. Work a further 11 rows without shaping. Cast off.

COLLAR
Using 4mm needles cast on 127sts and work 5cm in k1 p1 rib. Change to 3¼mm needles and work a further 2cm in k1 p1 rib. Cast off.

MAKING UP
Join shoulder, side and sleeve seams. Set in sleeve, making box pleat of excess material at shoulder level (see page 174).
Pin cast off edge of collar to wrong side of sweater, overlap collar by 1cm at front neck; stitch into position. Weave in any loose ends.

CARE INSTRUCTIONS
See ball tag and page 172.

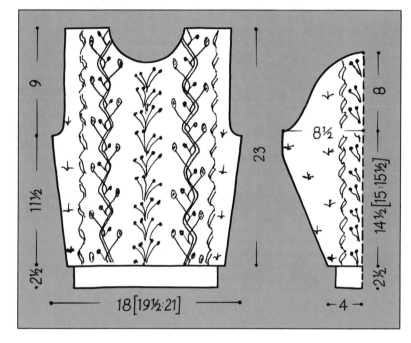

COTESBACH

THE ONLY DISADVANTAGE OF THIS EXTRA LONG CARDIGAN (OR SHORT COAT?) IS THE EXTRA TIME NEEDED BEFORE YOU CAST OFF! BUT I HOPE THE UNUSUAL CABLE PATTERN WILL KEEP YOU INTERESTED, AND THE GENEROUS LENGTH WILL BE STYLISH ON ANY FIGURE.

Shown on opposite page in white Chandos.

See diagram at end of pattern

SIZE cm(in)
To fit bust:

86–91(34–36)	91–102(36–40)
Actual size:	
97(38)	107(42)
Length from back neck:	
89(35)	91(36)
Sleeve seam:	
43(17)	44(17½)

MATERIALS
Chandos – 50g balls:

19	20
1 pair each of 3¼mm and 4mm needles	
3¾mm circular needle. Cable needle	
7 buttons	

TENSION
22sts and 28 rows = 10cm square on 4mm needles over stocking stitch. See page 9.

ABBREVIATIONS
See page 9.
tw4f = place next 2sts on cn, leave at front, p2, k2 from cn
tw4b = place next 2sts on cn, leave at back, k2, p2 from cn
c4f = place next 2sts on cn, leave at front, k2, k2 from cn
c4b = place next 2sts on cn, leave at back, k2, k2 from cn
tw6f = place next 4sts on cn, leave at front, p2, k4 from cn
tw6b = place next 2sts on cn, leave at back, k4, p2 from cn

BACK
Using 3¼mm needles cast on 119(131)sts and work in k1 p1 rib for 7 rows.
Row 8: rib 17(21) *inc, rib 2* 11 times, inc, rib 19(23) *inc, rib 2* 12 times rib to end *143(155)sts*
Change to 4mm needles and patt as follows:
Row 1: k15(19) *p1 k1 p1 tw4f p2 k4 p1 k1 p5 k4 p4 k4 p5 k1 p1 k4 p2 tw4b p1 k1 p1* k9(13) rep * to * k15(19)
NB The patt rep between * * on this and following rows will be worked again as referred to on sleeves and fronts.
Row 2 and alt rows: knit the k sts and purl the p sts as they present
Row 3: k15(19) *p1 k1 p3 c4f tw4f p1 k1 p5 c4f p4 c4b p5 k1 p1 tw4b c4b p3 k1 p1* k9(13) rep * to * k15(19)
Row 5: k15(19) *p1 k1 p1 tw4b tw4f k2 p1 k1 p5 k4 p4 k4 p5 k1 p1 k2 tw4b tw4f p1 k1 p1* k9(13) rep * to * k15(19)
Row 7: k15(19) *p1 k1 p1 k2 p4 c4f p1 k1 p5 c4f p4 c4b p5 k1 p1 c4b p4 k2 p1 k1 p1* k9(13) rep * to * k15(19)
Row 8: as row 2
These 8 rows form patt rep. Cont in patt until work measures 59(60)cm.
Shape armhole: cast off 5(6)sts beg next 2 rows. Dec 1st each end next 5(6) rows. Dec 1st each end next 7 alt rows *109(117)sts*
Cont without shaping until work measures 89(91)cm. Cast off.

SLEEVES
Using 3¼mm needles cast on 59sts and work 7 rows in rib as for back.
Row 8: *rib 5 inc* 9 times rib 5 *68sts*

*Opposite:
Coat, jacket or
cardigan? I'm not
sure but I know I like
the length on this
design, Cotesbach.*

COTESBACH

Change to 4mm needles and patt as for back between * *
Row 1: k8, work * to * from back, k8
Inc each end of every 4th row to 120(124)sts, working extra sts in stocking st.
Cont without shaping until work measures 43(45)cm
Shape sleevehead: and change centre of patt as follows:
Row 1: cast off 4(5)sts patt 45(46) p5 tw6f tw6b p5 patt to end
Row 2: cast off 4(5)sts knit the k sts and purl the p sts as they appear
Row 3: dec patt 43(44) p7 k8 p7 patt 43(44) dec
Row 4: dec patt to last 2sts dec
Row 5: dec patt 41(42) p7 tw4f tw4b p7 patt 41(42) dec
Row 6: as 4
Row 7: dec patt 39(40) p9 k4 p9 patt 39(40) dec
Row 8: dec each end on 2nd size only (102sts rem for both sizes)
Cont dec each end of next and every foll alt row. Instructions given for centre panel only. Please note that number of sts varies, owing to working the 'medallion'.
Row 9: p9 c4b p9
Row 10 and alt rows: knit the k sts and purl the p sts as they appear
Row 11: p9 k4 p9
Row 13: p7 c4b c4f p7
Row 15: p7 k8 p7
Row 17: p5 tw6b tw6f p5
Row 19: p5 k4 p4 k4 p5
Row 21: p3 tw6b p4 tw6f p3
Row 23: p3 k4 p3 k1 yrn, pick up loop between

sts and k it, then k1 p3 k4 p3
Row 25: p1 tw6b p3 k2 yrn k1 yrn k2 p3 tw6f p1
Row 27: p1 k4 p5 k7 p5 k4 p1
Row 29: as row 27
Row 31: p1 k4 p5 k2togb k3 k2tog p5 k4 p1
Row 33: p1 tw6f p3 k2togb k1 k2tog p3 tw6b p1
Row 35: p3 k4 p3, slip next st on cn, leave at front, p2tog, p1 from cn, p3 k4 p3
Row 37: p3 tw6f p4 tw6b p3
Row 39: p5 k4 p4 k4 p5
Row 41: p5 tw6f tw6b p5
Row 43: p7 k8 p7
Row 45: cast off 4sts, patt to centre panel, p7 tw4f tw4b p7, patt to end
Row 46: cast off 4sts, patt to end
Row 47: cast off 4sts, patt to centre panel, p9 k4 p9, patt to end
Row 48: as row 46
Row 49: cast off 4sts, patt to centre panel, p9 c4b p9, patt to end
Row 50: as row 46. Cast off.

POCKETS (2)
Using 4mm needles cast on 52sts. Work 15cm * to * from back. Leave sts on holder.

LEFT FRONT
Using 3¼mm needles cast on 59(67)sts and work 7 rows in rib as for back.
Row 8: rib 17(21) *inc, rib 2* 12 times rib 6(10) *71(79) sts*
Change to 4mm needles and patt as for back.
Row 1: k15(19) work * to * k4(8)
Cont until work measures 10(13)cm
Change centre panel patt to 'medallion' as on top of sleeve and work the 50 rows omitting shapings.
Row 1: patt 30(34) p5 tw6f tw6b p5 patt to end
Place pocket: k15(19), place next 52sts on holder, patt across 52sts of pocket, k4(8).
Cont in patt as for back until work measures 48(51)cm.
Shape neck: dec end of next and every foll 5th row at neck edge. Cont until work measures 59(60)cm.
Shape armhole: cast off 5(6)sts beg next row AT THE SAME TIME cont neck decs.
Dec armhole edge on next 5(6) rows, dec armhole edge on next 7 alt rows.
Cont dec neck edge only until 33(39)sts rem.
Cont without shaping until work measures 89(91)cm. Cast off.

RIGHT FRONT
Rib as for left front.
Increase row: rib 8(12) * inc rib 2* 12 times rib 15(19)
Change to 4mm needles and patt as for back.
Row 1: k4(8) work * to * k15(19)
Cont as for left front reversing all neck and armhole shapings.

POCKET TRIMS (2)
Pick up 52sts from holder and using 3¼mm

52

needles work 6 rows rib as for back, dec 1st at centre of 1st row of sts from holder. Cast off in rib.

BUTTON BAND
Using 3¼mm needles with right side facing and starting at first neck dec on left front, pick up evenly and knit 125sts to bottom of welt. Work 8 rows in k1 p1 rib. Cast off in rib.

BUTTONHOLE BAND
With right side facing and starting at bottom of welt on right front, pick up evenly and knit as for button band, ending at first neck dec. Rib 3 rows.
Row 4: rib 3 * yf k2tog rib 18* 6 times yf k2tog Rib 4 rows. Cast off in rib.

COLLAR
Join shoulder seams. Using 3¾mm circular needle, with right side facing and starting at first neck dec on right front, pick up evenly and knit 114sts up to shoulder, 57sts across back neck, and 114sts down left front to first neck dec *285sts*
Next row: rib 163, turn, s1 rib 40, turn, s1, rib 42, turn, s1 rib 44
Cont thus, work 2 more sts on each row until turn, s1 rib 56 has been worked.
Cont as before but work 4 more sts on each row, until turn s1 rib 96 has been worked.
Cont as before but work 6 more sts on each row until turn s1 rib 156 has been worked.
Cont as before but work 8 more sts on each row until turn s1 rib 252 has been worked; turn s1 rib to end. Rib 7 more rows. Cast off loosely in rib.

MAKING UP
Join side and sleeve seams. Ease sleeves into sleeveheads and stitch into position. Slipstitch pockets into place. Join button(hole) bands to collar. Weave in any loose ends. Sew on buttons.

CARE INSTRUCTIONS
See ball tag and page 172.

FINE RIB SKIRT

Shown on pages 15, 19 and 47 in white Chandos.

SIZE cm(in)
To fit hip:

	89–94(35–37)
Actual size:	
	96(38)
Length:	
	51(20)

MATERIALS
Chandos – 50g balls:

6
1 pair 4mm needles. Elastic for waistband

TENSION
22sts and 28 rows = 10cm square on 4mm needles over stocking stitch. See page 9.

ABBREVIATIONS
See page 9.
SPECIAL NOTE
The skirt is worked in one piece with a side seam; you could alternatively use a 4mm circular needle and work it in rounds so that it is seamless.

BACK AND FRONT (one piece)
Using 4mm needles cast on 232sts.
Row 1: *k1 p1* to end
Cont as set working in k1 p1 rib until work measures 51cm. Cast off in rib.

MAKING UP
Join side seam. Thread elastic through top of skirt. Weave in any loose ends.

CARE INSTRUCTIONS
See ball tag and page 172.

2

There was a very clear objective in my mind when planning the desgins for this chapter: to create a look which was unashamedly feminine in every respect. I have therefore used the softest and prettiest colours, the designs are elegant and yet informal, and the emphasis is on an unstructured and classical silhouette which is not going to go out of fashion tomorrow. Some of the designs are in plain stocking stitch, with just an original shape to draw them apart from the crowd; some of them incorporate stitch patterns of varying complexity to add that unmistakably hand-knitted feeling. In either case you should find one here which will prove a valuable addition to your wardrobe. I am frequently being asked for cardigans – which are a good bet if either you or the weather are feeling a bit indecisive – thus you will find that half the designs in this chapter are with buttons. This girl is wearing Barocco, featured on page 65.

CAVENDISH

T HE IDEA, AS YOU CAN SEE, IS A GRADUATION OF CABLES FROM THE BOLD 'PLAIT' WHICH IS REDUCED BIT BY BIT UNTIL ONLY A STITCH IS LEFT. THE RESULT IS A STYLISH CARDIGAN WHICH IS BOTH SIMPLE AND INTERESTING TO KNIT.

Shown on page 58 in eau-de-nil Chandos. For the long version shown on page 10 you would work approx. 150cm to the armhole and finish off as for the standard pattern.

See diagram at end of pattern

SIZE cm(in)
To fit bust:

81–86(32–34)	86–91(34–36)	97–102(38–40)

Actual size:

97(38)	104(41)	112(44)

Length from back neck:

76(30)	76(30)	76(30)

Sleeve seam:

44(17½)	44(17½)	47(18½)

MATERIALS
Chandos – 50g balls:

14	15	16

1 pair each of 3¼mm and 4mm needles

3¾mm circular needle for collar

Cable needle. Stitch holders. 7 buttons

TENSION
22sts and 28 rows = 10cm square on 4mm needles over stocking stitch. See page 9.

ABBREVIATIONS
See page 9.
t2f = knit into front of second st then first st, take both sts off together
t2b = knit into back of second st then first st, take both sts off together
c4f = place next 2sts on cn, leave at front of work, k2 then k2 sts from cn
c4b = place next 2 sts on cn, leave at back of work, k2 then k2 sts from cn
c6f = place next 3 sts on cn, leave at front of work, k3 then k3 sts from cn
c6b = place next 3sts on cn, leave at back of work, k3 then k3 sts from cn

BACK
Using 3¼mm needles cast on 101(109:117)sts and work 6cm in k1 p1 rib.
Increase row: rib 1(5:9) *rib 2 inc* 32 times, rib 4(8:12) *133(141:149)sts* ·
Change to 4mm needles and work as follows:
Row 1 and alt rows: (wrong side) *k3 p1* 2(3:4) times k3 p2 k3 p1 k3 p4 k3 p1 k3 p6 k3 p1 k3 p9 k3 p1 k3 p6 k1 p6 k3 p1 k3 p9 k3 p1 k3 p6 k3 p1 k3 p4 k3 p1 k3 p2 k3 *p1 k3* 2(3:4) times
Row 2: *p3 k1* 2(3:4) times p3 t2f p3 k1 p3 c4f p3 k1 p3 k6 p3 k1 p3 c6f k3 p3 k1 p3 k6 p1 k6 p3 k1 p3 k3 c6b p3 k1 p3 k6 p3 k1 p3 c4b p3 k1 p3 t2b p3 *k1 p3* 2(3:4) times
Row 4: *p3 k1* 2(3:4) times p3 t2f p3 k1 p3 k4 p3 k1 p3 c6f p3 k1 p3 k9 p3 k1 p3 c6f p1 c6b p3 k1 p3 k9 p3 k1 p3 c6b p3 k1 p3 k4 p3 k1 p3 t2b p3 *k1 p3* 2(3:4) times
Row 6: *p3 k1* 2(3:4) times p3 t2f p3 k1 p3 c4f p3 k1 p3 k6 p3 k1 p3 k3 c6b p3 k1 p3 k6 p1 k6 p3 k1 p3 c6f k3 p3 k1 p3 k6 p3 k1 p3 c4b p3 k1 p3 t2b p3 *k1 p3* 2(3:4) times
Row 8: *p3 k1* 2(3:4) times p3 t2f p3 k1 p3 k4 p3 k1 p3 k6 p3 k1 p3 k9 p3 k1 p3 k6 p1 k6 p3 k1 p3 k9 p3 k1 p3 k6 p3 k1 p3 k4 p3 k1 p3 t2b p3 *k1 p3* 2(3:4) times
Row 10: *p3 k1* 2(3:4) times p3 t2f p3 k1 p3 c4f p3 k1 p3 c6f p3 k1 p3 c6f k3 p3 k1 p3 c6f p1 c6b p3 k1 p3 k3 c6b p3 k1 p3 c6b p3 k1 p3 c4b p3 k1 p3 t2b p3 *k1 p3* 2(3:4 times)
Row 12: as row 8
Row 14: as row 6
Row 16: as row 4

Glossary of cable abbreviations (top right)
work, k2 then k2 sts from cn
c6f = place next 3 sts on cn, leave at front of work, k3 then k3 sts from cn
c6b = place next 3sts on cn, leave at back of work, k3 then k3 sts from cn

Following page: This design, Cavendish, is the down-to-earth version of the white coat shown on page 10.

CAVENDISH

Row 18: as row 2
Row 20: as row 8
Row 22: *p3 k1* 2(3:4) times p3 t2f p3 k1 p3
c4f p3 k1 p3 c6f p3 k1 p3 k3 c6b p3 k1 p3 c6f
p1 c6b p3 k1 p3 c6f k3 p3 k1 p3 c6b p3 k1 p3
c4b p3 k1 p3 t2b p3 *k1 p3* 2(3:4) times
Row 24: as row 8
These 24 rows form patt. Cont in patt until
work measures 51cm.
Shape armholes: cast off 4(5:6)sts beginning
next 2 rows. Dec each end next 4 rows. Dec each
end next and foll alt rows to 105(109:113)sts.
Cont without shaping until work measures
74cm.
Shape shoulders and neck: cast off 7(7:8)sts,
patt 35(36:36), cast off 21(23:25)sts, patt to
end.
On 42(43:44)sts:
Row 1: cast off 7(7:8)sts patt to end
Row 2: cast off 5 sts patt to end
Row 3: cast off 7(8:8)sts patt to end
Row 4: cast off 4sts patt to end
Row 5: cast off 8(8:8)sts patt to end
Row 6: cast off 3sts patt to end
Row 7: cast off
Rejoin yarn to rem sts at neck edge and work
rows 2–7 inclusive.

POCKET LININGS (2)
Using 4mm needles cast on 35sts and work 39
rows in stocking st.
Row 40: p2 *inc p5* 5 times inc p2 *41sts*
Leave sts on stitch holder.

LEFT FRONT
Using 3¼mm needles cast on 51(55:59)sts and
work 6cm in k1 p1 rib.
Increase row: rib 3(7:11) *inc rib 2* 16 times
67(71:75)sts
Change to 4mm needles and work as follows:
Row 1 and alt rows: (wrong side) k1 p6 k3 p1
k3 p9 k3 p1 k3 p6 k3 p1 k3 p4 k3 p1 k3 p2 k3
p1 k3 2(3:4) times
Row 2: *p3 k1* 2(3:4) times p3 t2f p3 k1 p3 c4f
p3 k1 p3 k6 p3 k1 p3 c6f k3 p3 k1 p3 k6 p1
Row 4: *p3 k1* 2(3:4) times p3 t2f p3 k1 p3 k4
p3 k1 p3 c6f p3 k1 p3 k9 p3 k1 p3 c6f p1
Row 6: *p3 k1* 2(3:4) times p3 t2f p3 k1 p3 c4f
p3 k1 p3 k6 p3 k1 p3 k3 c6b p3 k1 p3 k6 p1
Row 8: *p3 k1* 2(3:4) times p3 t2f p3 k1 p3 k4
p3 k1 p3 k6 p3 k1 p3 k9 p3 k1 p3 k6 p1
Row 10: *p3 k1* 2(3:4) times p3 t2f p3 k1 p3
c4f p3 k1 p3 c6f p3 k1 p3 c6f k3 p3 k1 p3 c6f p1
Row 12: as row 8
Row 14: as row 6
Row 16: as row 4
Row 18: as row 2
Row 20: as row 8
Row 22: *p3 k1* 2(3:4) times p3 t2f p3 k1 p3
c4f p3 k1 p3 c6f p3 k1 p3 k3 c6b p3 k1 p3 c6f p1
Row 24: as row 8
These 24 rows form patt. Cont in patt to
completion of row 40.
Row 41: (place pocket) patt 16(20:24) place
next 41sts on holder patt across 41sts of pocket,
patt 10

Cont in patt placing marker at button edge
when work measures 40cm. Cont until work
measures 51cm.
Shape armholes and neck: cast off 4(5:6)sts patt
to last 2 sts k2tog.
Work 1 row.
Row 3: dec each end of row
Row 4: dec at armhole edge
Row 5: dec each end of row
Row 6: as row 4
Row 7: as row 3
Row 8: patt
Repeat rows 7 and 8 until 44(45:46)sts rem.
Continue dec neck edge only on every alt row
until 30(31:32)sts rem. Work should measure
63(65:66)cm.
Shape shoulders: cast off 7(7:8)sts patt to end.
Work 1 row. Cast off 7(8:8)sts patt to end.
Work 1 row. Cast off 8(8:8)sts patt to end.
Work 1 row. Cast off.

RIGHT FRONT
Using 3¼mm needles cast on 51(55:59)sts and
work 6cm in k1 p1 rib.
Increase row: *rib 2, inc* 16 times, rib 3(7:11)
67(71:75)sts
Change to 4mm needles and work as follows:
Row 1 and alt rows: (wrong side) *k3 p1*
2(3:4) times k3 p2 k3 p1 k3 p4 k3 p1 k3 p6 k3
p1 k3 p9 k3 p1 k3 p6 k1
Row 2: p1 k6 p3 k1 p3 k3 c6b p3 k1 p3 k6 p3
k1 p3 c4b p3 k1 p3 t2b p3 *k1 p3* 2(3:4) times
Row 4: p1 c6b p3 k1 p3 k9 p3 k1 p3 c6b p3 k1
p3 k4 p3 k1 p3 t2b p3 *k1 p3* 2(3:4) times
Row 6: p1 k6 p3 k1 p3 c6f k3 p3 k1 p3 k6 p3
k1 p3 c4b p3 k1 p3 t2b p3 *k1 p3* 2(3:4) times
Row 8: p1 k6 p3 k1 p3 k9 p3 k1 p3 k6 p3 k1 p3
k4 p3 k1 p3 t2b p3 *k1 p3* 2(3:4) times
Row 10: p1 c6b p3 k1 p3 k3 c6b p3 k1 p3 c6b
p3 k1 p3 c4b p3 k1 p3 t2b p3 *k1 p3* 2(3:4)
times
Row 12: as row 8
Row 14: as row 6
Row 16: as row 4
Row 18: as row 2
Row 20: as row 8
Row 22: p1 c6b p3 k1 p3 c6f k3 p3 k1 p3 c6b
p3 k1 p3 c4b p3 k1 p3 t2b p3 *k1 p3* 2(3:4)
times
Row 24: as row 8
These 24 rows form patt. Cont in patt to
completion of row 40.
Row 41: (place pocket) patt 10, place next 41sts
on holder, patt across 41sts of pocket, patt
16(20:24).
Cont in patt placing marker at button edge
when work measures 40cm. Cont until work
measures 51cm
Work armhole and neck shaping by reversing
shapings of left front.

SLEEVES
Using 3¼mm needles cast on 49sts and work
6cm in k1 p1 rib.
Increase row: rib 3 *inc rib 1* 22 times, rib 2
71sts

Change to 4mm needles work patt as follows.
AT THE SAME TIME inc each end of every 5th
row to 109(113:117)sts, working extra sts in p3
k1 rib.
Row 1 and alt rows: (wrong side) k3 p1 k3 p4
k3 p1 k3 p6 k3 p1 k3 p9 k3 p1 k3 p6 k3 p1 k3
p4 k3 p1 k3
Row 2: p3 k1 p3 c4f p3 k1 p3 c6f p3 k1 p3 c6f
k3 p3 k1 p3 k6 p3 k1 p3 c4b p3 k1 p3
Row 4: p3 k1 p3 k4 p3 k1 p3 c6f p3 k1 p3 k9
p3 k1 p3 c6b p3 k1 p3 k4 p3 k1 p3
Row 6: p3 k1 p3 c4f p3 k1 p3 k6 p3 k1 p3 k3
c6b p3 k1 p3 k6 p3 k1 p3 c4b p3 k1 p3
Row 8: p3 k1 p3 k4 p3 k1 p3 k6 p3 k1 p3 k9 p3
k1 p3 k6 p3 k1 p3 k4 p3 k1 p3
Row 10: p3 k1 p3 c4f p3 k1 p3 c6f p3 k1 p3 c6f
k3 p3 k1 p3 c6b p3 k1 p3 c4b p3 k1 p3
Row 12: as row 8
Row 14: as row 6
Row 16: as row 4
Row 18: as row 2
Row 20: as row 8
Row 22: p3 k1 p3 c4f p3 k1 p3 c6f p3 k1 p3 k3
c6b p3 k1 p3 c6b p3 k1 p3 c4b p3 k1 p3
Row 24: as row 8
These 24 rows form patt. Cont inc to
109(113:117)sts. Cont without shaping until
work measures 44(44:47)cm.
Shape sleevehead: cast off 4(5:6)sts beg next 2
rows. Dec each end next 4 rows. Dec each end
next and every foll alt row until 75sts rem. Dec
each end every row until 55sts rem. Cast off 5sts
beg next 6 rows. Cast off.

POCKET TRIMS

Using 3¼mm needles work 6 rows in k1 p1 rib
across sts on holder. Cast off in rib.

BUTTON BAND

Using 3¾mm circular needle and with right side
facing and starting at marker on left front, pick
up and knit 125sts evenly to bottom of welt.
Work 8 rows in k1 p1 rib. Cast off in rib.

BUTTONHOLE BAND

With right side facing and starting at bottom of
welt on right front, pick up sts as for button
band, ending at marker.
Rib 3 rows.
Row 4: rib 3 * yf k2tog rib 18* 6 times yf k2tog
Rib 4 rows. Cast off in rib.

COLLAR

Join shoulder seams.

With right side facing and starting at marker on
right front, pick up and knit 114sts evenly up to
shoulder, 57sts across back neck, and 114sts
down left front to marker *285sts*
Next row: rib 163, turn
s1 rib 40, turn, s1, rib 42, turn, s1 rib 44, cont
thus, working 2 more sts on each row until turn,
s1 rib 56 has been worked.
Cont as before but work 4 more sts on each row,
until turn s1 rib 96 has been worked.
Cont as before but work 6 more sts on each row
until turn s1 rib 156 has been worked.
Cont as before but work 8 more sts on each row
until turn s1 rib 252 has been worked. Turn s1
rib to end.
Rib 7 more rows. Cast off loosely in rib.

MAKING UP

Join side and sleeve seams. Ease sleeves into
armholes and stitch into position. Slipstitch
pockets into place. Join button(hole) bands to
collar. Weave in any loose ends. Sew on buttons.

CARE INSTRUCTIONS

See ball tag and page 172.

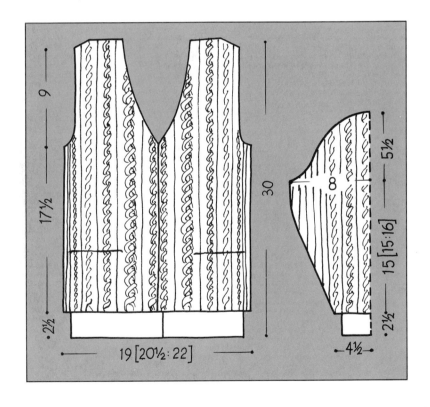

TUTU

ONCE AGAIN, THE MAXIMUM EFFECT FOR THE MINIMUM KNITTING IS THE AIM HERE; THIS SMALL FEMININE CARDIGAN IS MOSTLY IN STOCKING STITCH, BUT WHAT GIVES IT THE EDGE ARE THE CABLES WHICH NATURALLY GATHER IN THE FABRIC AROUND THE FOREARMS AND WAIST.

Shown on opposite page in blossom Chandos.

See diagram at end of pattern

SIZE cm(in)
To fit bust:

87–91(34–36)	97–102(38–40)
Actual size:	
97(38)	107(42)
Length from back neck:	
52(20½)	54(21½)
Sleeve seam:	
44(17½)	44(17½)

MATERIALS
Chandos – 50g balls:

10	11
1 pair each of 3¼mm and 4mm needles	
5 buttons	

TENSION
22sts and 28 rows = 10cm square on 4mm needles over stocking stitch. See page 9.

ABBREVIATIONS
See page 9.
c6 = place next 3sts on cn, leave at back, k3, then k3 from cn.
[ ] = repeat enclosed instructions number of times indicated
yrn = yarn round needle

BACK
Using 3¼mm needles cast on 88(98)sts and work as follows:
Row 1: p2 *p4 k6* 8(9) times p6

Row 2: k2 *k4 p6* 8(9) times k6
Row 3: p2 *p4 c6* 8(9) times p6
Row 4: as row 2
Rows 5–6: as rows 1–2
These six rows form patt rep. Cont until work measures 7cm. Change to 4mm needles and cont in patt until work measures minimum of 18(20)cm ending on row 5 (note number of rows) **.
Next row: k2 *k4 [p1, inc]3 times* 8(9) times k6 *112(125)sts*
Change to stocking st (next row knit) and cont until work measures 25(27)cm.
Inc each end next and every foll 8th row to 128(141)sts. Cont without shaping until work measures 51(53)cm.
Shape neck: k50(56) cast off 28(29)sts, k50(56). On 50(56)sts:
Row 1: purl
Row 2: cast off 5sts knit to end
Row 3: purl. Cast off.
Join yarn to rem sts and work to match.

LEFT FRONT
Using 3¼mm needles cast on 42(46)sts and work 7cm in cable rib. (*Row 1:* p2(6) *k6 p4* four times.)
Change to 4mm needles and cont rib as for back to **.
Next row: *k4 [p1, inc] 3 times *4 times k2(6) *54:58sts*
Change to stocking st and cont until work measures 25(27)cm.
Shape neck and armhole edge: (right side facing) inc, k51(55) dec. Cont in stocking st, inc armhole edge on every foll 8th(6th) row 7(9) more times and dec neck edge on every foll 4th row 16 more times to 45(51)sts. Cont without shaping until work measures 52(54)cm. Cast off.

TUTU

RIGHT FRONT

As left front reversing all shapings and noting row 1 of rib is *p4 k6* 4 times p2(6).

SLEEVES

Using 3¼mm needles cast on 44sts and work as follows:
Row 1: *p4 k6* 4 times p4
Rows 2–30: cont in cable rib as set, inc each end of every 6th row to 54sts working extra sts into patt.
Rows 31–59: Change to 4mm needles and cont with cable rib inc each end of every 4th row to 68sts.
Row 60: k1 *[p1 inc]3 times p4* 6 times [p1 inc] 3 times k1 *89sts*
Change to stocking st and inc each end every 3rd row to 131sts. Cont until work measures 44cm. Cast off.

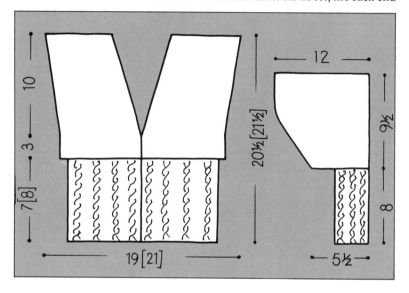

BUTTON BAND

Join shoulder seams. Using 3¼mm needles pick up 58(64)sts from hem to V shaping, 60sts along V shaping, 37(39) along back neck, 60sts along V shaping and 58(64)sts from V shaping to hem *273(287)sts*
Work 3 rows k1 p1 rib.
Row 4: rib 2 *dec, yrn, rib 12(13)* 4 times dec, yrn, rib to end
Work 2 more rows in rib. Cast off in rib.

MAKING UP

Make 21(23)cm side seam. Join sleeve seams and set in sleeves. Weave in any loose ends. Sew on buttons.

CARE INSTRUCTIONS

See ball tag and page 172.

BAROCCO

T HE CLASSIC YOKE OF THIS CARDIGAN IS A RELIABLY PRETTY SIL-
HOUETTE, AND WITH SUCH A VARIATION OF STITCH PATTERNS YOU
SHOULD RECEIVE PLENTY OF ADMIRATION FOR YOUR EFFORTS. THE
YOKE IS KNITTED ON A CIRCULAR NEEDLE AND YOU ARE WORKING SEVERAL
PATTERNS AT A TIME, ALTHOUGH NO INDIVIDUAL PATTERN IS AT ALL
COMPLEX.

Shown on page 67 in primrose and eau-de-nil Chandos.
Also shown on page 54 in blossom.
Also shown on page 26 in white.

See diagram at end of pattern

SIZE cm(in)
To fit bust:

81–86(32–34)	86–91(34–36)	91–97(36–38)

Actual size:

86(34)	91(36)	97(38)

Length from back neck:

58(23)	58(23)	58(23)

Sleeve seam:

43(17)	43(17)	43(17)

MATERIALS
Chandos – 50g balls:

12	13	14

1 pair each of 3¼mm and 4mm needles

3¾mm circular needle. Cable needle

8 small buttons

TENSION
22sts and 28 rows = 10cm square on 4mm needles over stocking stitch. See page 9.

ABBREVIATIONS
See page 9.
m = moss stitch
b = bobble by k1 p1 k1 into next st, turn, p3, turn, k3, turn, p3 turn, k3, take 2nd and 3rd sts

over first st
lb = large bobble by k1 p1 k1 p1 k1 into next st, turn, p5, turn, k5, turn, p5, turn, k5, take 2nd 3rd, 4th and 5th sts over first st
tw2 = knit into front of second st then k first st, taking both sts off together
c6f = place next 3sts on to cn and hold at front of work, k3, then k3 from cn
c4b = place next 2sts on to cn and hold at back of work, k2, then p2 from cn
c4f = place next 2sts on to cn and hold at front of work, p2, then k2 from cn
c6b = place next 3sts on to cn and hold at back of work, k3, then k3 from cn

BACK
Using 3¼mm needles cast on 111(119:127)sts and work 6cm in k1 p1 rib.
Increase row: rib 1(5:9) *inc rib 8* 12 times inc rib to end *124(132:140)sts*
Change to 4mm needles and patt as follows:
Row 1: m16(20:24) p2 k2 p3 k2 p2 k9 *p2 k2* twice p15 k2 p2 k2 p15 *k2 p2* twice k9 p2 k2 p3 k2 p2 m16(20:24)
Row 2: m16(20:24) k2 p2 k3 p2 k2 p9 *k2 p2* twice k15 p2 k2 p2 k15 *p2 k2* twice p9 k2 p2 k3 p2 k2 m16(20:24)
Row 3: m16(20:24) p2 tw2 p1 b p1 tw2 p2 c6f k3 p2 tw2 p2 tw2 p15 k2 p2 k2 p15 *tw2 p2* twice c6f k3 p2 tw2 p1 b p1 tw2 p2 m16(20:24)
Row 4: as row 2
Row 5: m16(20:24) p2 tw2 p3 tw2 p2 k9 *p2 tw2* twice p13 c4b p2 c4f p13 *tw2 p2* twice k9 p2 tw2 p3 tw2 p2 m16(20:24)
Row 6: m16(20:24) k2 p2 k3 p2 k2 p9 *k2 p2* twice k13 p2 k6 p2 k13 *p2 k2* twice p9 k2 p2 k3 p2 k2 m16(20:24)

Following page: This cardigan, Barocco, is also shown on pages 27 and 54. It is a fairly complex design but none of the individual stitch techniques are difficult.

Row 7: m16(20:24) p2 tw2 p1 b p1 tw2 p2 k3 c6b *p2 tw2* twice p7 k2 p2 c4b p6 c4f p2 k2 p7 *tw2 p2* twice k3 c6b p2 tw2 p1 b p1 tw2 p2 m16(20:24)

Row 8: m16(20:24) k2 p2 k3 p2 k2 p9 *k2 p2* twice k7 p2 k2 p2 k10 p2 k2 p2 k7 *p2 k2* twice p9 k2 p2 k3 p2 k2 m16(20:24)

Row 9: m16(20:24) p2 tw2 p3 tw2 p2 k9 *p2 tw2* twice p7 *k2 p2* 5 times k2 p7 *tw2 p2* twice k9 p2 tw2 p3 tw2 p2 m16(20:24)

Keeping edge 44(48:52)sts in patt as set (8 row patt – rows 2–9), work centre 36sts as follows:

Row 10: patt 44(48:52) as row 2 k7 *p2 k2* 5 times p2 k7 patt 44(48:52)

Row 11: patt 44(48:52) as row 3 p5 c4b p2 b p3 k2 p2 k2 p3 b p2 c4f p5 patt to end

Row 12: patt 44(48:52) k5 p2 k8 p2 k2 p2 k8 p2 k5 patt to end

Row 13: patt 44(48:52) p3 c4b p6 c4b p2 c4f p6 c4f p3 patt to end

Row 14: patt 44(48:52) k3 p2 k8 p2 k6 p2 k8 p2 k3 patt to end

Row 15: patt 44(48:52) p3 *k2 p2* twice c4b p6 c4f *p2 k2* twice p3 patt to end

Row 16: patt 44(48:52) k3 *p2 k2* twice p2 k10 *p2 k2* twice p2 k3 patt to end

Row 17: patt 44(48:52) p3 b p3 *k2 p2* 5 times k2 p3 b p3 patt to end

Rep rows 10–17 inclusive until work measures 38cm, ending with a wrong side row.

Shape armhole and back: cast off 5(6:7)sts at beg of next 2 rows. Dec each end of next 6 rows. Dec each end of alt rows to 100(102:104)sts.

Row 1: k2tog, patt 35(36:37), turn, s1, patt to end

Row 2: k2tog, patt 29(30:31), turn, s1, patt to end

Row 3: k2tog, patt 22(23:24), turn, s1, patt to end

Row 4: k2tog, patt 10(11:12), turn, s1, patt to end

Row 5: k2tog, patt 5(6:7), turn, s1, patt to end. Break yarn. Place 58(59:60)sts on holder.

Rejoin yarn to rem sts, patt to last 2sts, k2tog.

Row 2: patt 30(31:32), turn, s1, patt to last 2sts, k2tog

Row 3: patt 24(25:26), turn, s1, patt to last 2sts, k2tog

Row 4: patt 12(13:14), turn, s1, patt to last 2sts, k2tog

Row 5: patt 7(8:9), turn, s1, patt to last 2sts, k2tog. Break yarn. Place sts on holder. *90(92:94)sts*

RIGHT FRONT

Using 3¼mm needles, cast on 55(59:63)sts, and work 6cm in k1 p1 rib.

Increase row: *rib 5, inc* 8 times, rib to end *63(67:71)sts*

Change to 4mm needles and patt as follows:

Row 1: p2, k2, p15, *k2, p2* twice, k9, p2, k2, p3, k2, p2, m16(20:24)

Row 2: m16(20:24), k2, p2, k3, p2, k2, p9, *k2, p2* twice, k15, p2, k2

Row 3: p2, k2, p15, *tw2, p2* twice, c6f, k3, p2, tw2, p1, b, p1, tw2, p2, m16(20:24)

Row 4: as row 2

Row 5: p2, c4f, p13, *tw2, p2* twice, k9, p2, tw2, p3, tw2, p2, m16(20:24)

Row 6: m16(20:24), k2, p2, k3, p2, k2, p9, *k2, p2* twice, k13, p2, k4

Row 7: p4, c4f, p2, k2, p7, *tw2, p2* twice, k3, c6b, p2, tw2, p1, b, p1, tw2, p2, m16 (20:24)

Row 8: m16(20:24), k2, p2, k3, p2, k2, p9, *k2, p2* twice, k7, p2, k2, p2, k6

Row 9: *p2, k2* 3 times, p7, *tw2, p2* twice, k9, p2, tw2, p3, tw2, p2, m16(20:24)

Keeping 44(48:52)sts of side panel correct, work 19sts of front panel as follows:

Row 10: patt 44(48:52) as row 2, k7, *p2, k2* 3 times

Row 11: p2, k2, p3, b, p2, c4f, p5, patt 44(48:52) as row 3

Row 12: patt 44(48:52), k5, p2, k8, p2, k2

Row 13: p2, c4f, p6, c4f, p3, patt 44(48:52)

Row 14: patt 44(48:52), k3, p2, k8, p2, k4

Row 15: p4, c4f, *p2, k2* twice, p3, patt 44(48:52)

Row 16: patt 44(48:52), k3, *p2, k2* twice, p2, k6

Row 17: *p2, k2* 3 times, p3, b, p3, patt 44(48:52)

Rep rows 10–17 inclusive until work measures 38cm.

Shape armhole and front:

Row 1: patt

Row 2: cast off 5(6:7)sts, patt to end

Dec armhole edge every row to 54(55:58)sts

Medium and large sizes only: dec armhole edge on alt rows to (54:55)sts

Small size only:

Row 1: patt to last 2sts, k2tog

Row 2: k2tog, patt 33, turn, s1, patt to last 2sts, k2tog

Medium and large sizes only:

Row 1: patt to last 2sts, k2tog

Row 2: patt (35:36), turn, s1, patt to last 2sts, k2tog

All sizes:

Row 3: patt 29(30:31), turn, s1, patt to last 2sts, k2tog

Row 4: patt 24(25:26), turn, s1, patt to last 2sts, k2tog

Row 5: patt 14(15:16), turn, s1, patt to last 2sts, k2tog

Row 6: patt 11(12:13), turn, s1, patt to last 2sts, k2tog

Row 7: patt 7(8:9), turn, s1, patt to last 2sts, k2tog

Break yarn, leave sts on holder *46(47:48)sts*

LEFT FRONT

Rib and increase row as for right front.

Change to 4mm needles and patt as follows:

Row 1: m16(20:24), p2, k2, p3, k2, p2, k9, *p2, k2* twice, p15, k2, p2

Row 2: k2, p2, k15, *p2, k2* twice, p9, k2, p2, k3, p2, k2, m16(20:24)

Row 3: m16(20:24), p2, tw2, p1, b, p1, tw2, p2, c6f, k3, *p2, tw2* twice, p15, k2, p2

Row 4: as row 2

Row 5: m16(20:24), p2, tw2, p3, tw2, p2, k9, *p2, tw2* twice, p13, c4b, p2
Row 6: k4, p2, k13, *p2, k2* twice, p9, k2, p2, k3, p2, k2, m16(20:24)
Row 7: m16(20:24), p2, tw2, p1, b, p1, tw2, p2, k3, c6b, *p2, tw2* twice, p7, k2, p2, c4b, p4
Row 8: k6, p2, k2, p2, k7, *p2, k2* twice, p9, k2, p2, k3, p2, k2, m16(20:24)
Row 9: m16(20:24), p2, tw2, p3, tw2, p2, k9, *p2, tw2* twice, p7, *k2, p2* 3 times
Keeping 44(48:52)sts of side panel correct, cont as follows:
Row 10: *k2, p2* 3 times, k7, patt 44(48:52)
Row 11: patt 44(48:52), p5, c4b, p2, b, p3, k2, p2
Row 12: k2, p2, k8, p2, k5, patt 44(48:52)
Row 13: patt 44(48:52), p3, c4b, p6, c4b, p2
Row 14: k4, p2, k8, p2, k3, patt 44(48:52)
Row 15: patt 44(48:52), p3, *k2, p2* twice, c4b, p4
Row 16: k6, p2, *k2, p2* twice, k3, patt 44(48:52)
Row 17: patt 44(48:52), p3, b, p3, *k2, p2* 3 times
Rows 10–17 form patt. Cont until work measures 38cm
Shape armhole: cast off 5(6:7)sts at beg of next row. Work one row. Dec armhole edge on every row to 54(55:58)sts.
Medium and large sizes only: dec armhole edge on alt rows to (54:55)sts.
Small size only: row 1: k2tog, patt 34, turn, s1, patt to last 2sts, k2tog.
Medium and large sizes only: row 1: k2tog, patt (34:35), turn, s1, patt to end.
All sizes:
Row 2: k2tog, patt 28(29:30), turn, s1, patt to end
Row 3: k2tog, patt 23(24:25), turn, s1, patt to end
Row 4: k2tog, patt 13(14:15), turn, s1, patt to end
Row 5: k2tog, patt 10(11:12), turn, s1, patt to end
Row 6: k2tog, patt 6(7:8), turn, s1, patt to end
Row 7: k2tog, patt 2(3:4), turn, s1, patt to end
Break yarn, leave sts on holder 46(47:48)sts

SLEEVES

Using 3¼mm needles, cast on 58(61:64)sts and work 6cm in k1 p1 rib.
Next row: rib 1, *rib 2, inc* 18(19:20) times, rib 3 76(80:84)sts
Change to 4mm needles and patt as follows:
Row 1: m6(8:10), p2, k2, p2, k9, *p2, k2* twice, p6, k2, p2, k2, p6, *k2, p2* twice, k9, p2, k2, p2, m6(8:10)
Row 2: m6(8:10), k2, p2, k2, p9, *k2, p2* twice, k6, p2, k2, p2, k6, *p2, k2* twice, p9, k2, p2, k2, m6(8:10)
Row 3: m6(8:10), p2, tw2, p2, c6f, k3, *p2, tw2* twice, p6, k2, p2, k2, p6, *tw2, p2* twice, c6f, k3, p2, tw2, p2, m6(8:10)
Row 4: as row 2
Row 5: m6(8:10), p2, tw2, p2, k9, *p2, tw2* twice, p4, c4b, p2, c4f, p4, *tw2, p2* twice, k9, p2, tw2, p2, m6(8:10)
Row 6: m6(8:10), k2, p2, k2, p9, *k2, p2* twice, k4, p2, k6, p2, k4, *p2, k2* twice, p9, k2, p2, k2, m6(8:10)
Row 7: m6(8:10), p2, tw2, p2, k3, c6b, *p2, tw2* twice, p2, c4b, p6, c4f, p2, *tw2, p2* twice, k3, c6b, p2, tw2, p2, m6(8:10)
Row 8: m6(8:10), k2, p2, k2, p9, *k2, p2* twice, k2, p2, k10, p2, k2, *p2, k2* twice, p9, k2, p2, k2, m6(8:10)
Row 9: m6(8:10), p2, tw2, p2, k9, *p2, tw2* twice, *p2, k2* 4 times, p2, *tw2, p2* twice, k9, p2, tw2, p2, m6(8:10)
Row 10: m6(8:10), k2, p2, k2, p9, *k2, p2* twice, *k2, p2* 4 times, k2, *p2, k2* twice, p9, k2, p2, k2, m6(8:10)
Row 11: m6(8:10), p2, tw2, p2, c6f, k3, *p2, tw2* twice, p2, b, p3, k2, p2, k2, p3, b, p2, *tw2, p2* twice, c6f, k3, p2, tw2, p2, m6(8:10)
Rep rows 4–11 inclusive, inc each end of next row and every foll 8th row to 92(98:104)sts, working extra sts in moss stitch. Cont until work measures 43cm.
Shape armhole: cast off 5(6:7)sts at beg of next 2 rows. Dec each end of next 6 rows. Dec each end of alt rows until 60sts remain. Leave on holder.

YOKE

Using 3¾mm circular needle, and with right side facing, slip sts from holders as follows: right front, right sleeve, back, left sleeve, left front (work back and forth NOT circular) *302(306:310)sts*
Rows 1–3: moss st
Row 4: (small size) *k9, k2tog* 27 times, k5 *275sts*
(medium size) *k12, k2tog* 21 times, k12 *285sts*
(large size) *k18, k2tog* 15 times, k10 *295sts*
Row 5: k7, *lb, k9* 26(27:28) times, lb, k7
Row 6: purl
Row 7: p2tog, p5, *tw2, p8* 26(27:28) times, tw2, p6
Row 8: m5, *k1, p2, k1, m6* 26(27:28) times, k1, p2, k1, m5
Row 9: m5, *p1, tw2, p1, m6* 26(27:28) times, p1, tw2, p1, m5
Row 10: as row 8
Rows 11–12: as rows 9–10
Row 13: k6, *p2tog, k8* 26(27:28) times, p2tog, k6 *247(256:265)sts*
Row 14: k1, *p2, k7* 27(28:29) times, p2, k1
Row 15: k2, *lb, k8* 27(28:29) times, lb, k1
Row 16: as row 14
Row 17: p1, *tw2, p7* 27(28:29) times, tw2, p1
Row 18: as row 14
Row 19: as row 17
Row 20: as row 14
Row 21: p1, *tw2, p3, lb, p3* 27(28:29) times, tw2, p1
Row 22: k1, *p2, k2tog, k1, p2, k2* 27(28:29) times, p2, k1 *220(228:236)sts*
Row 23: p1, *tw2, p2, tw2, p2* 27(28:29)

times, tw2, p1
Row 24: k1, *k2tog, k2, p2, k2* 27(28:29) times, k2tog, k1 *192(199:206)sts*
Row 25: p4, *tw2, p5* 26(27:28) times, tw2, p4
Row 26: k4, *p2, k5* 26(27:28) times, p2, k4
Row 27: as row 25
Row 28: as row 26
Row 29: p4, *tw2, p2tog, p3* 26(27:28) times, tw2, p4 *166(172:178)sts*
Row 30: k4, *p2, k4* 26(27:28) times, p2, k4
Row 31: p4, *tw2, p4* 26(27:28) times, tw2, p4
Row 32: as row 30
Row 33: *p1, p2tog, p1, tw2* 27(28:29) times, p1, p2tog, p1 *138(143:148)sts*
Row 34: *k3, p2* 27(28:29) times, k3
Row 35: p3, *tw2, p3* 27(28:29) times
Row 36: as row 34
Row 37: *p1, p2tog, tw2* 27(28:29) times, p1, p2tog *110(114:118)sts*
Row 38: *k2, p2* 27(28:29) times, k2
Row 39: *p2, p2tog* 27(28:29) times, p2 *83(86:89)sts*
Leave sts on holder.

BUTTON BAND
Using 3¼mm needles, pick up 134sts along left front edge.
Work 5 rows in k1 p1 rib. Cast off.

BUTTONHOLE BAND
Pick up sts as for button band. Work one row k1 p1 rib.
Row 2: rib 3, *cast off 2sts, rib 17* 6 times, cast off 2sts, rib to end
Row 3: cast on 2sts where cast off in row before
Rows 4–5: rib
Cast off.

NECKBAND
Using 3¼mm needles, pick up 5sts from buttonhole band, rib across neck sts, pick up 5sts from button band. Work one row rib.
Row 2: rib 2, cast off 2sts, rib to end
Row 3: rib, casting on 2sts where cast off in row before
Rows 4–5: rib. Cast off.

MAKING UP
Join small raglan seams. Join side and sleeve seams. Weave in any loose ends. Sew on buttons.

CARE INSTRUCTIONS
See ball tag and page 172.

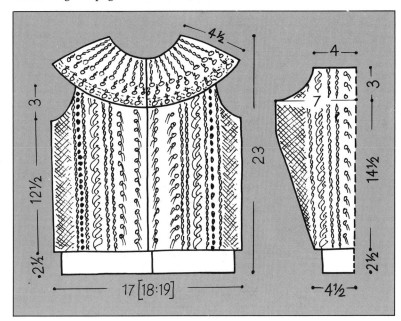

ROSEMOOR

THIS IS A SIMPLE AND GENEROUS SHAPE TAPERING GENTLY TO THE WAIST AND ALL IN STOCKING STITCH FOR THE EASIEST POSSIBLE PATTERN; OF COURSE YOU COULD ALWAYS ADD YOUR OWN STITCH DESIGN IF YOU FIND IT TOO PLAIN!

Shown on opposite page in gold Dragonfly.

See diagram at end of pattern

SIZE cm(in)
One size to fit up to bust:

102(40)

Actual size:

130(51)

Length from back neck:

58(23)

MATERIALS
Dragonfly – 50g balls:

10

1 pair each of 3¼mm, 3¾mm, 4mm needles

4 buttons

TENSION
22sts and 28 rows = 10cm square on 4mm needles over stocking stitch. See page 9.

ABBREVIATIONS
See page 9.

BACK
Using 3¼mm needles cast on 89sts and work 6cm in k1 p1 rib.
Increase row: rib 3 * inc, rib 8 * 9 times, inc, rib 4 *99sts*
Change to 4mm needles and stocking st, inc each end of 5th and every foll 4th row to 143 sts. Work 3 rows.
Rows 93–94: cast off 8sts beg of each row.
Work without shaping to row 146.
Row 147: k46, cast off 35sts, k46
Dec at neck edge of every row to 43sts. Cast off.

Rejoin yarn to other side at neck edge and work to match taking care shapings are at neck edge.

FRONT
Work as for back to row 92.
Row 93: cast off 8sts, k61, cast off 5sts, k69
Row 94: cast off 8sts
Work without shaping to row 130.
Row 131: cast off 4sts
Row 132: patt
Row 133: cast off 4sts
Rows 134–138: dec at neck edge on every row
Row 139: patt
Rows 140–148: dec at neck edge on alternate rows
Row 151: cast off
Work other side to match.

COLLAR
Join shoulder seams.
Using 3¼mm needles (wrong side facing) pick up and knit 25sts up front neck, 42sts across back neck, 25sts down front neck *92sts*
Work 6 rows in k1 p1 rib. Change to 3¾mm needles and work 6 rows in rib. Change to 4mm needles and work 6 rows in rib. Cast off in rib.

BUTTON BAND
Using 3¼mm needles pick up and knit 28sts along left side opening. Work 7 rows in k1 p1 rib. Cast off in rib.

BUTTONHOLE BAND
Using 3¼mm needles pick up and knit 28sts along right side opening. Work 3 rows in k1 p1 rib.
Row 4: rib 3 * yrn, dec, rib 5 * three times yrn, dec, rib 2
Work 3 rows rib. Cast off in rib.

Opposite:
Both Rosemoor, on the right, and Pronto, are basically in stocking stitch, which is all you really need for the silky Dragonfly yarn. The pattern for Pronto is on page 73.

ARMHOLE EDGING
Using 3¼mm needles pick up and knit 93sts around armhole edging IGNORING 8sts of armhole cast off. Work 7 rows in k1 p1 rib.

MAKING UP
Join side seams. Stitch armhole edging to sweater at underarm. Place buttonhole band over button band and stitch lower edges to sweater. Weave in any loose ends. Sew on buttons.

CARE INSTRUCTIONS
See ball band, and page 172.

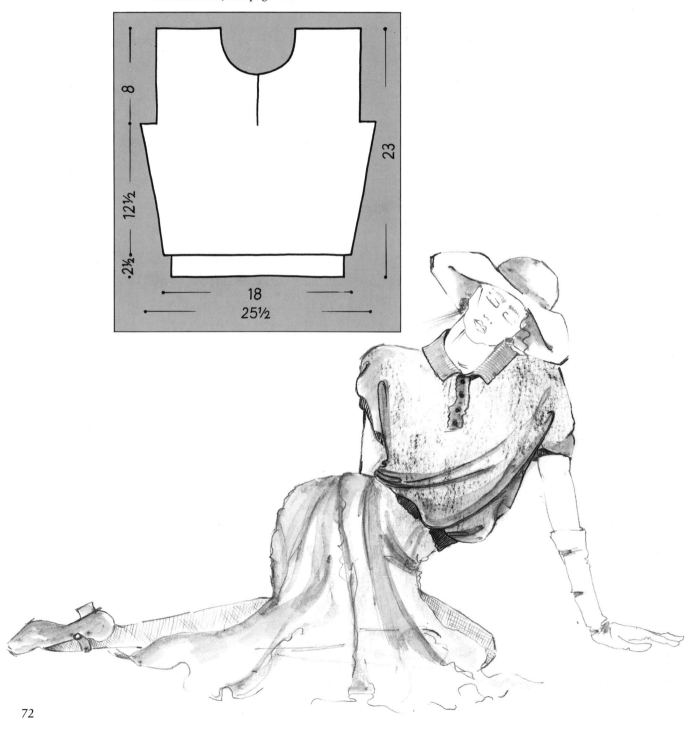

PRONTO

THE SILHOUETTE OF THIS DESIGN RELIES ON THE INCREASE ROW AFTER THE CABLES TO TURN THE FITTED WAIST INTO A LOOSE TOP HALF. OTHERWISE THE PATTERN IS NOT AT ALL COMPLICATED AND IT WILL WORK WELL AS AN EVENING SWEATER, A SUMMER TOP OR PART OF A TWINSET.

Shown on page 71 in silver Dragonfly.

See diagram at end of pattern

SIZE cm(in)
To fit bust:

82–86(32–34)	91–96(36–38)	102–107(40–42)

Actual size:

91(36)	101(40)	111(43½)

Length from back neck:

48(19)	51(20)	53(21)

MATERIALS
Dragonfly – 50g balls:

6	7	8

1 pair each of size 3¼mm and 4mm needles. Cable needle.

3 buttons

TENSION
22sts and 28 rows = 10cm square on 4mm needles over stocking stitch. See page 9.

ABBREVIATIONS
See page 9.
c6 = place next 3sts on cn, leave at back, k3, then k3 from cn
[ ] = repeat enclosed instructions number of times indicated

BACK
Using 3¼mm needles cast on 78(88:98)sts and work as follows:
Row 1: p2 *p4 k6* 7(8:9) times p6
Row 2: k2 *k4 p6* 7(8:9) times k6
Row 3: p2 *p4 c6* 7(8:9) times p6
Row 4: as row 2
Rows 5–6: as rows 1–2

These 6 rows form patt rep. Cont until work measures 7cm. Change to 4mm needles and cont in patt until work measures minimum of 15(18:20)cm ending on row 5 of patt repeat.
Next row: k2 *k4 [p1 inc] 3 times* 7(8:9) times k6 *99:112:125sts*
Change to stocking st (next row knit) and cont until work measures 22(25:27)cm.
Shape armhole: cast off 4sts beg next 2 rows. Inc each end every foll 5th row to 109(122:135)sts. Cont without shaping until work measures 44(47:49)cm ending on a purl row.
Shape shoulders and neck:
Row 1: cast off 4(5:6)sts, k38(43:48), cast off 25(26:27)sts, k42(48:54)
Row 2: cast off 4(5:6)sts, work to end
Row 3: cast off 2(3:4)sts, work to end
Row 4: as 2
Row 5: cast off 2sts, work to end
Row 6: as row 2
Row 7: as row 5
Row 8: as row 2
Row 9: dec work to end
Rows 10–11: as rows 8–9. Cast off.
Rejoin yarn to rem sts at neck edge and work rows 3–1 . Cast off.

FRONT
As back until work measures 28(31:33)cm.
Shape neck opening: cast off centre 5(6:5)sts. Cont in stocking st increasing every 5th row to 52(58:64)sts. Cont without shaping until work measures 41(44:46)cm, ending at neck edge.
Row 1: cast off 4(5:5)sts work to end
Row 2: patt
Row 3: as row 1
Rows 4–7: dec neck edge every row
Row 8: patt
Row 9: dec neck edge

Rows 10–11: as rows 8–9
Row 12: cast off 4(5:6)sts. Work to end
Row 13: as row 9
Rows 14–19: as rows 12–13 3 times
Row 20: cast off 6sts, work to end
Row 21: patt
Cast off. Rejoin yarn to rem sts at neck edge and work other side to match.

ARMBANDS
Join shoulder seams.
Using 3¼mm needles pick up 99sts around armhole omitting cast off sts. Work 3 rows in k1 p1 rib. Cast off.

BUTTON BAND
Using 3¼mm needles pick up 25sts along neck opening. Work 6 rows k1 p1 rib, cast off.

BUTTONHOLE BAND
As * to * above. Work 2 rows k1 p1 rib.
Row 3: rib 6 *yrn, dec rib 7* twice, rib 1
Work 3 more rows rib. Cast off.

NECKBAND
Using 3¼mm needles pick up 5sts across buttonhole band, 22sts from front neck, 45(48:51)sts across back neck, 22sts from front and 5sts from button band *99(102:105)sts*
Work 5 rows rib, making further buttonhole on row 3. Cast off in rib.

MAKING UP
Join side seams, catch armbands to cast off armhole sts. Catch button and buttonhole bands to neck cast off sts. Weave in any loose ends. Sew on buttons.

CARE INSTRUCTIONS
See ball band and page 142.

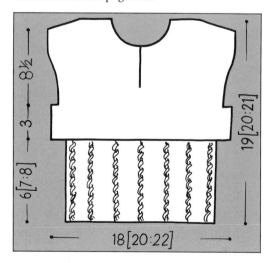

This design, Beauchamp, has a classic feeling to it, but you will see that the silhouette is far from ordinary. The pattern is on the following pages and it is also shown in a sleeveless version on page 31.

BEAUCHAMP

THIS IDEA DERIVES FROM THE BASIC SADDLE-SLEEVE SHAPE, BUT BY PICKING OUT THE SADDLE PANEL IN A CABLE PATTERN IT APPEARS TO ACHIEVE THE IMPOSSIBLE: A CABLE GOING SIDEWAYS. THE CARDIGAN HAS CONVENTIONAL ARMHOLE SHAPING, AND THE SLEEVELESS VERSION IS INCREASED AFTER THE ARMHOLE TO FORM A CAP SLEEVE.

Shown on previous page in primrose Chandos (cardigan version)
Also shown on page 31 in white Chandos (sleeveless version)

See diagram at end of pattern

SIZE cm(in)
To fit bust:

86-91(34-36)	94-99(37-39)	102-107(40-42)
Actual size:		
97(38)	104(41)	112(44)
Length from back neck:		
64(25¼)	64(25¼)	64(25¼)
Sleeve seam:		
43(17)	43(17)	44(17½)

MATERIALS
Chandos – 50g balls:

sleeveless version:		
10	11	12
cardigan version:		
12	13	14

1 pair each of 3¼mm and 4mm needles

Cable needle. Stitch holders. 10 buttons

TENSION
22sts and 28 rows = 10cm square on 4mm needles over stocking stitch. See page 9.

ABBREVIATIONS
See page 9.
c6b = place next 3sts on to cn, leave at back of work, k3, then k3 from cn

c6f = place next 3sts on to cn, leave at front of work, k3, then k3 from cn

BACK
Using 3¼mm needles cast on 91(99:107)sts and work 7cm in k1 p1 rib.
Change to 4mm needles and stocking st. Inc each end every 8th row to 107(115:123)sts.
Shape armhole:
Sleeveless version: work 8 rows. Cast on 2sts beginning next 16 rows *139(147:155)sts*
Cont until work measures 53cm.
Cardigan version: cont without shaping until work measures 38cm. Cast off 4(5:6)sts beg next 2 rows. Dec each end next 4 rows. Dec each end next and foll alt rows to 83(87:91)sts. Cont until work measures 53cm.
Shape shoulder:
Sleeveless version: cast off 7sts beg next 10 rows. Cast off 8(10:12)sts beg next 4 rows. Cast off.
Cardigan version: cast off 4(5:5)sts beg next 8 rows. Cast off 7(5:7)sts beg next 2 rows.
On 37sts work 20 rows stocking st without shaping. Cast off.

POCKETS (2)
Using 4mm needles cast on 25sts and work 30 rows stocking st. Leave on holder.

LEFT FRONT
Using 3¼mm needles cast on 41(45:49)sts and work 7cm in k1 p1 rib.
Change to 4mm needles and stocking st.
Inc 1st at side edge and dec 1st at front edge on every 8th row 8 times (64 rows), AT THE SAME TIME, place pocket lining as follows on *row 31:*
Pocket row: k8(10:12), slip next 25sts on to a

holder and in their place, k across sts of one pocket lining, k to end.

Sleeveless version: (after 64 rows)
Work 8 rows without shaping so ending at side edge. Cast on 2sts at beg of next and foll 7 alt rows, AT THE SAME TIME, dec at front edge on every 8th row from previous dec until 51(55:59)sts rem. Work without shaping until front measures 53cm, ending at side edge.
Shape shoulder: cast off 7sts at beg of next and foll 4 alt rows, and 8(10:12)sts at beg of foll 2 alt rows.

Cardigan version:
Keeping side edge straight (after 64 rows), cont to dec at front edge on every 8th row until front measures 38cm, ending at side edge.
Shape armhole: cast off 4(5:6)sts at beg of next row. Still dec at front edge on every 8th row from previous dec, dec 1 st at armhole edge on next 4 rows then next and foll 3(4:5) alt rows. Keeping armhole edge straight, dec at front edge as before until 23(25:27)sts rem. Work without shaping until front measures 53cm, ending at side edge.
Shape shoulder: cast off 4(5:5)sts at beg of next and foll 3 alt rows. Work 1 row. Cast off.

RIGHT FRONT
Work to match left front reversing shapings.

YOKE (sleeveless version only)
Using 4mm needles cast on 53sts and work in patt as follows:
Row 1: p2 k6 p2 k4 p2 k2 p2 k6 p1 k6 p2 k2 p2 k4 p2 k6 p2
Row 2: k2 p6 k2 p3 k2 p3 k2 p6 k1 p6 k2 p3 k2 p3 k2 p6 k2
Row 3: p2 k6 p2 k2 p2 k4 p2 k6 p1 k6 p2 k4 p2 k2 p2 k6 p2
Row 4: k2 p6 k2 p1 k2 p4 k3 p6 k1 p6 k3 p4 k2 p1 k2 p6 k2
Row 5: p2 c6b p4 k4 p4 c6b p1 c6f p4 k4 p4 c6f p2
Row 6: k2 p6 k3 p4 k2 p1 k2 p6 k1 p6 k2 p1 k2 p4 k3 p6 k2
These 6 rows form patt repeat. Cont in patt until work fits across shoulder shaping (approx 23:25:27cm). Note number of rows *
Next row: cast off 26sts, patt to end
Work further 18cm in half patt.
Next row: cast on 26sts, patt to end
Work * number of rows. Cast off.

SLEEVES (cardigan version only)
Using 3¼mm needles cast on 49(51:53)sts and work 7cm in k1 p1 rib.
Increase row: rib 2(3:4) *inc, rib 3* 11 times, inc, rib 2(3:4) 61(63:65)sts
Change to 4mm needles and patt as follows (right side):
Row 1: k4(5:6) p2 k6 p2 k4 p2 k2 p2 k6 p1 k6

p2 k2 p2 k4 p2 k6 p2 k4(5:6)
Row 2: p4(5:6) k2 p6 k2 p3 k2 p3 k2 p6 k1 p6 k2 p3 k2 p3 k2 p6 k2 p4(5:6)
Row 3: k4(5:6) p2 k6 p2 k2 p2 k4 p2 k6 p1 k6 p2 k4 p2 k2 p2 k6 p2 k4(5:6)
Row 4: p4(5:6) k2 p6 k2 p1 k2 p4 k3 p6 k1 p6 k3 p4 k2 p1 k2 p6 k2 p4(5:6)
Row 5: inc k3(4:5) p2 c6b p4 k4 p4 c6b p1 c6f p4 k4 p4 c6f p2 k3(4:5) inc
Row 6: p5(6:7) k2 p6 k3 p4 k2 p1 k2 p6 k1 p6 k2 p1 k2 p4 k3 p6 k2 p5(6:7)
Cont in 6 row cable patt inc each end of every foll 4th row to 103(105:107)sts working extra sts in stocking st. Cont without shaping until work measures 43(43:44)cm, ending on a wrong side row.
Shape sleevehead: cast off 4(5:6)sts beg next 2 rows. Dec each end next 4 rows. Dec each end next and every foll 4th row to 77sts. Dec each end next 6 rows. Cast off 3sts beginning next 4 rows to 53sts. On 53sts work 11½(12:12½)cm. Cast off.

BUTTONHOLE BAND
Excluding welt divide front edge into 8, marking with pins
Using 3¼mm needles pick up 18sts along welt and 16sts along each division *146sts*
Work as follows:
Row 1: rib 16, turn
Row 2: s1 rib 13 k2tog
Row 3: k2tog rib 29, turn
Row 4: s1 rib 27 k2tog
Row 5: k2tog rib 43, turn
Row 6: s1 rib 43
Row 7: p2tog rib 58, turn
Row 8: s1 rib 58
Row 9: k2tog rib 73, turn
Row 10: s1 rib 73
Row 11: p2tog rib 88, turn
Row 12: s1 rib 88
Row 13: rib 105, turn
Row 14: s1 rib 104
Row 15: rib 121, turn
Row 16: s1 rib 120
Row 17: rib across all sts *139sts*
Rows 18–19: rib
Row 20: (buttonholes) rib 4 *cast off 2 rib 18* 4 times cast off 2, rib 53
Row 21: rib 53 *cast on 2 rib18* 4 times cast on 2 rib 4
Rows 22–41: rib
Rows 42–43: as rows 20–21
Rows 44–47: rib. Cast off in rib

BUTTON BAND
Excluding welt divide front edge into 8, marking with pins as for buttonhole band.
With right side facing, pick up 16sts from shoulder to 1st marker. Work as follows:
Row 1: s1 rib 14 p1

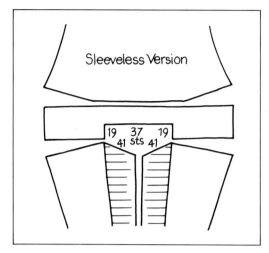

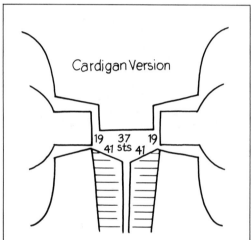

Row 2: p2tog rib 14, pick up 16sts to next marker, turn
Row 3: s1 rib 28 p2tog
Row 4: p2tog rib 28 pick up 16sts to next marker, turn
Row 5: s1 rib 42 p2tog
Row 6: rib 44 pick up 16sts to next marker, turn
Row 7: s1 rib to last 2sts k2tog
Row 8: rib 59 pick up 16sts, turn
Row 9: s1 rib to last 2sts p2tog
Row 10: rib 74 pick up 16sts, turn
Row 11: as row 7
Row 12: rib 89 pick up 16sts, turn
Row 13: s1 rib to end
Row 14: rib 105 pick up 16sts, turn
Row 15: s1 rib to end
Row 16: rib 121 pick up 18sts across welt
Rows 17–47: rib. Cast off in rib

COLLAR
Sleeveless version:
Join yoke to back and front shoulders (see diagram left).
Cardigan version:
Set in shoulders and sleeves (see diagram left).
Both versions: Using 3¼mm needles and with wrong side facing pick up 41sts across button band rib, 19sts across shoulder, 37sts back neck, 19sts across shoulder and 41 across buttonhole band rib *157sts*
Work 20 rows k1 p1 rib. Cast off in rib.

ARMBANDS (sleeveless version only)
Using 3¼mm needles, pick up 40sts across stocking st around armhole, 36sts across saddle pattern, 40sts across stocking st *116sts*
Work 5 rows in k1 p1 rib. Cast off in rib.

POCKET TRIMS
Using 3¼mm needles, work 6 rows k1 p1 rib across the 25sts from holder. Cast off in rib.

MAKING UP
Join side and sleeve seams. Slipstitch pockets into position on inside. Slipstitch pocket tops into position. Weave in any loose ends. Sew on buttons.

CARE INSTRUCTIONS
See ball tag and page 172.

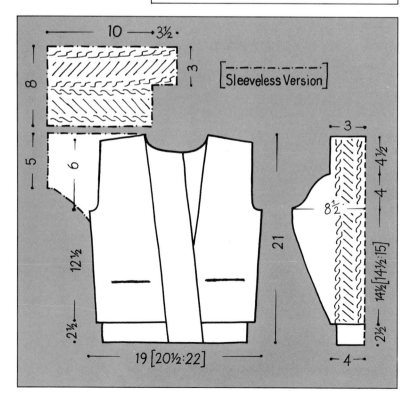

GLOUCESTER

T HE VERSATILITY OF THE BRITISH FAIRISLE TRADITION IS EXEMPLIFIED
HERE IN THE SOFT FEMININE COLOURS, BUT OF COURSE THE DESIGN
WOULD WORK EQUALLY WELL IN SHARPLY CONTRASTING BRIGHTS.

*Shown above in bluebell Chandos, with pattern
in ivory, silver and gold Dragonfly.
Also shown as children's version on page 22 in
ivory Chandos with the same highlights.*

See diagram at end of pattern

SIZE Childs cm(in)
To fit bust/chest:

1	2	3
56–61(22–24)	66–71(26–28)	76–81(30–32)
Actual size:		
64(25)	74(29)	84(33)
Length from back neck:		
41(16)	46(18)	60(23½)
Sleeve seam:		
30(12)	38(15)	43(17)

SIZE Adults cm(in)
To fit bust/chest:

4	5	6
86–91(34–36)	91–97(36–38)	102–107(40–42)
Actual size:		
94(37)	104(41)	114(45)
Length from back neck:		
60(23½)	60(23½)	60(23½)
Sleeve seam:		
43(17)	44(17½)	44(17½)

SPECIAL NOTE
The child's sizes 1 and 2 (see page 22) are
worked with a drop shoulder, the teenage/adult
sizes with a fitted sleeve. The pattern divides to
accommodate both versions at the armhole and
sleevehead shaping.

GLOUCESTER

MATERIALS
Chandos and Dragonfly – 50g balls:

1	2	3	4	5	6

Main colour M (bluebell):

6	7	9	11	12	13

Contrast A (ivory):

1	1	2	2	2	2

Contrast B (gold):

1	1	2	2	2	2

Contrast C (silver):

1	1	2	2	2	2

1 pair each of 3¼mm and 4mm needles

(Also 4½mm needles, see under 'Tension')

TENSION
22sts and 28 rows = 10cm square on 4mm needles over stocking stitch. See page 9. Note that the tension square is over stocking stitch. The tendency of the pattern to 'pull in' has been allowed for, but if your fairisle knitting comes out tight, it is recommended to knit these sections on one size bigger needle.

ABBREVIATIONS
See page 9. Where asterisks * * are not followed by one figure, repeat the instructions continuously to the end of the row.

BACK
Using 3¼mm needles and M cast on 66(76:86:90:102:114)sts and work 5(5:7:7:7:7)cm in k1 p1 rib.
Increase row:
Sizes 1(2:3) rib 10(6:2) *inc, rib 8* 5(7:9) times, inc, rib 10(6:2) *72(84:96)sts*
Sizes 4(5:6) rib 2(8:14) *inc, rib 4* 17 times, inc, rib 2(8:14) *108(120:132)sts*
Change to 4mm needles and patt as follows:
Row 1: using M knit
Row 2: using M purl
Rows 3–4: as rows 1–2
Row 5: knit 1M *2C, 4M* to last 5sts, 2C, 3M
Row 6: purl 3M *2C, 4M* to last 3sts, 2C, 1M
Rows 7–8: using M knit
Row 9: using A *k1, s1* to last 2sts, k2
Row 10: using A k2, *yf, s1, yb, k1* to end
Rows 11–12: as rows 7–8
Row 13: knit *4M, 2C* to end
Row 14: purl *2C, 4M* to end
Rows 15–20: as rows 7–12
Rows 21–22: as rows 5–6
Rows 23–26: as rows 1–4
Row 27: knit *3M, 1B* to end
Row 28: purl 2B *1M, 3B* to last 2sts, 1M, 1B
Row 29: knit *3B, 1M* to end
Row 30: purl 2M *1B, 3M* to last 2sts, 1B, 1M
Row 31: as 29
Row 32: as row 28
Row 33: as row 27
Row 34: as row 2
Rows 35–38: as rows 1–4
Row 39: knit *5C, 1M* to end

Row 40: purl 2M *3C, 3M* to last 4sts, 3C, 1M
Row 41: knit 1M *3C, 3M* to last 5sts, 3C, 2M
Row 42: purl 3M *1C, 5M* to last 3sts, 1C, 2M
Rows 43–46: as rows 39–42 using A for C
Rows 47–50: as rows 39–42 using B for C
Rows 51–54: as rows 1–4
Row 55: using A *k3, s1* to last 4sts, k4
Row 56: using A k4, *yf, s1, yb, k3* to end
Row 57: using A knit
Rows 58–59: using M knit
Rows 60–61: using C knit
Row 62: using M knit
Rows 63–64: using B as rows 55–56
These 64 rows form patt rep. Cont in patt until work measures approximately 41(46:38:38:38:38)cm, ending on row 44(60:30:30:30:30) of patt
*Sizes 1 and 2 go to * * to shape neck*
Sizes 3(4:5:6) shape armhole
Shape armhole: cast off 2(4:6:8)sts at beg next 2 rows. Dec each end of next 4 rows. Dec each end of next and foll alt rows to 80(84:86:88)sts. Cont in patt without shaping until work measures 60cm, ending with a wrong side row.
* * **Shape neck and shoulders:** (all sizes) cast off 5(6:6:6:6:6)sts, patt 19(23:20:21:21:21), cast off 24(26:28:30:32:34)sts, patt 24(29:26:27:27:27).
On 24(29:26:27:27:27)sts:
Row 1: cast off 5(6:6:6:6:6)sts, patt to end
Row 2: cast off 2sts, patt to end
Rows 3–4: as rows 1–2
Row 5: cast off 5(6:5:6:6:6)sts, patt to end
Row 6: patt
Row 7: cast off
Rejoin yarns to rem sts at neck edge and work rows 2–7 to match.

FRONT
As back until work measures 36(40:52:52:52:52)cm.
Shape neck: patt 30(35:33:34:34:34), cast off 12(14:14:16:18:20)sts, patt 30(35:33:34:34:34).
On 30(35:33:34:34:34)sts: dec neck edge on next 4(4:6:6:6:6) rows.
Dec neck edge on next and foll alt rows to 20(25:22:23:23:23)sts. Continue in patt to match back length at shoulder.
Shape shoulder:
Row 1: with wrong side facing cast off 5(6:6:6:6:6)sts, patt to end
Row 2: patt
Rows 3–4: as rows 1–2
Row 5: cast off 5(6:5:6:6:6)sts, patt to end
Row 6: as row 2
Row 7: cast off
With wrong side facing, rejoin yarns to rem sts at neck edge and work to match.

SLEEVES
Using 3¼mm needles and M cast on 38(38:46:46:50:50)sts and work 5(5:5:5:6:6)cm in k1 p1 rib.

Increase row: *rib 2, inc* to last
2(2:4:4:2:2)sts, rib to end
50(50:60:60:66:66)sts
Change to 4mm needles and patt. Starting on
row 51(51:39:39:39:39) of fairisle, inc each end
of 5th and every foll 6(4:6:6:5:5) row to
70(76:90:94:100:106)sts. Cont until work
measures approximately
31(38:43:43:44:44)cm, ending with row
64(22:30:30:30:30).
Shape sleevehead: sizes 3:4:5:6. Cast off
2(4:6:8)sts at beg of next 2 rows. Dec each end
of next and foll alt rows (except during patt
rows 55–64 when dec on rows 55, 59 and 63
only), to 66(66:68:68)sts. Cast off 8sts at beg
next 6 rows.
Cast off.
Shape sleevehead: sizes 1 and 2. Cast off 4sts
beg next 14 rows.
Cast off.

NECKBAND
Join right shoulder seam.
Using 3¼mm needles and M pick up
16(16:20:24:24:24)sts from side neck,
12(14:14:16:18:20)sts from centre front neck,
16(16:20:24:24:24)sts from side neck and
32(34:36:38:40:42)sts from back neck
76(80:90:102:106:110)sts
Work 5cm in k1 p1 rib. Cast off in rib.

MAKING UP
Join left shoulder seam and neckband. Set in
sleeves. Join side and sleeve seams. Fold
neckband in half to inside and slipstitch into
position. Weave in any loose ends.

CARE INSTRUCTIONS
See ball tag and page 172.

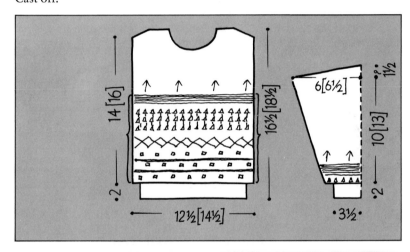

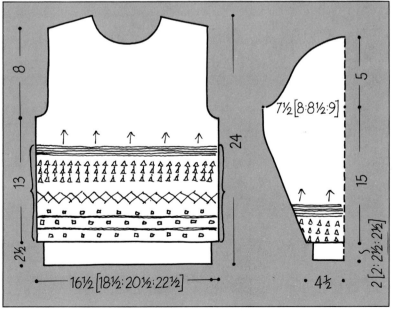

MADRIGAL

A LONG AND UNSTRUCTURED SHAPE OF CLASSIC PROPORTIONS, THIS ONE HAS THE ADDED INTEREST OF A VARIETY OF 'SAMPLER' STITCH PATTERNS; EASY AND ELEGANT, I HOPE YOU WILL AGREE.

Shown on opposite page in blossom Chandos.

See diagram at end of pattern

SIZE cm(in)
To fit bust:

86−96(34−38)	96−107(38−42)
Actual size:	
102(40)	112(44)
Length from back neck:	
67(26½)	68(27)
Sleeve seam:	
42(16½)	43(17)

MATERIALS
Chandos – 50g balls:

13	14

1 pair each of 3¼mm and 4mm needles

TENSION
22sts and 28 rows = 10cm square on 4mm needles over stocking stitch. See page 9.

ABBREVIATIONS
See page 9.
mb = make bobble by k1 p1 k1 into next st, turn, p3, turn k3, then take second and third sts over first st on right-hand needle
p2tog/p3tog = purl next 2/3sts together
[ ] = repeat enclosed instructions number of times indicated

BACK
Using 3¼mm needles cast on 107(115)sts and work 6cm in k1, p1 rib.
Change to 4mm needles and work as follows:
Increase row: k8(3) * inc, k8* 10(12) times, inc, k8(3) *118(128) sts*
Rows 1−3: knit

Row 4: p2(3) * yrn, p2tog, p2 * to last 4(5)sts yrn p2tog p2(3)
Rows 5−8: knit
Row 9: purl
Row 10: knit
Row 11: p1(6) * k1, p23 * to last 21(2)sts, k1, p20(1)
Row 12: k20(1) * p1, k23 * to last 2(7)sts, p1, k1(6)
Row 13: p0(p4, mb) * p1, k1, p1, mb, p19, mb * to last 22(3)sts, p1, k1, p1. *Size 1:* mb p18
Row 14: as row 12
Rows 15−18: as rows 11−14
Row 19: p9(14) * k1, p23 * to last 13(18)sts, k1, p12(17)
Row 20: k12(17) * p1, k23 * to last 10(15)sts, p1, k9(14)
Row 21: p7(12) * mb, p1, k1, p1, mb, p19 * to last 15(20)sts, mb, p1, k1, p1, mb p10(15)
Row 22: as row 20
Rows 23−26: as rows 19−22
Row 27: p17(22) * k1, p23 * to last 5(10)sts, k1, p4(9)
Row 28: k4(9) * p1, k23 * to last 18(23)sts, p1, k17(22)
Row 29: p15(20) * mb, p1, k1, p1, mb, p19 * to last 7(12)sts, mb, p1, k1, p1, mb, p2(7)
Row 30: as row 28
Rows 31−34: as rows 27−30
Row 35: purl
Rows 36−41: knit
Row 42: as row 4
Rows 43−46: knit
Row 47: k11(p4, k12) * p24, k12 * to last 35(40)sts p24 k11(k12, p4)
Row 48: p11(k4,p12) * k12[k1, p1, k1, into next st, p3tog] 3 times, p12 * to last 35(40)sts k12 [k1 p1 k1 into next st p3tog] 3 times, p11(p12, k4)
Row 49: as row 47
Row 50: p11(k4,p12) * k12 [p3tog, k1, p1, k1, into next st] 3 times, p12 * to last 35(40)sts

Opposite:
The stitch patterns on this design, Madrigal, go in horizontal bands, so you have only got one at a time to think about.

k12[p3tog, k1, p1, k1 into next st] 3 times,
p11(p12,k4)
Rows 51–54: as rows 47–50
Rows 55–56: as rows 47–48
Row 57–62: knit
Row 63: * k3, p2 * to last 3sts, k3
Row 64: k1, *p3, k2 * to last 2sts, p2
Row 65: k1 * p2, k3 * to last 2sts, p2
Row 66: p1 * k2,p3 * to last 2sts, k2
Row 67: p1, * k3, p2 * to last 2sts, k2
Row 68: * p3, k2 * to last 3sts, p3
Row 69: k2, * p2, k3 * to last st, p1
Row 70: * k2, p3 * to last 3sts, k2, p1
Row 71: * p2 k3 * to last 3sts, p2, k1
Row 72: p2, * k2, p3 * to last st, k1
Rows 1–72 form patt rep. Cont rep from row 1
until work measures 65(66)cm
Working in garter stitch (every row knit),
continue for a further 2cm.
Shape shoulders: cast off 12(13)sts beg next 4

rows and 12(15)sts beg foll 2 rows. Cast off.

FRONT
As back until work measures 61(62)cm.
Shape neck: patt 51(56), cast off 16sts, patt to
end. *On 51(56)sts:* dec at neck edge on next 8
rows, then next 7 alt rows *36(41)sts.*
When work measures 65(66)cm, work in garter
st for a further 2cm.
Shape shoulders as for back. Cast off.
Rejoin yarn to neck edge of remaining sts and
work other side to match.

SLEEVES
Using 3¼mm needles cast on 47sts and work
6cm in k1, p1 rib.
Change to 4mm needles and work as follows:
Increase row: inc, * p2, inc, p1, inc * 9 times, p1
66sts
Inc each end of every 5th row to 100sts, work in
body patt but noting that rows 1–56 only of
repeat are worked throughout.
Cont without shaping until work measures
42(43)cm.
Shape sleevehead: cast off 5sts beg of next 16
rows. Cast off.

NECKBAND
Join right shoulder seam. Using 3¼mm needles
and starting from top of left front pick up and
k24sts down left front 16sts across centre front,
24sts up right front and 46sts across back neck
110sts
Work 5cm in k1, p1 rib.
Cast off in rib.

MAKING UP
Join left shoulder seam. Fold neckband in half to
inside and slipstitch into position. Stitch sleeves
into position.
Weave in any loose ends. Sew side and sleeve
seams.

CARE INSTRUCTIONS
See ball tag and page 172.

BURLINGTON

T HIS DESIGN HAS A SADDLE SHOULDER PICKED OUT WITH KNITTED RIDGES WHICH ARE REPEATED ON THE PATCH POCKETS. IT IS A CLASSIC CARDIGAN SHAPE AND I WOULD SUGGEST IT IS WORN WITH SHOULDER PADS.

Shown on page 87 in walnut Chandos.

See diagram at end of pattern

SIZE cm(in)
To fit bust:

86–91(34–36)	91–96(36–38)	102–107(40–42)
Actual size:		
97(38)	104(41)	112(44)
Length from back neck:		
69(27)	69(27)	69(27)
Sleeve seam:		
41(16)	42(16½)	43(17)

MATERIALS
Chandos – 50g balls:

12	13	14
1 pair each of 3¼mm and 4mm needles		
Stitch holders. 8 buttons		

TENSION
22sts and 28 rows = 10cm square on 4mm needles over stocking stitch. See page 9.

ABBREVIATIONS
See page 9.

BACK
Using 3¼mm needles cast on 97(105:113)sts and work 5cm k1 p1 rib.
Increase row: rib 3(7:11) *inc, rib 8* 10 times, inc, rib 3(7:11) *108(116:124)sts*
Change to 4mm needles and stocking st. Cont until work measures 42cm.
Shape armhole: cast off 5(6:6)sts beg next 2 rows. Dec each end next 2(4:4) rows. Dec each end next and foll alt rows to 82(84:86)sts. Cont without shaping until work measures 61cm.
Shape shoulders: cast off 5sts beg next 4 rows.
Cast off 5(6:6)sts beg next 2 rows.
Cast off 6sts beg next 2 rows.
On 40(40:42)sts: work 18 rows without shaping. Cast off.

LEFT FRONT
Using 3¼mm needles cast on 47(51:55)sts and work 5cm in k1 p1 rib.
Increase row: rib 5(7:9) *inc, rib 8* 4 times, inc, rib 5(7:9) *52(56:60)sts*
Change to 4mm needles and stocking st and cont to 42cm.
Shape armhole: cast off 5(6:6)sts beg next row. Work 1 row. Dec armhole edge on next 2(4:4) rows. Dec armhole edge on next and foll alt rows to 39(40:41)sts. Cont to 61cm.
Shape shoulders and neck: right side facing
Row 1: cast off 5sts work to end
Row 2: cast off 10sts work to end
Row 3: as row 1
Row 4: cast off 4(4:5)sts work to end
Row 5: cast off 5(6:6)sts work to end
Row 6: cast off 4(4:4)sts work to end
Row 7: cast off

RIGHT FRONT
As left reversing all shapings.

SLEEVES
Using 3¼mm needles cast on 49(51:53)sts and work 5cm in k1 p1 rib.
Increase row: rib 0(1:2) *inc, rib 5* 8 times inc, rib 0(1:2) *58(60:62)sts*
Change to 4mm needles and patt as follows:
Rows 1–4: stocking st
Row 5: knit, inc each end
Row 6: knit
These 6 rows form patt rep. Cont in patt inc

Following pages: Burlington, on the left, and Seville, on the sofa, are both timeless classical silhouettes, but there the similarity ends. The cardigan is a simple stocking stitch design and the sweater uses a variety of stitch details. The pattern for Seville is on page 88.

each end every 5th row to 92(94:96)sts (ie rows 10, 15, 20, 25, etc).
Cont until work measures 41(42:43)cm.
Shape sleevehead: cast off 5(6:6)sts beg next 2 rows.
Dec each end next 4 rows.
Dec each end next and every foll alt row to 30(30:32)sts. Work 35(37:37) rows without shaping. Cast off.

POCKETS (2)

Using 4mm needles cast on 32sts. Work 34 rows in sleeve patt. Change to 3¼mm needles and work 6 rows in k1 p1 rib. Cast off in rib.

BUTTON BAND

Left front with right side facing. Using 3¼mm needles pick up 168sts along left front. Work 5 rows in k1 p1 rib. Cast off in rib.

BUTTONHOLE BAND

Right front with right side facing. Using 3¼mm needles pick up 168sts along right front. Work 2 rows in k1 p1 rib.
Row 3: rib 2 *yrn, dec, rib 21* 7 times, yrn, dec, rib 3. Work 2 more rows rib. Cast off in rib.

COLLAR

Using 4mm needles cast on 125(127:129)sts. Work 5cm in k1 p1 rib. Change to 3¼mm needles and work 6 rows k1 p1 rib. Cast off in rib.

MAKING UP

Join saddle shoulders as diagram page 174. Join side and sleeve seams. Set in sleevehead and stitch in position. Weave in any loose ends. Place patch pockets in centre of each front, slipstitch into position. Sew cast-off edge of collar to wrong side of neck edge. Sew on buttons.

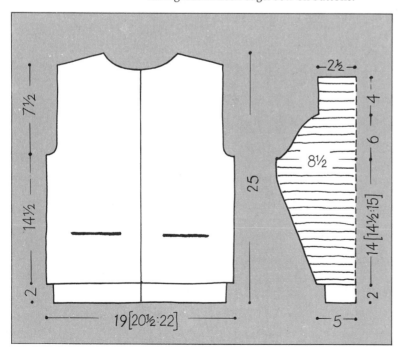

SEVILLE

T HE PLEATED SLEEVEHEAD, NEAT LITTLE COLLAR AND SLIGHTLY
SHAPED SIDE SEAMS GIVE THIS DESIGN A VERY ELEGANT SHAPE
WHICH IS ACCENTUATED BY THE CABLE PATTERN. IT WOULD ALSO
LOOK VERY CHIC WORN WITH A BELT AND A FULL SKIRT.

Shown on page 87 in silver grey Chandos.

See diagram at end of pattern

SIZE cm(in)
To fit bust:

86–91(34–36)	91–96(36–38)	102–107(40–42)
Actual size:		
94(37)	101(40)	109(43)
Length from back neck:		
59(23)	60(23½)	61(24)
Sleeve seam:		
45(17½)	45(17½)	46(18)

MATERIALS
Chandos – 50g balls:

11	12	13
1 pair each of 3¼mm and 4mm needles		
Cable needle		

TENSION
22sts and 28 rows = 10cm square on 4mm
needles over stocking stitch. See page 9.

ABBREVIATIONS
See page 9.
tw2r = twist 2sts to right by knitting into second
st and purling into back of first st, slip both sts
off needle together
tw2l = twist 2sts to left by purling into back of
second st and knitting into front of first st, slip
both sts off needle together
c2r = cable 2sts to right by passing needle in
front of first st, knit second st, knit first st and
slip both sts off needle together
c2l = cable 2sts to left by passing needle behind

first st, knit second st, knit first st, slip both sts
off needle together
[ ] = repeat instructions later in pattern as shown
c6b = place next 3sts on cn, leave at back of
work, k3 then k3 from cn
c6f = place next 3sts on cn, leave at front of
work, k3 then k3 from cn

BACK
Using 3¼mm needles cast on 91(99:107)sts and
work 7cm in k1 p1 rib.
Increase row: rib 10(14:18) *inc, rib 7* 8 times,
rib to end *99(107:115)sts*
Change to 4mm needles and patt as follows:
Row 1: *k2 p2* 4(5:6) times, c2r [p5 k2 p5] c2r
p2 *k1 p1* 5 times, p1 k9 p2 *k1 p1* 5 times,
p1 c2l rep [ ] again, c2l *p2 k2* 4(5:6) times
Row 2: *p2 k2* 4(5:6) times [*p2 k5* twice p2]
k3 *p1 k1* 4 times k2 p9 k3 *p1 k1* 4 times k2
rep [ ] again *k2 p2* 4(5:6) times
Row 3: *p2 k2* 3(4:5) times p4 c2r [p4 tw2r
tw2l p4] c2r p2 *k1 p1* 5 times p1 c6b k3 p2
k1 p1 5 times p1 c2l rep [ ] again c2l p4 *k2
p2* 3(4:5) times
Row 4: *k2 p2* 3(4:5) times k4 [p2 k4 p1 k2 p1
k4 p2] k3 *p1 k1* 4 times k2 p9 k3 *p1 k1* 4
times k2 rep [ ] again k4 *p2 k2* 3(4:5) times
Row 5: *k2 p2* 4(5:6) times c2r [p3 tw2r p2
tw2l p3] c2r p2 *k1 p1* 5 times p1 k9 p2 *k1
p1* 5 times p1 c2l rep [ ] again c2l *p2 k2*
4(5:6) times
Row 6: *p2 k2* 4(5:6) times [p2 k3 p1 k1 p2 k1
p1 k3 p2] k3 *p1 k1* 4 times k2 p9 k3 *p1 k1*
4 times k2 rep [ ] again *k2 p2* 4(5:6) times
Row 7: *p2 k2* 3(4:5) times p4 c2r [p2 *tw2r*
twice *tw2l* twice p2] c2r p2 *k1 p1* 5 times
p1 k9 p2 *k1 p1* 5 times p1 c2l rep [ ] again c2l
p4 *k2 p2* 3(4:5) times
Row 8: *k2 p2* 3(4:5) times k4 [p2 k2 p1 k1 p1

k2 p1 k1 p1 k2 p2] k3 *p1 k1* 4 times k2 p9 k3
p1 k1 4 times k2 rep [ ] again k4 *p2 k2*
3(4:5) times
Row 9: *k2 p2* 4(5:6) times c2r [p3 tw2r p2
tw2l p3] c2r p2 *k1 p1* 5 times p1 k3 c6f p2
k1 p1 5 times p1 c2l rep [ ] again c2l *p2 k2*
4(5:6) times
Row 10: *p2 k2* 4(5:6) times [p2 k3 p1 k4 p1
k3 p2] k3 *p1 k1* 4 times k2 p9 k3 *p1 k1* 4
times k2 rep [ ] again *k2 p2* 4(5:6) times
Row 11: *p2 k2* 3(4:5) times p4 c2r [p2 tw2r
p4 tw2l p2] c2r p2 *k1 p1* 5 times p1 k9 p2
k1 p1 5 times p1 c2l rep [ ] again c2l p4 *k2
p2* 3(4:5) times
Row 12: *k2 p2* 3(4:5) times k4 [p2 k2 p1 k6
p1 k2 p2] k3 *p1 k1* 4 times k2 p9 k3 *p1 k1*
4 times k2 rep [ ] again k4 *p2 k2* 3(4:5) times
These 12 rows form the patt rep. Cont in patt;
inc at each end of next and every foll 8(7:6)th
row to 111(121:131)sts, working extra sts into
edge pattern. Cont without shaping until work
measures 36(37:37)cm.
Shape armhole: cast off 3(4:5)sts beg next 2
rows. Dec each end next 6(6:8) rows. Dec each
end next and every alt row to 85(89:93)sts.
Cont without shaping until work measures
59(60:61)cm.
Shape shoulders: cast off 7sts beg next 4 rows.
Cast off 7(7:8)sts beg next 2 rows and 7(8:8)sts
beg next 2 rows. Cast off.

FRONT

As back until work measures 52(53:53)cm.
Shape neck: patt 36(37:39)sts, cast off
13(15:15), patt 36(37:39).
On 36(37:39)sts: dec neck edge on alt rows to
28(29:30)sts.
Work 1(1:3) rows or 2(2:4) rows depending on
which side of the neck you are knitting, to match
back at shoulder.
Shape shoulder: cast off 7sts beg next and foll
alt row. Work 1 row. Cast off 7(7:8)sts beg next
row. Work 1 row. Cast off.
Rejoin yarn to rem sts, work to match.

SLEEVES

Using 3¼mm needles cast on 49sts and work
7cm in k1 p1 rib.
Increase row: rib 1 * inc, rib 3* 12 times *61sts*
Change to 4mm needles and patt as follows:
Row 1: k1 p2 *k2 p2* twice c2r p2 *k1 p1* 5
times p1 k9 p2 *k1 p1* 5 times p1 c2l *p2 k2*
twice p2 k1.
Cont in patt as set, 39sts central panel, plus edge
pattern. Do not include the 'chevron' patt as on

back and front.
Inc at each end of every 4th row to
99(101:103)sts, working extra sts into edge
pattern. Cont without shaping until work
measures 45(45:46)cm.
Shape sleevehead: cast off 3(4:5)sts beg next 2
rows. Dec each end of next and following alt
row to 49sts. Cast off 6sts at beg next 4 rows.
Cast off.

COLLAR

Using 4mm needles cast on 121(127:133)sts.
Work 5cm k1 p1 rib. Change to 3¼mm needles
and work further 8 rows in rib. Cast off loosely
in rib.

MAKING UP

Sew shoulder seams together. Set in sleeve by
folding back moss st panels either side of central
cable to form a pleat on the *outside* of the sleeve,
see diagram page 174. Pin into position ensuring
sleeve fits armhole. Sew sleeves firmly into
armholes. Sew side and sleeve seams. Pin collar
into position as shown in photo and sew
carefully and firmly into position with an
invisible flat seam. Weave in any loose ends.

CARE INSTRUCTIONS

See ball tags and page 172.

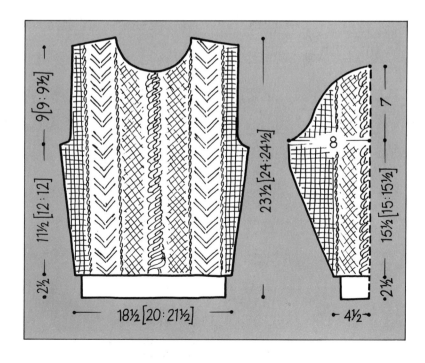

3

Back to the photography studio and handknitting updated for the 1980s. This chapter is all about bold punchy designs which won't be forgotten in a hurry, and which fully exploit all the technical possibilities of texture and colour. Once again there are some very easy ones, and also some more complex ones. You should be able to find a sweater to match your more extrovert moods on days when words like 'understated' and 'classical' do not describe what you want to wear. These sweaters are uncompromisingly loud and immodest.

ACROBAT

THIS DESIGN REQUIRES 33 COLOUR CHANGES IN EVERY SINGLE ROW. NO, I'M AFRAID THAT WAS NOT A MISPRINT. IDEALLY YOU SHOULD USE 34 SEPARATE STRANDS OR BOBBINS TO ACHIEVE THIS, BUT YOU COULD TAKE THE MAIN COLOUR ACROSS THE BACK OF THE CONTRASTS AND YOUR WIDEST LOOP WOULD BE ONLY 6 STITCHES. ALTERNATIVELY YOU COULD MAKE IT IN JUST BLACK AND WHITE; THIS WOULD BE VERY STRIKING AND THE KNITTING WOULD THEN BECOME AS EASY AS A CONVENTIONAL FAIRISLE.

Shown on page 94 in black and multi colours of Chandos.

See diagram at end of pattern

SIZE cm(in)
To fit bust/chest up to:

107(42)	

Actual size:

117(46)	

Length from back neck:

69(27)	

Sleeve seam:

51(20)	

MATERIALS
Chandos – 50g balls:

M black:		11
A poppy:	×	1
B fuchsia:	●	2
C cobalt:	/	2
D turquoise:	V	1
E teal:	⬤	1

1 pair each of 3¼mm and 4mm needles

Following page: Think twice before starting the man's sweater, Acrobat, it is not easy! The girl's sweater, Collage, also shown on page 98, is by contrast much simpler than it appears; the pattern is on page 97.

TENSION
22sts and 28 rows = 10cm square on 4mm needles over stocking stitch. See page 9.

ABBREVIATIONS
See page 9.

SPECIAL NOTE
This sweater is knitted using the block knitting technique, see page 173. Plain areas on the graph are reverse stocking stitch in black; always work changeover colour row in knit to avoid second colour loop on right side of work. Where possible knit in loose ends to avoid excess weaving in.

BACK
Using 3¼mm needles and M cast on 112sts and work 7cm in k1 p1 rib.
Increase row: rib 3, * inc, rib 7 * 13 times, inc, rib 4 *126sts*
Change to 4mm needles and follow graph (on opposite page). Cont as follows:
Using M knit. Change to moss st and continue until work measures 66cm.***
Shape shoulders and neck: cast off 9sts at beg next 2 rows. Cast off 7sts at beg next 4 rows.
Row 7: cast off 7sts, moss 11sts, cast off 44sts, moss 18sts
On 18sts: cast off 7sts, moss to end. Cast off 2sts, moss to end. Cast off. Rejoin yarn to rem sts at neck edge. Cast off 2sts, moss to end. Cast off.

FRONT
As back to 9 rows less than ***.

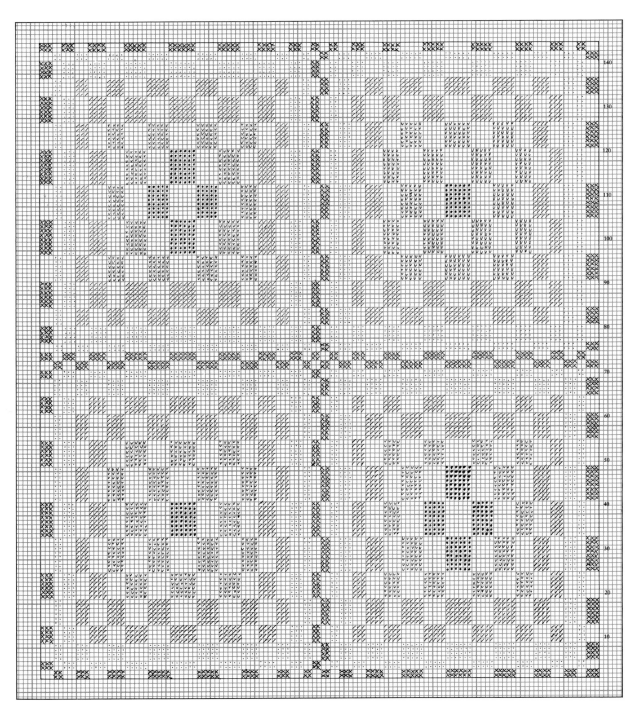

Shape neck: moss 51sts, cast off 24sts, moss 51sts.
On 51sts:
Rows 1–8: moss st, dec neck edge
Row 9: cast off 9sts, moss to last 2sts, dec
Row 10: dec, moss to end
Row 11: cast off 7sts, moss to last 2sts, dec
Row 12: as row 10
Row 13: cast off 7sts, moss to end

Row 14: moss
Rows 15–16: as rows 13–14. Cast off.
Rejoin yarn to rem sts and work to match.

SLEEVES
Using 3¼mm needles and M cast on 48sts and
work 6cm k1 p1 rib.
Increase row: rib 2, * inc, rib 3 * 11 times, inc,
rib 1 *60sts*

ACROBAT

Change to 4mm needles and work in basket stitch pattern as follows:

Row 1: knit
Row 2: k3, * p6, k6 * 4 times, p6, k3
Row 3: p3, * k6, p6 * 4 times, k6, p3
Row 4: as row 2
Row 5: inc, p2, * k6, p6 * 4 times, k6, p2, inc

Row 6: k4, * p6, k6 * 4 times, p6, k4
Row 7: p4, * k6, p6 * 4 times, k6, p4
Row 8: as row 6
Row 9: inc, knit to last st, inc
Row 10: p5, * k6, p6 * 4 times, k6, p5
Row 11: k5, * p6, k6 * 4 times, p6, k5
Row 12: as row 10
Row 13: inc, k4, * p6, k6 * 4 times, p6, k4, inc
Row 14: * p6, k6 * 5 times, p6
Row 15: * k6, p6 * 5 times, k6
Row 16: as row 14

These 16 rows form patt rep. Cont in patt, inc each end of next and every foll 4th row until work measures approx 51cm, ending with row 8 or 16. Cast off loosely.

NECKBAND
Join right shoulder. Using 3¼mm needles and M pick up 18sts from side front neck, 24sts from centre front, 18sts from side neck and 52sts from back neck *112sts*
Work 11 rows in k1 p1 rib.
Cast off loosely in rib.

MAKING UP
Join left shoulder seam and neckband. Fold neckband in half to inside and slipstitch into position. Set in sleeves and stitch into position. Join side and sleeve seams. Weave in any loose ends.

CARE INSTRUCTIONS
See ball tag and page 172.

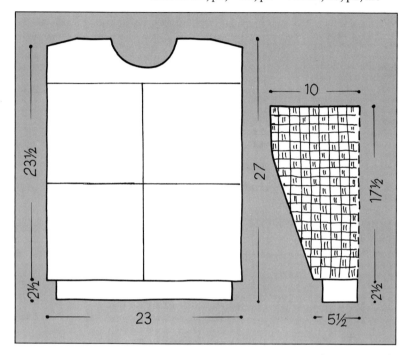

COLLAGE

THE IMMEDIATE REACTION TO THIS DESIGN IS THAT IT IS IMPOSSIBLY DIFFICULT. BUT WHEN YOU REALISE YOU DON'T HAVE A SINGLE MID-ROW COLOUR CHANGE THROUGHOUT (THE COLOUR PATTERNS ARE ALL MADE WITH SLIPPED STITCHES) IT BECOMES CONSIDERABLY EASIER. EACH SQUARE IS PICKED UP FROM THE PREVIOUS ONE AND KNITTED SEPARATELY, ONE AT A TIME.

Shown on page 98 in monochrome Chandos colours.
Also shown on page 94 in bright Chandos colours.

See diagram at end of pattern

SIZE cm(in)
To fit bust:

	81–97(32–38)

Actual size:

	101(40)

Length from back neck:

	68(27)

Sleeve seam:

	46(18)

MATERIALS
Chandos – 50g balls:

MONOCHROME VERSION

silver	5
flannel	4
white	4
black	4

BRIGHT VERSION

fuchsia	4
turquoise	4
poppy	3
teal	3
cobalt	3

1 pair each of 3¼mm and 4mm needles

TENSION
22sts and 28 rows = 10cm square on 4mm needles over stocking stitch. See page 9.

SPECIAL NOTE
The success of this garment depends upon careful knitting. The following may help with this. Each edge stitch must be worked (not slipped at beginning of row and knitted on return). Picking up must be even and rough guides are given in pattern. DO NOT break yarns until section is completed, carry colours up side of work. A, B, C refer to sequence of colours in section (ie A – 1st, B – 2nd, C – 3rd). COLOUR COMBINATIONS ARE BELOW.

COLOUR COMBINATIONS FOR MONOCHROME VERSION

1a: A = white	B = silver	C = black
1b: A = flannel	B = black	C = silver
2a: A = silver	B = flannel	C = black
2b: A = black	B = white	C = silver
2c: A = silver	B = black	C = white
3a: A = black	B = silver	C = flannel
3b: as 1a		
4a: as 2c		
4b: as 2a		
4c: as 2b		
5a: A = silver	B = black	C = white
5b: A = black	B = silver	C = flannel

Yoke colours

A = silver	Welts (front and back): black
B = black	Neckband: silver
C = flannel	
D = white	

Sleeve 1 cuff: flannel Part 1: as 1b Part 2: as 2b
Sleeve 2 cuff: white Part 1: as 1a Part 2: as 2c

Following page: This design, Collage, is also shown on page 94 in a mixture of bright colours. You will be surprised at the relative simplicity of the pattern.

COLOUR COMBINATIONS FOR BRIGHT VERSION

1a: A = teal   B = turquoise   C = fuchsia
1b: A = poppy   B = fuchsia   C = turquoise
2a: A = poppy   B = cobalt   C = turquoise
2b: A = cobalt   B = teal   C = fuchsia
2c: A = fuchsia   B = teal   C = poppy
3a: A = turquoise B = cobalt   C = fuchsia
3b: A = teal   B = poppy   C = cobalt
4a: as 2b
4b: as 2c
4c: as 2a
5a: as 2a
5b: A = turquoise B = fuchsia   C = cobalt

Yoke colours
A = teal   Welts (front and back):
B = poppy   turquoise
C = turquoise   Neckband: fuchsia
D = fuchsia

Sleeve 1 cuff: teal   Part 1: as 1b   Part 2: as 2b
Sleeve 2 cuff: cobalt   Part 1: as 1a   Part 2: as 2a

ABBREVIATIONS

See page 9.
k2togb/p2togb = knit/purl next 2sts tog through backs of sts
In the following instructions the figures in the first set of brackets refer to row numbers; those in the second set refer to knitting instructions. For example, for row 37 using A **k25**, s1, turn. See bold figures below.

BACK

With 3¼mm needles cast on 90sts and work 7cm in k1 p1 rib. Change to 4mm needles. Purl 1 row.

Section 1
Base Triangle 1a
Rows 1(13:25:37:49:61): using A k1(9:17:25:33:41)s1, turn
Rows 2(14:26:38:50:62): using A p2(10:18:26:34:42) turn
Rows 3(15:27:39:51:63): using A k3(11:19:27:35:43) s1, turn
Rows 4(16:28:40:52:64): using A p4(12:20:28:36:44) turn
Rows 5(17:29:41:53): using B k5(13:21:29:37) turn
Rows 6(18:30:42:54): using B k5(13:21:29:37) turn
Rows 7(19:31:43:55): using C k2 *s1, k1* 2(6:10:14:18) times, turn
Rows 8(20:32:44:56): using C *k1, yf, s1, yb* twice (6:10:14:18) times, k2, turn
Rows 9(21:33:45:57): using B k7(15:23:31:39) turn
Rows 10(22:34:46:58): using B k7(15:23:31:39) turn
Rows 11(23:35:47:59): using A *k1 s1* 4(8:12:16:20) times, turn
Rows 12(24:36:48:60): using A p8(16:24:32:40) turn
Row 65: using A k21, k2togb, k22

Base Triangle 1b
Work rows 1–65 again using new colour combination.

Section 2
Side Triangle 2a
Row 1: (wrong side facing and using A) p1, s1, turn
Row 2: k1, inc, turn
Row 3: inc, p1, p2tog, s1, turn
Row 4: using B k2tog, yf, s1, yb, k1, inc, turn
Row 5: using B p5, s1, turn
Row 6: using A k2tog, k1, yf, s1, yb, k1, inc, turn
Row 7: using A p6, s1, turn
Row 8: using C k2tog, k2, s1, k1, inc, turn
Row 9: using C *p3, s1* twice, turn
Row 10: using C k2tog, k2, s1, k2, inc, turn
Row 11: using C p1 *p3, s1* twice, turn
Rows 12(22:32:42:52:62): using A k2tog, k6(12:18:24:30:36) inc, turn
Rows 13(23:33:43:53:63): using A inc, p7(13:19:25:31:37) p2tog, s1, turn
Rows 14(24:34:44:54:64): using B k2tog, *yf, s1, yb, k1* 4(7:10:13:16:19) times, inc, turn
Rows 15(25:35:45:55:65): using B p11(17:23:29:35:41) s1, turn
Rows 16(26:36:46:56:66): using A k2tog, *k1, yf, s1, yb* 4(7:10:13:16:19) times, k1, inc, turn
Rows 17(27:37:47:57:67): using A p12(18:24:30:36:42) s1, turn
Rows 18(38:58): using C k2tog, k2 *s1, k3* 2(5:8) times, inc, turn
Rows 19(39:59): using C p5, s1 *p3, s1* 2(5:8) times, turn
Rows 20(40:60): using C k2tog, k2 *s1, k3* 2(5:8) times, k1, inc, turn
Rows 21(41:61): using C p6, s1 *p3, s1* 2(5:8) times, turn
Rows 28(48:68): using C k2tog, k2 *s1, k3* 3(6:9) times, s1, k1, inc, turn
Rows 29(49:69): using C *p3, s1* 5(8:11) times, turn
Rows 30(50:70): using C k2tog, k2 * s1, k3* 3(6:9) times, s1, k2, inc, turn
Rows 31(51:71): using C p1 *p3, s1* 5(8:11) times, turn
Row 72: using A k2tog, k43, turn
Row 73: using A p44
Centre Diamond 2b (wrong side facing and using A)
Pick up 45sts p-wise along base triangle 1b (8sts per patt rep + 5sts); s1 from base triangle 1a, turn
Row 1: k2tog, k44, turn
Row 2: p44, p2tog, s1, turn
Row 3: using B k2tog *yf, s1, yb, k1* 22 times, turn
Row 4: using B p45, s1, turn
Row 5: using A k2tog *k1, yf, s1, yb* 21 times, k2, turn
Row 6: using A p45, s1, turn
Row 7: using C k2tog, k2 * s1, k3* 10 times, s1, k1, turn
Row 8: using C p1 *s1, p3* 11 times, s1, turn
Rows 9–10: as rows 7–8

Rows 11–71: repeat rows 1–10 6 more times then row 1 again
Row 72: using A *p21, p2tog* twice
Side Triangle 2c (wrong side facing and using A)
Pick up 45sts along base triangle 1a (8sts per patt rep + 5sts)
Rows 1(11:21:31:41:51:61): using A k2tog k43(37:31:25:19:13:7) turn
Rows 2(12:22:32:42:52:62): using A p42(36:30:24:18:12:6) p2tog, turn
Rows 3(13:23:33:43:53:63): using B k2tog *k1, yf, s1, yb* 20(17:14:11:8:5:2) times, k1, turn
Rows 4(14:24:34:44:54:64): using B p42(36:30:24:18:12:6) turn
Rows 5(15:25:35:45:55:65): using A k2tog *k1, yf, s1, yb* 19(16:13:10:7:4:1) times, k2, turn
Rows 6(16:26:36:46:56:66): using A p41(35:29:23:17:11:5) turn
Rows 7(27:47): using C k2tog, k1 *s1, k3* 9(6:3) times, s1, k1, turn
Rows 8(28:48): using C p1 *s1, p3* 9(6:3) times, s1, p2, turn
Rows 9(29:49): using C k2tog *s1, k3* 9(6:3) times, s1, k1, turn
Rows 10(30:50): using C p1 *s1, p3* 9(6:3) times, s1, p1, turn
Rows 17(37:57): using C k2tog *k3, s1* 8(5:2) times, k1, turn
Rows 18(38:58): using C p1 *s1, p3* 8(5:2) times, p1, turn
Rows 19(39:59): using C k2tog, k2 *s1, k3* 7(4:1) times, s1, k1, turn
Rows 20(40:60): using C p1 *s1, p3* 8(5:2) times, turn
Row 67: using C k2tog, k1, s1, k1, turn
Row 68: using C p1, s1, p2, turn
Row 69: using C k2tog, s1, k1, turn
Row 70: using C p1, s1, p1, turn
Row 71: using A k2tog, k1, turn
Row 72: using A p2tog

Section 3
Diamond 3a (right side facing and using A)
k1 from 2c and pick up 44sts along straight edge of 2c (6sts per patt rep + 2sts): s1 from 2b, turn
Row 1: p2togb, p44, turn
Row 2: k44, k2togb, s1, turn
Row 3: as row 1
Row 4: using B k44, k2togb, turn
Row 5: using B k45, turn
Row 6: using C *k1, s1* 22 times, k2togb, turn
Row 7: using C *k1, yf, s1, yb* 22 times, k1, turn
Rows 8–9: as rows 4–5
Row 10: using A k1, *k1, s1* 21 times, k1, k2togb, turn
Row 11: using A p45, turn
Row 12: using A k44, k2togb, s1, turn
Rows 13–60: work rows 1–12 4 more times
Rows 61–63: as rows 1–3
Row 64: using A *k21, k2togb* twice
Diamond 3b (right side facing and using A)
Pick up 45sts along the edge of 2b (6sts per patt rep + 3sts) s1 from 2a, turn

Repeat rows 1–64 from 3a noting colour changes.

Section 4
As second section noting different colour combinations.

Section 5
NB When casting off, the st on the RHS needle is included in the instructions.
Top Triangle 5a (right side facing and using A)
k1 from 4c: pick up 44sts along 4c (6sts per patt rep + 2sts) s1 from 4b, turn
Rows 1(13:25:37:49): using A p2togb, p44(36:28:20:12) turn
Rows 2(14:26:38:50): using A cast off 2sts k42(34:26:18:10) k2togb, s1, turn
Rows 3(15:27:39:51): using A p2togb, p42(34:26:18:10) turn
Rows 4(16:28:40:52): using B cast off 1st k41(33:25:17:9): k2togb, turn
Rows 5(17:29:41:53): using B k42(34:26:18:10) turn
Rows 6(18:30:42:54): using C cast off 1st *s1, k1* 19(15:11:7:3) times, s1, k2togb, turn
Rows 7(19:31:43:55): using C *k1, yf, s1, yb* 20(16:12:8:4) times, k1, turn
Rows 8(20:32:44:56): using B cast off 1st k39(31:23:15:7) k2togb, turn
Rows 9(21:33:45:57): using B k40(32:24:16:8) turn
Rows 10(22:34:46:58): using A cast off 1st *k1, s1* 18(14:10:6:2) times, k1, k2togb, turn
Rows 11(23:35:47:59): using A p39(31:23:15:7) turn
Rows 12(24:36:48:60): using A cast off 2sts k36(28:20:12:4) k2togb, s1, turn
Row 61: using A p2togb, p4, turn
Row 62: using A cast off 2sts, k2, k2togb, s1, turn
Row 63: using A p2togb, p2tog, turn
Row 64: using A k3togb
Top Triangle 5b (right side facing and using A)
k1 from 5a: pick up 44sts along 4b (6sts per patt rep + 2sts) s1 from 4a, turn
Repeat rows 1–64 as 5a. Fasten off. #

BACK YOKE
† Using 4mm needles and A pick up 119sts across top triangles (11sts per patt rep + 4sts and centre st). Work as follows:
Row 1: using A purl
Row 2: using B *k3, s1* to last 3sts, k3
Row 3: using B *p3, s1* to last 3sts, p3
Rows 4–5: as rows 2–3 †
Row 6: using A knit
Row 7: using C purl
Rows 8–11: using D as rows 2–5
Row 12: using C knit
Row 13: using B purl
Rows 14–17: using A as rows 2–5
Row 18: using B knit
Row 19: using D purl
Rows 20–23: using C as rows 2–5
Row 24: using D knit
Row 25: as row 1

Row 26: using B *k3, s1* 11 times, k1, cast off 29sts, k1 *s1, k3* 11 times
Row 27: patt as set
Row 28: cast off 5sts, patt to end
Rows 29–30: as rows 27–28. Cast off. Rejoin yarns to rem sts and work to match.

FRONT

Work as for back to #. Work † to † as back yoke. Keeping patts and colours as back yoke shape neck as follows:
Patt 50, cast off 19sts, patt 50. Cast off 2sts at neck edge on next 2 alt rows. Dec neck edge on next 4 rows. Dec neck edge on next and foll alt rows to 35sts. Work to match back. Cast off. Rejoin yarns to rem sts and work to match.

SLEEVE 1

Using 3¼mm needles cast on 49sts and work 7cm in k1 p1 rib.
Increase row: rib 1, *inc, rib 3* to end *61sts*
Change to 4mm needles and patt as follows.
Part 1
Rows 1–4: using A stocking st. Inc each end row 4

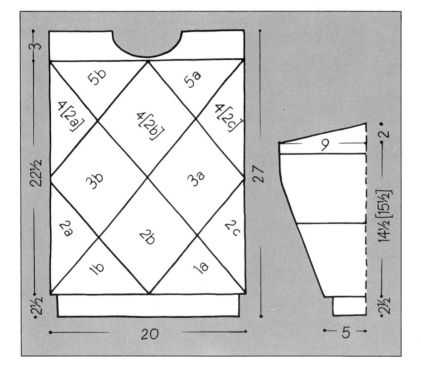

Rows 5–6: using B knit
Row 7: using C *k1, s1* to last st, k1
Row 8: using C inc, *yf, s1, yb, k1* to end, inc into last st
Rows 9–10: using B knit
Row 11: using A *k1, s1* to last st, k1
Row 12: using A purl, inc at each end
Rows 1–12 form the patt rep. Cont keeping patt correct inc each end every 4th row until 91sts (5 repeats)
Part 2
Change the colour combination.
Rows 1–2: using A stocking
Row 3: using B *k1, yf, s1, yb* to last st, k1
Row 4: using B purl, inc at each end
Row 5: using A *k1, yf, s1, yb* to last st, k1
Row 6: using A purl
Row 7: using C k2 *s1, k3* to last 3sts, s1, k2
Row 8: using C inc, p1 *s1, p3* to last 3sts, s1, p1, inc
Row 9: using C *k3, s1* to last 3sts, k3
Row 10: using C *p3, s1* to last 3sts, p3
Rows 1–10 form patt rep. Cont keeping patt correct, inc every 4th row to 111sts. Cont without shaping until work measures 42cm. Change to teal or silver depending on version, knit 1 row. Working colours and patt as for back yoke (NB match slip st to slip st in rows 7–10 of previous patt). Work 6 rows.
Rows 7–24: keeping patt and colours correct cast off 4sts beg each row.
Cast off.

SLEEVE 2

Shapings and stitches as Sleeve 1 noting different colour combinations.

NECKBAND

Join right shoulder seam. Using 3¼mm needles pick up 22sts from side front neck, 19sts from centre front neck, 22sts from side front neck and 51sts from back neck *114sts*
Work 7cm in k1 p1 rib. Cast off loosely in rib.

MAKING UP

Join left shoulder seam and neckband. Fold neckband in half to inside and slipstitch into position. Set in sleeves. Join side and sleeve seams. Weave in any loose ends.

CARE INSTRUCTIONS

See ball tag and page 172.

HELTER SKELTER

YOU SAW THIS DESIGN ON THE INSIDE FRONT COVER, AND HERE IT IS AGAIN IN MUCH BRIGHTER COLOURS LOOKING VERY DIFFERENT. TO INCREASE THE IMPACT OF THE POPPY CABLES I HAVE KNITTED THE SECTIONS WITH THIN BLACK STRIPES IN COBALT OR TEAL INSTEAD OF POPPY AS IT SAYS IN THE PATTERN. MAKE YOUR OWN CHOICE.

Shown above in bright Chandos colours and on title page in pastel Chandos colours.

See diagram at end of pattern

SIZE cm(in)
To fit bust:

86–91(34–36)	97–102(38–40)
Actual size:	
97(38)	104(41)
Length from back neck:	
58(23)	58(23)
Sleeve seam:	
42(16½)	43(17)

MATERIALS
Chandos – 50g balls:

A cobalt	(eau-de-nil)	(walnut):
6		7
B turquoise	(primrose)	(blossom):
2		2
C poppy	(white)	(white):
2		2
D black	(silver)	(silver):
2		2
E teal	(bluebell)	(primrose):
2		2

1 pair each of 3¼mm and 4mm needles

Cable needle. 3 large buttons or
8 small buttons. 20cm Velcro for fastening

TENSION
22sts and 28 rows = 10cm square on 4mm
needles over stocking stitch. See page 9.

ABBREVIATIONS
See page 9 and on chart.

BACK
Using 3¼mm needles and A cast on 103(111)sts
and work 10cm in kl pl rib.
Change to 4mm needles and stocking stitch,
starting with a purl row.
Work 67 rows.
Cast off 3sts at beg next 2 rows and continue as
follows:
Rows 1–2: using C stocking stitch
Row 3: using D knit
Row 4: using D *kl pl* to last st, kl.
Rows 5–6: as 1–2
Row 7: using D, knit, inc at both ends
Row 8: as 4
Rows 9–16: as 1–8
Rows 17–20: as 1–4
Rows 21–24: using B, stocking stitch, inc at
each end row 23
Rows 25–26: as 3–4
Rows 27–38: using B, stocking stitch, inc at
each end row 31
Rows 39–48: using A, stocking st, inc at each
end rows 39 and 47
Row 49: as row 3
Rows 50–51: using D, moss st
Rows 52–60: using E, stocking st, inc at each
end row 55
Row 61: as row 3
Rows 62–63: using D moss st, inc at each end
row 63 *113(121)sts*
Rows 64–68: using A, stocking st

Shape shoulders: using A cast off 5(6)sts next 6
rows. Cast off 12sts beg next 4 rows. Cast off.

SLEEVES
Using 3¼mm needles and A cast on 47sts. Work
6cm in k1 p1 rib.
Increase row: rib 2 *inc, rib 5* 7 times, inc,
rib 2 *55sts*
Change to 4mm needles and stocking st. Inc at
each end of every foll 4th row to 97sts, AT THE
SAME TIME when the work measures
15(16)cm work colour sequence (rows 1–63) as
for back. Cont in stocking st using A until work
measures 42(43)cm. Cast off.

LEFT FRONT
Wind off 3 small balls of C. These will be used
as the 'strands' of the cable pattern.
**NB You can carry yarn across the back of '1
strand' of cable but not '2 strands' of cable. Twist
yarns when changing colour to prevent holes.
When using D, the first row is always stocking
st (k or p) and thereafter in moss st as on back,
to avoid loops forming on the colour change.**
Using 3¼mm needles and A cast on 63(67)sts
and work 10cm in k1 p1 rib.
Increase row: rib 21(25) *inc, rib 2* 5 times, rib
27 *68(72)sts*
Change to 4mm needles. Work wrong side row
as follows: place next 15sts on holder (front
band) using B p13, C p3, B p7, C p6 ('2
strands'), E p24(28). Now follow the graph
opposite from row 2.

RIGHT FRONT
Rib as for left front.
Increase row: rib 27, *inc, rib 2* five times, rib
21(25) *68(72)sts*
Change to 4mm needles. Work wrong side row
as follows: using A p24(28), C p6 ('2 strands'),
C p7, C p3('1 strand'), C pl3. Leave last 15sts on
holder. Now follow the graph from row 2.

BUTTON BAND (right front)
Place 15sts from holder of right front on 4mm
needles. Right side facing, using C, knit 1 row.
Change to moss st and work 65 rows.
Next row: cast off 7sts and moss to end. Cont in
moss st decreasing at neck edge of every
following 5th row to 1st. Fasten off.

BUTTON BAND (left front)
Work as for right front, reversing shapings.

COLLAR
Carefully join front bands to fronts. Join
shoulder seams. Using 4mm needles and A and
with wrong side facing, pick up 59sts evenly
along left V shaping, 36sts across back neck and
59sts along right V shaping. Work 15 rows moss
st. Change to C and knit 1 row. Change to moss
st and work 5 rows. Cast off in moss.

MAKING UP
Join side seams. Join sleeve seams leaving 1cm
open at armhole edge. Ease sleeves into armhole
stitching open 1cm across armhole cast off.

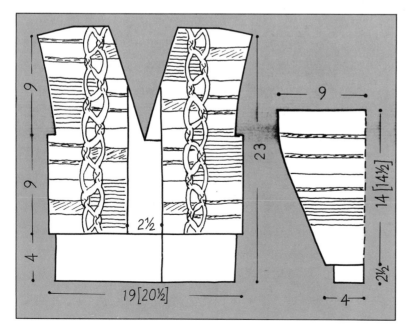

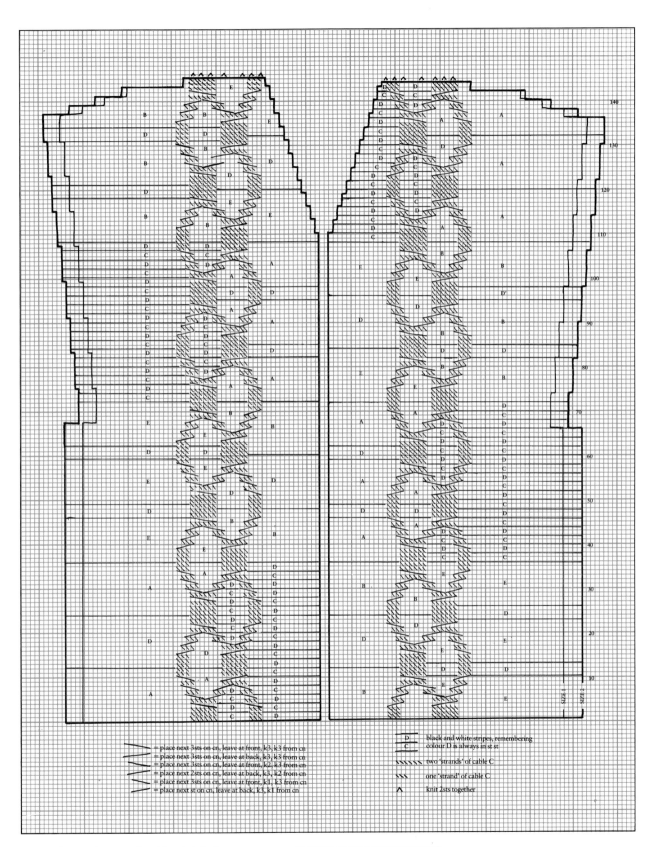

= place next 3sts on cn, leave at front, k3, k3 from cn
= place next 3sts on cn, leave at back, k3, k3 from cn
= place next 3sts on cn, leave at front, k2, k3 from cn
= place next 2sts on cn, leave at back, k3, k2 from cn
= place next 3sts on cn, leave at front, k1, k3 from cn
= place next st on cn, leave at back, k3, k1 from cn

D
C = black and white stripes, remembering colour D is always in st st

= two 'strands' of cable C

= one 'strand' of cable C

Λ = knit 2sts together

Sew Velcro strip to underside of right button band and top side of left band, on the edge nearest the fastening. Sew on buttons to right-hand band.

CARE INSTRUCTIONS
See ball tag and page 172.

GERONIMO

THERE IS ANOTHER WAY OF ARRANGING THE COLOURS HERE, WHICH I PARTICULARLY RECOMMEND: TRY KNITTING THE BLACK AND WHITE STRIPES IN FUCHSIA AND POPPY, OR TURQUOISE AND COBALT, LIKE THE LITTLE TRIANGLES, AND THEN DO THE LITTLE TRIANGLES ALL IN BLACK AND WHITE STRIPES.

Shown on opposite page in black and white and multi-colours of Chandos.

See diagram at end of pattern

SIZE cm(in)
To fit bust:

84–89(33–35)	91–96(36–38)	99–104(39–41)

Actual size:

94(37)	102(40)	107(43)

Length from back neck:

64(25)	64(25)	64(25)

Sleeve seam:

42(16½)	43(17)	44(17½)

MATERIALS
Chandos – 50g balls:

A white:

5	6	6

B black:

6	7	7

C cobalt:

1	1	1

D turquoise:

1	1	1

E fuchsia:

1	1	1

F poppy:

1	1	1

1 pair each of 3¼mm and 4mm needles

TENSION
22sts and 28 rows = 10cm square on 4mm needles over stocking stitch. See page 9.

ABBREVIATIONS
See page 9.

BACK
Using 3¼mm needles and B cast on 93(99:107)sts and work 7cm in k1 p1 rib.
Increase row: rib 4(1:5), *inc, rib 5* 14(16:16) times, inc, rib 4(1:5) *108(116:124)sts*
Change to 4mm needles and work as follows:
Rows 1–10: Using B stocking st
Row 11: Using A knit
Rows 12–20: Using A moss st
Rows 1–20 form patt rep. Cont to end of row 120
Inc each end of next and every foll 8th row to 120(128:136)sts. Cont to end of row 180.
Shape neck:
Row 181: k48(52:56), cast off 24sts, k48(52:56)
Row 182: on 48(52:56)sts, patt
Row 183: cast off 5sts, patt to end
Rows 184–187: as rows 182–183
Row 188: cast off
Rejoin yarn to rem sts at neck edge and work to match.

FRONT
Rib as for back.
Change to 4mm needles and using block knitting technique follow graph I. See opposite page.

LEFT SLEEVE
Using 3¼mm needles and B cast on 47sts and work 6(7:8)cm in k1 p1 rib.
Increase row: rib 1, *inc, rib 3* 11 times, inc, rib 1 *59sts*
Change to 4mm needles and graph II. See page 108 and work rows 1–60.

Opposite:
There is a simple device in this design, Geronimo, where the stripes are split down the middle to emphasize the geometric effect.

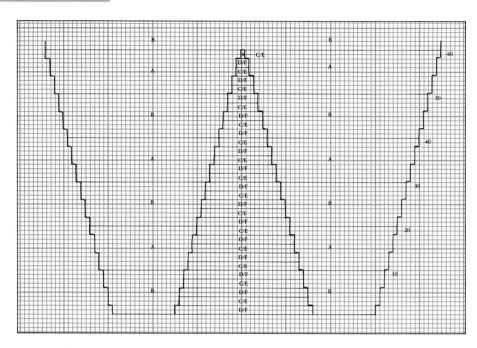

Rows 61–110: cont in black and white stripe patt inc every 4th row to 109sts. Cast off.

RIGHT SLEEVE

Rib as for left sleeve.
Change to 4mm needles and work 50 rows in black and white stripes (as back), AT THE SAME TIME inc each end of row 3 and every foll 4th row.

Row 51: using A inc, k42, using C k1, using A k42, inc.

Using row 51 to position coloured triangle, turn left sleeve graph upside down for triangle shapings, at the same time cont black and white stripes and inc as for left sleeve.
Cast off.

NECKBAND

Join right shoulder seam.
Using 3¼mm needles and B pick up 25sts from side neck, 14sts from centre front neck, 25sts from side neck and 58sts from back neck.
122sts
Work 5cm in k1 p1 rib.
Cast off in rib.

MAKING UP

Join left shoulder seam and neckband. Fold neckband in half to inside and slipstitch into position. Set in sleeves and stitch into position. Join side and sleeve seams. Weave in any loose ends.

CARE INSTRUCTIONS

See ball tag and page 172.

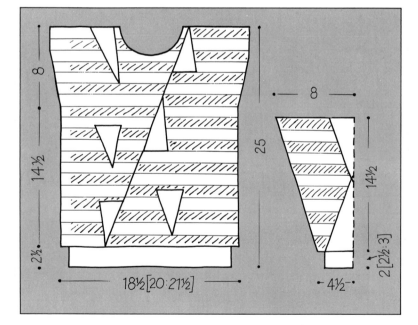

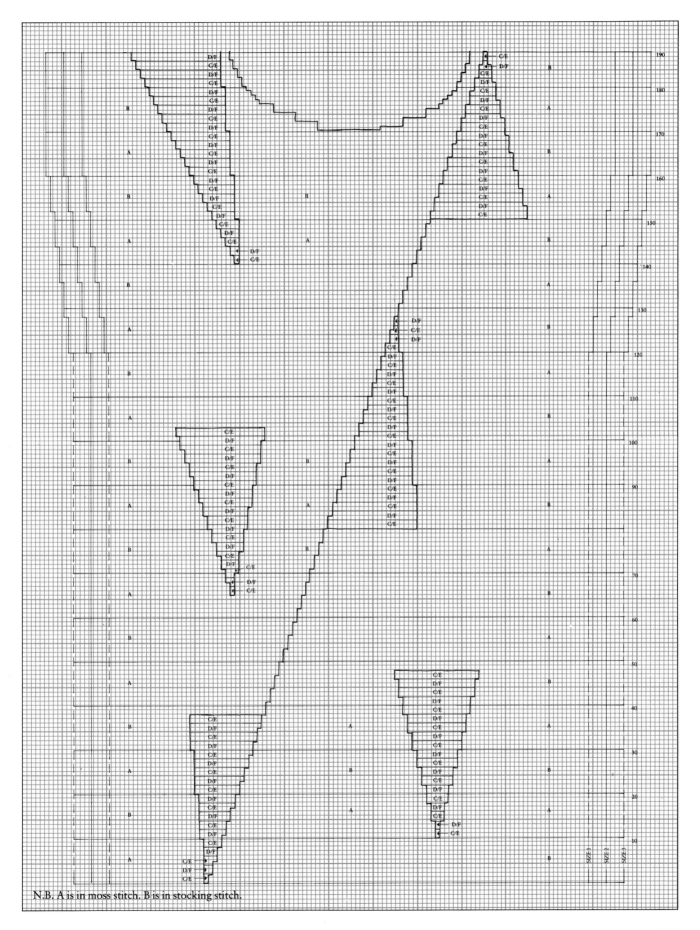

N.B. A is in moss stitch. B is in stocking stitch.

109

BRITANNIA

YOU WILL NOTICE THAT THE OUTER HEBRIDES ARE NOT KNITTED IN THE PHOTOGRAPH, BUT THEY DO APPEAR ON THE GRAPH. THIS IS BECAUSE I WAS THINKING OF SIMPLICITY OF KNITTING AT THE DESIGN STAGE, BUT AFTERWARDS THIS SEEMED A BIT HARD ON THE ISLANDERS THEMSELVES. THE ORKNEYS HAVE DISAPPEARED INTO THE NECKLINE, I'M AFRAID, AND IRELAND ... WELL, WHOEVER THOUGHT KNITWEAR DESIGN COULD GET INTO POLITICS? SERIOUSLY, IT WOULD GET CUT IN HALF BY THE SIDE SEAM, AND IT'S ALL OR NOTHING, REALLY, ISN'T IT?

Shown opposite in black and white Chandos.

See diagram at end of pattern

SIZE cm(in)
To fit bust:

81–86(32–34)	86–91(34–36)	91–96(36–38)

Actual size:

89(35)	96(38)	104(41)

Length from back neck:

80(31½)	80(31½)	80(31½)

Sleeve seam:

44(17½)	44(17½)	44(17½)

MATERIALS
Chandos – 50g balls:

M black:

10	11	12

C white:

2	2	2

1 pair each of 3¼mm, 3¾mm and 4mm needles

TENSION
22sts and 28 rows = 10cm square on 4mm needles over stocking stitch. See page 9.

ABBREVIATIONS
See page 9.

FRONT
Using 3¼mm needles and M cast on 88(96:104)sts and work 5cm in k2 p2 rib. (Every row *k2 p2*.)
Increase row: rib 3(7:11), *inc, rib 8* 9 times, inc, rib 3(7:11) *98(106:114)sts*
Change to 4mm needles and stocking st. Work from graph (see page 113). When work measures 58cm, shape armhole as follows, noting that you must have no more than 34 rows left to complete from the graph. If your tension is slightly tight and at 58cm you have not reached row 144 (marked *), continue without shaping until * in order to complete the graph before neck shaping commences. If your tension is slightly loose, at 58cm you will already be beyond *, in which case commence armhole and complete the graph.
Shape armhole at * or after.
Cast off 2(3:5)sts beg next 2 rows. Dec each end next 2(4:4) rows. Dec each end next and foll alt rows to 78(80:82)sts. Cont until work measures 70cm.
Shape neck: k29(30:31), cast off 20sts, k29(30:31).
On 29(30:31)sts:
Row 1: patt
Row 2: cast off 5sts, work to end
Row 3: patt
Row 4: cast off 2sts, patt to end
Row 5: patt
Rows 6–15: as rows 4–5 5 times
Row 16: dec patt to end
Row 17: patt
Rows 18–23: as rows 16–17 three times
Rows 24–29: patt
Cast off

BRITANNIA

Rejoin yarns to rem sts at neck edge and work rows 2–29. Cast off.

BACK
Work as front omitting motif.

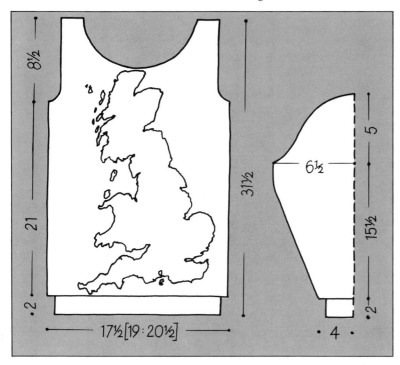

SLEEVES
Using 3¼mm needles and M cast on 40(42:44)sts and work 5cm in k2 p2 rib.
Increase row: rib 0(2:4) *inc, rib 3* to end *50(52:54)sts*
Change to 4mm needles and stocking stitch. Inc each end every 8th row to 70(72:74)sts. Cont without shaping until work measures 44cm.
Shape sleevehead: cast off 2sts beg next 4 rows. Dec each end next and every foll 4th row to 48(50:52)sts. Cast off 5sts beg next 6 rows. Cast off.

NECKBAND
Join one shoulder seam. Using 4mm needles and M pick up 34sts from side neck, 20sts centre neck and 34sts side neck on both back and front *176sts*
Work 3 rows k2 p2 rib. Change to 3¾mm needles and work 4 rows rib. Change to 3¼mm needles and work 6 rows rib. Cast off firmly in rib.

MAKING UP
Join second shoulder seam, side seams and sleeve seams. Set in sleeves and stitch into position. Weave in any loose ends.

CARE INSTRUCTIONS
See ball tag and page 172.

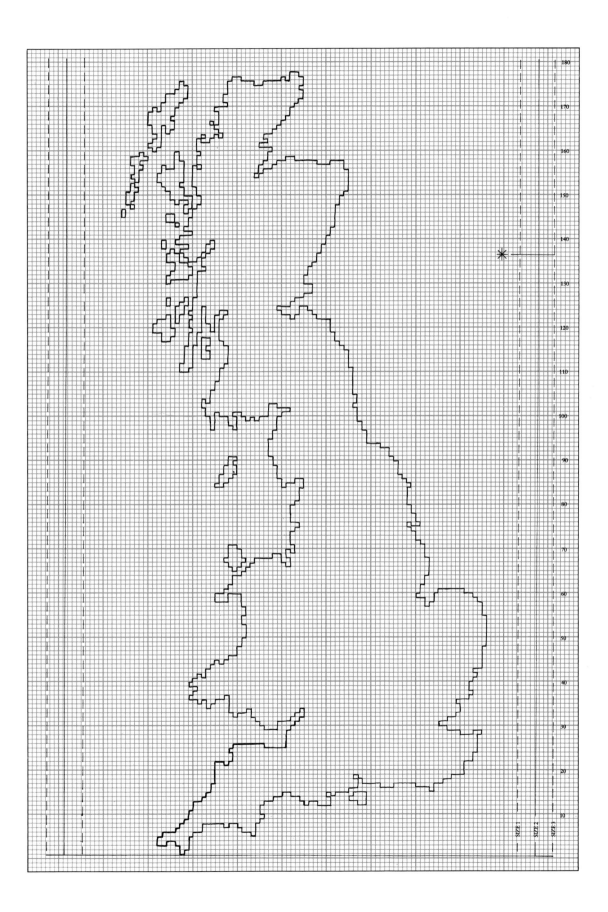

KIMO

IT IS OFTEN THE COMBINATION OF TEXTURED STITCHES AND COLOUR DETAILS WHICH REALLY MAKES A DESIGN UNDOUBTEDLY HAND-KNITTED. KIMO IS THUS BROUGHT TO LIFE BY THE CONTRAST OF THE STRIPES AGAINST THE CENTRAL CABLE PANEL. NOTICE HOW, IN THE SLEEVE-LESS VERSION, THE COLOURS OF THE STRIPES PICK OUT THE FLECK COLOURS IN THE TWEED.

Shown on opposite page in eskimo Chicago and black and flannel Chandos (sleeved version). Also shown on page 162 in midnight Chicago and teal and turquoise Chandos (sleeveless version).

See diagram at end of pattern

SIZE cm(in)
To fit bust:

89–94(35–37)	96–102(38–40)	104–109(41–43)
Actual size:		
96(38)	104(41)	112(44)
Length from back neck:		
67(26½)	67(26½)	67(26½)
Sleeve seam:		
43(17)	43(17)	44(17½)

MATERIALS
Chicago and Chandos – 50g balls
cardigan: (sleeveless version)

M:	Chicago eskimo (midnight)		
	15(10)	16(11)	17(12)
A:	Chandos black (teal)		
	1(1)	1(1)	1(1)
B:	Chandos flannel (turquoise)		
	1(1)	1(1)	1(1)

1 pair each of 5mm and 6mm needles.

5mm circular needle. Cable needle. 8 buttons

TENSION
14sts and 20 rows = 10cm square on 6mm needles over stocking stitch. See page 9.

Opposite:
The tweedy cardigan, Kimo, is also shown as a sleeveless version on page 162. Try working the stripes in brightly contrasting colours if you want to be noticed!

ABBREVIATIONS
See page 9.
t2l = knit into back of second stitch, then knit first st, slipping both sts off needle tog
t2r = knit into front of second stitch, then knit first st, slipping both sts off needle tog
c6b = place next 3sts on cn, leave at back of work, k3 then k3 from cn
c6f = place next 3sts on cn, leave at front of work, k3, then k3 from cn
pup = pick up loop between sts and purl into back of loop
puk = pick up loop between sts and knit into back of loop
yrn = yarn round needle

SPECIAL NOTE
Chandos is knitted DOUBLE (ie 2 ends together).

BACK
Using 5mm needles and M cast on 68(72:76)sts and work 10 rows in k1 p1 rib.
Change to 6mm needles and work 114 rows in stocking st. Place markers each end of row 60 on sleeveless version.
Shape shoulders: cast off 5sts beg next 6 rows. Cast off 4(5:6)sts beg next 4 rows. Cast off.

SLEEVES
Using 5mm needles and M cast on 38sts and work 5cm in k1 p1 rib.
Increase row: rib 2 *inc rib 3* to end 47sts
Change to 6mm needles and stocking st. Inc each end 11th and every foll 4th row to 73(75:77)sts. Continue without shaping until work measures 43(43:44)cm.
Shape sleevehead: cast off 4sts beg next 14 rows. Cast off.

LEFT FRONT

Using 5mm needles and M cast on 39(41:43)sts and work 9 rows in k1 p1 rib.

Increase row:
Row 10: rib 1(2:3) *inc rib 8* 4 times, inc, rib 1(2:3) 44(46:48)sts

Change to 6mm needles and work 52 rows in stocking st.

Start stripe inset and neck shaping. Wind off small balls of yarn (see page 173) in each colour (use Chandos DOUBLED). Use block knitting technique, working in stocking st:

Row 1: 13(15:17)M, 15A, 14M, k2togM
Row 2: 15M, 15A, 13(15:17)M
Row 3: 28(30:32)M, 15A
Row 4: p2togA, 14A, 27(29:31)M
Row 5: 12(14:16)M, 15B, 15M
Row 6: 15M, 15B, 12(14:16)M
Row 7: 26(28:30)M, 14B, k2togB
Row 8: 15B, 26(28:30)M

(*** sleeveless jacket version – see page 162, place markers at armhole edge.)

These 8 rows form colour change rep. Cont as set, dec front edge on every 3rd row and keeping the front edge panel at 15sts. Cont to row 62 *23:25:27sts*

Shape shoulder: cast off 5sts beg next and foll 2 alt rows. Cast off 4(5:6)sts beg next and foll 2 alt rows.

RIGHT FRONT

Rib as for left front.

Increase row:
Row 10: rib 2(4:6) *inc, rib 6* 3 times, *inc, rib 2* 5 times, inc 48(50:52)sts

Change to 6mm needles and patt as follows:
Row 1: p1 k1 p2 t2l p2 k9 p2 t2r p2 k1 p1 k23(25:27)
Row 2: p24(26:28) k3 p2 k2 p9 k2 p2 k3 p1
Row 3: p1 k1 p2 t2l p2 c6b k3 p2 t2r p2 k1 p1 k23(25:27)

Row 4: as row 2
Rows 5–8: as rows 1–2
Row 9: p1 k1 p2 t2l p2 k3 c6f p2 t2r p2 k1 p1 k23(25:27)
Row 10: as row 2
Rows 11–12: as rows 1–2
Rows 13–48: as rows 1–12 three times
Rows 49–51: as rows 1–3
Row 52: p24(26:28) k3 p2tog k2 *p2 p2tog* twice p1 k2 p2tog k3 p1. Start colour inset and neck shaping
Row 1: k2togM 14M 15A 13(15:17)M
Cont as for left front reversing all shapings, keeping stripe pattern correct as left front.

COLLAR AND BUTTON BANDS

Join shoulder seams. Using 5mm circular needle and M pick up 52sts along right front cable panel, 60sts along striped panel, 23sts from back neck, 60sts along striped panel and 52sts from left front plain panel. *247sts*
Work as follows:
NB Always slip first stitch after 'turn'. This is counted in instructions.
Row 1: *k1 p1* 97 times k1 turn
Row 2: rib 143 turn
Row 3: rib 135 turn
Row 4: rib 127 turn
Row 5: rib 119 turn
Row 6: rib 111 turn
Row 7: rib 42 pup k1 pup rib 25 pup k1 pup rib 34 turn
Row 8: rib 34 k1 p1 k1 rib 25 k1 p1 k1 rib 34 turn
Row 9: rib 34 p1 k1 p1 rib 25 p1 k1 p1 rib 30 turn
Row 10: rib 30 k1 p1 k1 rib 25 k1 p1 k1 rib 30 turn
Row 11: rib 30 puk rib 3 puk rib 25 puk rib 3 puk rib 26 turn
Row 12: rib 87 turn
Row 13: rib 83 turn
Row 14: rib 79 turn
Row 15: rib 22 pup rib 5 pup rib 25 pup rib 5 pup rib 18 turn
Row 16: rib 18 k1 rib 5 k1 rib 25 k1 rib 5 k1 rib 18 turn
Row 17: rib 18 p1 rib 5 p1 rib 25 p1 rib 5 p1 rib 14 turn
Row 18: rib 14 k1 rib 5 k1 rib 25 k1 rib 5 k1 rib 14 turn
Row 19: rib 14 puk rib 7 puk rib 25 puk rib 7 puk rib 10 turn
Row 20: rib 63 turn
Row 21: rib 59 turn
Row 22: rib 55 turn
Row 23: rib 6 pup rib 9 pup rib 25 pup rib 9 pup rib 2 turn
Row 24: rib 2 k1 rib 9 k1 rib 25 k1 rib 9 k1 rib 2 turn
Row 25: rib 2 p1 rib 9 p1 rib 25 p1 rib 9 p1 rib to end
Row 26: rib 110 k1 rib 9 k1 rib 25 k1 rib 9 k1 rib 110
Row 27: rib 3 *yrn dec rib 14* 3 times yrn dec rib 57 [puk rib 11 puk] rib 25 rep [] again rib 57

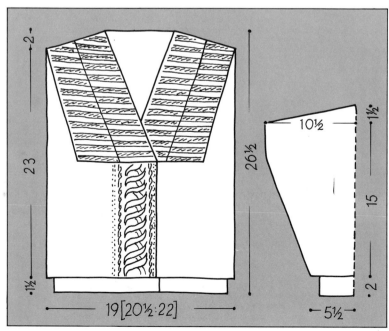

19[20½:22]

23

2

1½

26½

15

10½

1½

5½

2

dec yrn rib 14 3 times dec yrn rib 3
Rows 28–29: rib across all sts
Cast off in rib.

ARMHOLE EDGING (for sleeveless version)
Using 5mm needles and M pick up 91sts
between markers. ***
Row 1: rib 88 turn
Row 2: rib 85 turn
Row 3: rib 82 turn
Row 4: rib 79 turn
Row 5: rib to end
Cast off in rib.

MAKING UP
Set in sleeves. Join side and sleeve seams. Weave
in any loose ends. Sew on buttons.

CARE INSTRUCTIONS
See ball tag and page 172.

HERCULES

THE BOLD GRID DESIGN IN THIS PATTERN WOULD ALSO LOOK VERY EFFECTIVE KNITTED IN JUST ONE COLOUR, AS THE SQUARES ARE FORMED BY THE TEXTURED STITCHES; BUT IN FLANNEL AND WHITE THE EFFECT IS HIGHLIGHTED FURTHER. THIS SWEATER WOULD BE EQUALLY GOOD ON A GIRL.

Shown on opposite page in flannel and white Chandos.

See diagram at end of pattern

SIZE cm(in)

To fit up to chest:	
	107(42)
Actual size:	
	112(44)
Length from back neck:	
	71(28)
Sleeve seam:	
	53(21)

MATERIALS

Chandos – 50g balls:

A flannel:	
	8
B white:	
	8
1 pair each of 3¼mm and 4mm needles	
Cable needle	

TENSION

22sts and 28 rows = 10cm square on 4mm needles over stocking stitch. See page 9.

ABBREVIATIONS

See page 9.
c6b = place next 3sts on cn, leave at back of work, k3, then knit 3sts on cn;
c6f = place next 3sts on cn, leave at front of work, k3, then knit 3sts on cn;
[] = repeat instructions enclosed within brackets.

BACK

Using 3¼mm needles and A cast on 121sts and work 6cm in k1 p1 rib.
Increase row: rib 5 *inc rib 10* 10 times, inc, rib 5. *132sts.*
Change to 4mm needles and patt.
Row 1: [Using B k3 *p1 k5* 6 times p1 k3], using A k46 rep [] again.
Row 2: [using B p4 *k1 p5* 6 times] p3, using A p46 rep [] again k1 p2.
Row 3: using B k1 [*p1 k5* 6 times] p1 k2 c6b, using A k40 c6f, using B k4 rep [] again.
Row 4: using B [*k1 p5* 6 times] k1 p3 p3A p3B p40A p3B p3A, using B p3 rep [] again k1.
Row 5: using B [*k5 p1* 6 times] k4 k3A k3B k40A k3B k3A, using B k2 p1 rep [] again k1.
Row 6: using B p2 *k1 p5* 6 times k1 p1 p3A p3B p40A p3B p3A, using B *p5 k1* 6 times p4.
Row 7: using B k3 [*p1 k5* 6 times p1] k3A k3B k40A k3B k3A, using B rep [] again k3.
Row 8: using B p4 [*k1 p5* 6 times] p3A p3B p40A p3B p3A, using B p1 rep [] again k1 p2.
Row 9: as row 3.
Row 10: using B *k1 p5* 7 times p1, using A p46, using B p6 *k1 p5* 6 times k1.
Row 11: using B *k5 p1* 6 times k7, using A k46, using B *k5 p1* 7 times k1.
Row 12: using B p2 *k1 p5* 6 times k1 p4, using A p46, using B p8 *k1 p5* 5 times k1 p4.
Rows 13–60: as rows 1–12 4 times.
Row 61: k86B 3A 43B.
Row 62: k40B p3B p3A k86B.
Row 63: k86B c6f k40B.
Row 64: k40B p3A p3B k86B.
Row 65: k89B 3A 40B.
Row 66: as row 64.
Row 67: using A k43 using B k3 *k5 p1* 6 times k7 using A k43.
Rows 68–126: as set (stocking st, cable,

Opposite:
The man's sweater, Hercules, is a strong and simple design which would work well in a wide variety of colours. The girl is wearing a lengthened version of Tristan, the pattern is on page 152.

diagonal, cable, stocking st.).
Row 127: k40B 3A 89B.
Row 128: k86B p3B p3A k40B.
Row 129: k40B c6b k86B.
Row 130: k86B p3A p3B k40B.
Row 131: k43B k3A k86A.
Row 132: as row 130.
Row 133: as row 1.
Cont with patt (rows 2–60) inc each end of
every 8th row to 146sts, working extra sts in
diagonal patt.
Cont as set until work measures 71cm. Cast off.

FRONT
As back to 28 rows less than finished length.

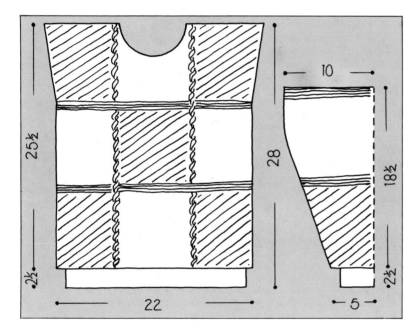

Shape neck:
cast off centre 16sts. Cast off 2sts at
neck edge on next 2 alt rows. Dec neck edge on
next 8 alt rows. Work 7 rows. Cast off.
Rejoin yarn to rem sts and work to match.

SLEEVES
Using 3¼mm needles and A cast on 49sts and
work 7cm in k1 p1 rib.
Increase row: rib 2 *inc rib 3* 11 times, inc,
rib 2 *61 sts.*
Change to 4mm needles and B.
Row 1: p1 *k5 p1* 10 times.
Row 2: p1 *k1 p5* 10 times.
Row 3: k4 *p1 k5* 9 times p1.
Moving the diagonal pattern 1st to the right on
every row, inc each end of next and every
following 4th row until sleeve measures 28cm,
working inc sts into patt and ending wrong side
row. Knit 6 rows inc as before. Change to A and
stocking stitch, inc as before until there are
119sts. Work straight until sleeve measures
51cm, ending wrong side row. Change to B and
knit 6 rows. Cast off loosely.

NECKBAND
Join right shoulder seam.
Using 3¼mm needles and A pick up 30sts from
side front neck, 16sts centre front, 30sts from side
front neck and 44sts from back neck. *120sts.*
Work 6cm in k1 p1 rib. Cast off in rib. Fold in
half to inside and slipstitch into position.

MAKING UP
Join left shoulder seam and neckband. Set in
sleeves. Join side and sleeve seams. Fold
neckband in half to inside and slipstitch into
position. Weave in any loose ends.

CARE INSTRUCTIONS
See ball tag and page 172.

CRUSOE

VERY OFTEN THE MOST STRIKING DESIGNS ARE THE SIMPLEST, AND HERE INDEED IS ONE SUCH CASE. THE SILHOUETTE IS QUITE SKINNY-SLEEVED AND FITTING, SO IT FOLLOWS THE LINE OF THE BODY, AND YOU MAY NOTICE THAT THE WHITE STRIPES ARE WIDER THAN THE BLACK TO SOFTEN THE HORIZONTAL EFFECT. THE PATTERN ALSO INCLUDES A VERSION IN A SHORTER LENGTH.

Shown on page 121 in black and white Chandos.

See diagram at end of pattern

SIZE cm(in)
To fit bust:

81–84(32–34)	86–91(34–36)	91–96(36–38)
Actual size:		
89(35)	97(38)	104(41)
Length from back neck: LONG:		
76(30)	76(30)	76(30)
Length from back neck: SHORT:		
67(26½)	67(26½)	67(26½)
Sleeve seam:		
44(17½)	44(17½)	44(17½)

MATERIALS
Chandos – 50g balls:

Black M: LONG:		
7	7	8
Black M: SHORT:		
6	6	7
White C: LONG:		
6	6	7
White C: SHORT:		
5	5	6

1 pair each of 3¼mm, 3¾mm, 4mm needles

TENSION
22sts and 28 rows = 10cm square on 4mm needles over stocking stitch. See page 9.

ABBREVIATIONS
See page 9.

BACK AND FRONT
Using 3¼mm needles and M cast on 88(96:104)sts and work 5cm in k2 p2 rib.
Increase row: rib 3(7:11) *inc, rib 8* 9 times, inc, rib 3(7:11) *98(106:114)sts*
Change to 4mm needles, stocking st and stripe patt. Working 14 rows C, 12 rows M, cont until work measures 54cm for long version or 45cm for short version.
Shape armhole: cast off 2(3:5)sts beg next 2 rows. Dec each end next 2(4:4) rows. Dec each end next and foll alt rows to 78(80:82)sts. Cont until work measures 66cm (long) or 57cm (short).
Shape neck: k29(30:31), cast off 20sts, k29(30:31).
On 29(30:31)sts:
Row 1: patt
Row 2: cast off 5sts, work to end
Row 3: patt
Row 4: cast off 2sts, patt to end
Row 5: patt
Rows 6–15: as rows 4–5 5 times
Row 16: dec patt to end
Row 17: patt
Rows 18–23: as rows 16–17 3 times
Rows 24–29: patt. Cast off.
Rejoin yarns to remaining sts at neck edge and work rows 2–29. Cast off.

SLEEVES
Using 3¼mm needles and M cast on 40(42:44)sts and work 5cm in k2 p2 rib.
Increase row: rib 0(2:4) *inc, rib 3* to end. *50(52:54)sts*

Following page: This stripy jersey, Crusoe, is perhaps one of the easiest designs in the book, and also one of the loudest.

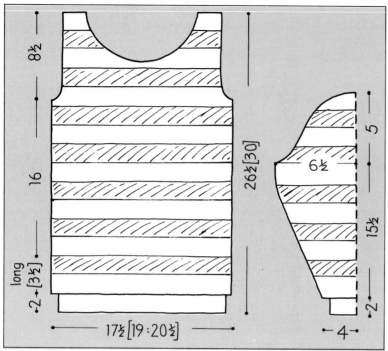

Change to 4mm needles and stripe patt. Inc each end every 8th row to 70(72:74)sts. Cont without shaping until work measures 44cm.
Shape sleevehead: cast off 2sts beg next 4 rows. Dec each end next and every foll 4th row to 48(50:52)sts. Cast off 5sts beg next 6 rows. Cast off.

NECKBAND
Join one shoulder seam. Using 4mm needles and M pick up 34sts from side neck, 20sts centre neck and 34sts side neck on both back and front. *176sts.*
Work 3 rows k2 p2 rib. Change to 3¾mm needles and work 4 rows rib. Change to 3¼mm needles and work 6 rows rib. Cast off firmly in rib.

MAKING UP
Join second shoulder seam, side seams and sleeve seams. Set in sleeves and stitch into position. Weave in any loose ends.

CARE INSTRUCTIONS
See ball tag and page 172.

KALEIDOSCOPE

T HIS ONE, LIKE COLLAGE, USES THE 'ENTRELAC' KNITTING TECHNIQUE TO FORM THE DIAMONDS, AND SLIPPED STITCHES IN THE INDIVIDUAL SECTIONS TO FORM THE COLOUR PATTERNS, SO YOU NEVER NEED TO CHANGE COLOUR IN THE MIDDLE OF A ROW TO KNIT THIS SWEATER. IF YOU CAN PICK UP STITCHES ALONG THE EDGE OF A SQUARE, YOU CAN DO IT!

Shown on page 127 in bright Chandos colours.

See diagram at end of pattern

SIZE cm(in)
One size only to fit bust:

81–97(32–38)	

Actual size:

104(41)	

Length from back neck:**

63.5(25)	

Sleeve seam:

45(47½)	

**SPECIAL NOTE: The pattern works out 7½cm (3in) longer than shown in the photograph.

MATERIALS
Chandos – 50g balls:

A black:	
	5

B poppy:	
	4

C fuchsia:	
	2

D cobalt:	
	2

F teal:	
	2

H turquoise:	
	2

One pair each of 3¼mm and 4mm needles

TENSION
22sts and 28 rows = 10cm square on 4mm needles over stocking stitch, see page 9.

ABBREVIATIONS
See page 9.
ML = insert right-hand needle through work (from front to back) under the purl st of 2 rows before, yrn, pull through (make loop).
PMLO = pass made loop over
p2togb = p next 2sts tog through back of sts
k2togb = k next 2sts tog through back of sts

BACK AND FRONT
Using 3¼mm needles and A cast on 91sts and work 7cm in k1 p1 rib.
Increase row: rib 3 *inc rib 6* 12 times, inc rib 3 *104sts*
Section 1
Change to 4mm needles and purl 1 row. Work base triangles as follows:
Using A
Row 1: k1 s1 turn
Row 2: p2
Row 3: k3 s1 turn
Row 4: p4
Using B
Row 5: k5 s1 turn
Row 6: p6
Row 7: k1 p1 k3 p1 k1 s1 turn
Row 8: p8
Using A
Row 9: k1 *ML k1 PMLO k3* twice s1 turn
Row 10: p10
Row 11: *k3 p1* twice k3 s1 turn
Row 12: p12
Using B
Row 13: *k3 ML k1 PMLO* twice k5 s1 turn
Row 14: p14

Following page: You will not get lost in a crowd wearing this design, Kaleidoscope, which you can easily change to incorporate your favourite colours.

Row 15: k1 *p1 k3* 3 times p1 k1 s1 turn
Row 16: p16
Using A
Row 17: k1 *ML k1 PMLO k3* 4 times s1 turn
Row 18: p18
Row 19: *k3 p1* 4 times k3 s1 turn
Row 20: p20
Using B
Row 21: *k3 ML k1 PMLO* 5 times k5 s1 turn
Row 22: p22
Row 23: k1 *p1 k3* 4 times p1 k1 s1 turn
Row 24: p24
Using A
Row 25: k1 *ML k1 PMLO k3* 6 times s1 turn
Row 26: p26
Row 27: k27 s1 turn
Repeat rows 2–27 3 more times ending last
repeat k26.
Section 2
(2a) Side triangles and diamonds. Wrong side
facing:
Using C
Row 1: inc, yf s1 turn
Row 2: k2tog inc
Using D
Row 3: inc yb sl yf p2tog turn
Row 4: p1 yb s1 yf p1 k1
Row 5: inc p2 p2tog s1 turn
Row 6: k2tog k3 inc
Using F
Row 7: inc *yb s1 yf p1* twice p2tog turn
Row 8: k1 *p1 yb s1 yf* twice p1 k1
Row 9: inc p5 p2tog s1 turn
Row 10: k2tog k6 inc
Using H
Row 11: inc *yb s1 yf p1* 3 times yb s1 yf p2tog
turn
Row 12: *p1 yb s1 yf* 4 times p1 k1
Row 13: inc p8 p2tog s1 turn
Row 14: k2tog k9 inc
Using C
Row 15: inc *yb s1 yf p1* 5 times p2tog turn
Row 16: k1 *p1 yb s1 yf* 5 times p1 k1
Row 17: inc p11 p2tog s1 turn
Row 18: k2tog k12 inc
Using D
Row 19: inc *yb s1 yf p1* 6 times yb s1 yf p2tog
turn
Row 20: *p1 yb s1 yf* 7 times p1 k1
Row 21: inc p14 p2tog s1 turn
Row 22: k2tog k15 inc
Using F
Row 23: inc *yb s1 yf p1* 8 times p2tog turn
Row 24: k1 *p1 yb s1 yf* 8 times p1 k1
Row 25: inc p17 p2tog s1 turn
Row 26: k2tog k18 inc
Using H
Row 27: inc *yb s1 yf p1* 9 times yb s1 yf p2tog
turn
Row 28: *p1 yb s1 yf* 10 times p1 k1
Row 29: inc p20 p2tog s1 turn
Row 30: k2tog k21 inc
Using C
Row 31: inc *yb s1 yf p1* 11 times p2tog turn
Row 32: k1 *p1 yb s1 yf* 11 times p1 k1
Row 33: inc p23 p2tog s1 turn

Row 34: k2tog k24 inc
Row 35: p26 p2tog do not break yarn pick up 27sts along edge of base triangle s1 turn

(2b) Diamonds
Using C
Row 1: k2tog k26 turn
Using D
Row 2: *p1 yb s1 yf* 13 times p2tog turn
Row 3: *p1 yb s1 yf* 13 times p1 turn
Row 4: p26 p2tog s1 turn
Row 5: k2tog k26 turn
Using F
Row 6: p1 *p1 yb s1 yf* 12 times p1 p2tog turn
Row 7: k1 *p1 yb s1 yf* 12 times p1 k1 turn
Row 8: p26 p2tog s1 turn
Row 9: k2tog k26 turn
Using H
Rows 10–13: as rows 2–5
Using C
Rows 14–17: as rows 6–9
Using D
Rows 18–21: as rows 2–5
Using F
Rows 22–25: as rows 6–9
Using H
Rows 26–29: as rows 2–5
Using C
Rows 30–33: as rows 6–9
Using D
Rows 34–35: as rows 2–3
Row 36: p26 p2tog pick up 27sts across base triangle, s1 turn
Repeat section (2b) twice, (rows 1–36), omitting s1 on last row of last rep keeping colour sequence correct.
NB: subsequent diamonds will start and finish with different colours.

(2c) Side triangle:
Using H
Row 1: k2tog k25
Using C
Row 2: *p1 yb s1 yf* 12 times p2tog
Row 3: *p1 yb s1 yf* 12 times p1
Row 4: p23 p2tog
Row 5: k2tog k22
Using D
Row 6: p1 *p1 yb s1 yf* 10 times p2tog
Row 7: *p1 yb s1 yf* 10 times p1 k1
Row 8: p20 p2tog
Row 9: k2tog k19
Using F
Rows 10–13: patt and dec as set
Using H
Rows 14–17: patt and dec as set
Using C
Rows 18–21: patt and dec as set
Using D
Rows 22–25: patt and dec as set
Using F
Rows 26–29: patt and dec as set
Using H
Rows 30–33: patt and dec as set
Row 34: p2tog

Section 3 Diamonds
Right side facing.
Using A k1 from side triangle, pick up 26sts

along side triangle (2c) s1 turn
Using A
Row 1: p2togb p26 turn
Row 2: *k3 p1* 6 times k2 k2togb s1 turn
Row 3: as row 1
Using B
Row 4: *k3 ML k1 PMLO* 6 times k2 k2togb s1 turn
Row 5: p2togb p26 turn
Row 6: *k1 p1 k2* 6 times k1 p1 k2togb s1 turn
Row 7: as row 5
Using A
Row 8: *k1 ML k1 PMLO k2* 6 times k1 ML k1 PMLO k2togb s1 turn
Rows 9–24: as rows 1–8 3 times
Row 25: as row 1
Row 26: k26 k2togb s1 turn
Row 27: p2togb p26
Row 28: k27, pick up 27sts along (2b) s1 turn
Work rows 1–28 again omitting s1 at end of last rep. Work sections 2 and 3 again then section 2.

Section 4 Top triangles
Right side facing
Using A, k1 pick up 26sts along 2c s1 turn
Row 1: p2togb p26 turn
Row 2: cast off 2sts, *p1 k3* 5 times p1 k2 k2togb s1 turn
Row 3: p2togb p24 turn
Using B
Row 4: cast off 2sts k2 ML k1 PMLO *k3 ML k1 PMLO* 4 times k2 k2togb s1 turn
Row 5: p2togb p22 turn
Row 6: cast off 2sts k2 p1 *k3 p1* 4 times k2togb s1 turn
Row 7: p2togb p20 turn
Rows 8–25: cont in patt and dec as set
Row 26: cast off 2sts k2togb s1 turn
Row 27: p2togb turn
Repeat rows 1–27 3 more times. Fasten off.

BACK YOKE

Using 4mm needles and C pick up 113sts across back (28sts each triangle and 1st at centre back).
Using C
Row 1: purl
Row 2: knit
Using D
Rows 3–4: *p1 yb s1 yf* to last st p1
Row 5: purl
Row 6: knit
Using F
Row 7–8: k1 *p1 yb s1 yf* to last 2sts p1 k1
Row 9: purl
Row 10: knit
Using H
Rows 11–14: as rows 3–6
Keeping patt correct and using C
Rows 15–16: cast off 8sts beg each row
Row 17: cast off 8sts patt 27, cast off 27 patt 35
On 35sts:
Row 18: cast off 8sts patt to end
Using D
Row 19: cast off 6sts patt to end
Row 20: as row 18
Row 21: cast off 5sts patt to end

Row 22: cast off
Rejoin yarn to rem sts and work to match.

FRONT YOKE
Pick up as for back yoke
Using C
Row 1: purl
Row 2: k47 turn
Keeping patt correct as for back yoke, cast off 2sts neck edge on next 4 alt rows, then dec neck edge on next 7 alt rows. AT THE SAME TIME work shoulder shaping as for back. (Cast off 8sts on 4 alt rows.)
Place centre 19sts on pin. Work rem sts to match.

SLEEVES
Using 3¼mm needles and A cast on 49sts and work 7cm in k1 p1 rib.
Increase row: rib 1 *inc rib 3* *61sts*
Change to 4mm needles
Patt A
Using black
Row 1: knit
Row 2: purl
Row 3: k2 *p1 k3* to last 3sts p1 k2
Row 4: inc purl to last st inc
Using poppy
Row 5: k3 *ML k1 PMLO k3* to end
Row 6: purl
Row 7: k1 *p1 k3* to last 2sts p1 k1
Row 8: as row 4
Using black
Row 9: k2 *ML k1 PMLO k3* end last repeat k2
Row 10: purl
Row 11: k4 *p1 k3* to last st k1
Row 12: as row 4
Using poppy
Row 13: k1 *ML k1 PMLO k3* end last repeat k1
Row 14: purl
Row 15: *k3 p1* to last 3sts k3
Row 16: as row 4
Using black
Row 17: k4 *ML k1 PMLO k3* to last st k1
Row 18: purl
Rows 19–20: as rows 3–4
Rows 21–24: as rows 5–8
Rows 25–27: as rows 9–11
Using C
Row 28: inc purl to last st inc
Row 29: knit
Using D
Rows 30–31: *p1 yb s1 yf* to last st p1
Rows 32–33: as rows 28–29

Using F
Rows 34–37: as rows 30–33
Using H
Rows 38–41: as rows 30–33
Using C
Rows 42–43: as rows 30–31
Row 44: as row 28 *83sts*
Rep rows 1–44 again noting row 3 is k1*p1 k3* etc to keep continuity of pattern *105sts*
Start row 1 again noting row 3 is k4 *p1 k3* etc (cont black/poppy patt to end of sleeve). Inc to 115sts. Cont until work measures 45cm without shaping.
Shape sleevehead: keeping patt correct cast off 5sts beg next 16 rows. Cast off.

NECKBAND
Join right shoulder seam. Using 3¼mm needles and A pick up 28sts side front neck, knit across 19sts centre front neck, pick up 28sts side front neck and 53sts across back neck. *128sts.* Work 5cm k1 p1 rib. Cast off in rib.

MAKING UP
Join left shoulder seam and neckband. Fold neckband in half to inside and slipstitch into position. Ease sleevehead into position and stitch into place. Join side and sleeve seams. Weave in any loose ends.

CARE INSTRUCTIONS
See ball tag and page 172.

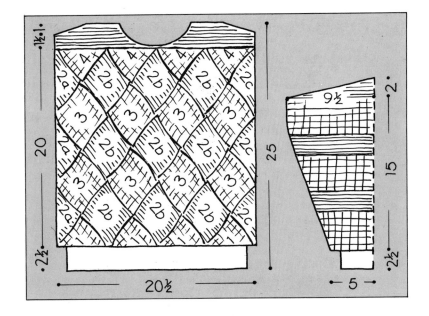

SPARKS

THIS IS A VERY EASY CARDIGAN, OR JACKET, AND A VERY VERSATILE DESIGN AS OF COURSE YOU COULD USE ANY PREFERRED COLOUR FOR THE STRIPES, AND ALSO DIFFERENT COLOURED BUTTONS LIKE IN APPLEJACK (PAGES 147 AND 167). BEING ALL IN STOCKING STITCH, THIS SHOULD NOT CAUSE YOU ANY PROBLEMS TO KNIT.

Shown on page 130 in eskimo Chicago and flannel Chandos. Shown on page 134 in blaze Chicago and midnight Chicago (omitting shoulder stripes).

See diagram at end of pattern

SIZE cm(in)
To fit bust:

89–94(35–37)	96–102(38–40)	104–109(41–43)
Actual size:		
97(38)	104(41)	112(44)
Length from back neck:		
59(23)	59(23)	59(23)
Sleeve seam:		
43(17)	43(17)	44(17½)

MATERIALS
Chicago and Chandos – 50g balls:

M eskimo (blaze):		
13	14	15
C flannel (midnight):		
2	2	2
1 pair each of 5mm and 6mm needles		
7 buttons. Stitch holder		

NB Chandos is used SINGLE, and Chicago DOUBLE, throughout.

TENSION
14sts and 20 rows = 10cm square on 6mm needles over stocking stitch. See page 9.

ABBREVIATIONS
See page 9.

Previous page:
The girl in the red hat is wearing Sparks, a bold and easy design shown again on page 134. The design on the right is Hanover, equally strong and simple, which you will also see on page 151, the pattern is on page 155.

BACK
Using 5mm needles and M cast on 64(68:72)sts and work 6cm in k2 p2 rib.
Increase row: rib 7(9:11) *inc, rib 15* 3 times, inc, rib 8(10:12) *68(72:76)sts*
Change to 6mm needles and stocking st. Cont until work measures 28cm.
Shape armhole: cast off 1(2:3)sts beg next 2 rows. Dec each end alt rows to 56(58:60)sts. Cont without shaping until work measures 51cm.
Shape shoulders: cast off 4sts beg next 6 rows, cast off 3(4:5)sts beg next 2 rows. On 26sts work further 5cm without shaping. Cast off.

POCKET
Using 6mm needles and M cast on 13sts and work 9cm in stocking st. Leave on holder.

LEFT FRONT
Using 5mm needles and M cast on 30(32:34)sts and work 6cm in k2 p2 rib.
Increase row: rib 2(3:4) *inc rib 11* twice inc rib 3(4:5) *33(35:37)sts*
Change to 6mm needles and stocking st. Cont until work measures 28cm.
Shape armhole: cast off 1(2:3)sts beg next row. Dec armhole edge on alt rows to 27(28:29)sts. Cont without shaping until work measures 41cm.
Place pocket: k7(8:8) place next 13sts on holder, knit 13 across pocket, k7(7:8), cont until work measures 51cm, ending at armhole edge.
Shape neck and shoulders:
Row 1: cast off 4sts and work to end.
Row 2: cast off 6sts and work to end.
Row 3: as row 1.
Row 4: cast off 3sts, work to end.
Rows 5–6: as rows 3–4. Cast off.

RIGHT FRONT

As left front reversing all shapings and omitting pocket.

SLEEVES

Using 5mm needles and M cast on 38sts and work 6cm in k2 p2 rib.
Increase row: rib 2 * inc, rib 3* to end. *47sts*
Change to 6mm needles and stocking st. Inc each and every foll 4th row to 67(69:71)sts. Cont without shaping until work measures 40cm.
Change to stripe patt (optional) as follows:
Working in stocking st, 2 rows C (when using Chandos as C use DOUBLE ie 2 ends together). 4 rows M, thus giving a 6 row repeat.
Cont without shaping until work measures 43(43:44)cm.
Shape sleevehead: cast off 1(2:3)sts beg next 2 rows. Dec each end alt rows to 51sts. Work 3 rows. Dec each end next and every foll 4th row to 43sts. Work 1 row. Cast off 4sts beg next 6 rows. On 19sts work a further 12cm without shaping. Cast off.

POCKET TRIM

Using 5mm needles and C (when using Chandos as C use DOUBLE), knit across pocket sts, inc 1st at end. Work 3 rows k2 p2 rib. Cast off in rib.

COLLAR

Using 6mm needles and C (when using Chandos as C use DOUBLE) cast on 82sts. Work 7cm in k2 p2 rib. Change to 5mm needles and cont until work measures 10cm.
Cast off in rib.

BUTTON BAND

Using 5mm needles and M pick up 82sts evenly along left front, work 5 rows in k2 p2 rib.
Cast off in rib.

BUTTONHOLE BAND

Pick up as for button band on right front, work 2 rows k2 p2 rib.
Row 3: rib 4 * yrn, dec, rib 10* 6 times, yrn dec rib 4.
Work 2 rows rib. Cast off in rib.

MAKING UP

Join saddle shoulder seams (see diagram page 174), join side and sleeve seams. Set in sleeves and stitch into position. Slipstitch pocket into position. Pin collar right sides together around neck omitting buttonhole band. Overstitch into position. Weave in any loose ends. Sew on buttons.

CARE INSTRUCTIONS

See ball tag and page 172.

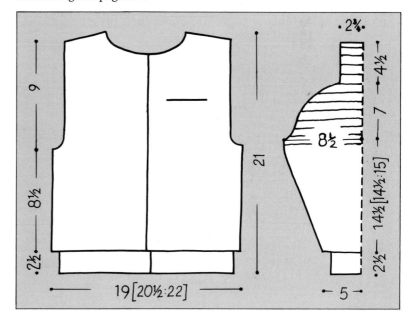

133

4

Let's not forget perhaps the most important function of a handknitted pullover — to keep you warm. And these ones will; they were photographed in St James's Park in London on one of the coldest days of the year, so they're not exactly new to the job. Some are in chunky Chicago tweed, some are in double thickness Chandos, and they're all in bright and vivacious colours. The Chicago lends itself naturally to quick and easy stitches, and the Chandos is just right for big bold cables and other details of texture. The bold and simple shapes of the designs in this chapter will work well in many colours, so you can choose the design from one page and the colour from another. This one is Sparks, featured on page 132.

JUNIPER

T HERE IS AN UNUSUAL CABLE IN THIS OVERSIZED JERSEY, WHERE ONE STRAND OF MOSS STITCH IS WOVEN IN WITH THE STOCKING STITCH. THE SHAPE IS INSPIRED BY AN OLD-FASHIONED FISHERMAN'S SMOCK, BUT JUST MADE SEVERAL SIZES LARGER; TRY IT IN WHITE TO ECHO THAT TRADITIONAL FEELING.

Shown on page 139 in poppy Chandos.

See diagram at end of pattern

SIZE cm(in)
To fit bust:

86–94(34–37)	96–104(38–41)	106–112(42–44)

Actual size:

106(42)	114(45)	122(48)

Length from back neck:

75(29½)	75(29½)	75(29½)

Sleeve seam:

41(16)	42(16½)	43(17)

MATERIALS
Chandos – 50g balls:

21	22	23

1 pair 6½mm needles. Cable needle

TENSION
15sts and 20 rows = 10cm square on 6½mm needles over stocking stitch using yarn DOUBLE (ie 2 ends together). See page 9.

ABBREVIATIONS
See page 9.
c2l = knit into back of second st, then knit first st
c2r = knit into front of second st, then knit first st, slipping both sts off needle tog
NB All cables are over 3sts moss stitch and 3sts stocking stitch.
To simplify pattern writing:
c6b = place 3sts on cn, leave at back of work, and *either* moss 3 (check sts just knitted on RH needle and work to match), then k3 from cn, *or* k3, moss 3 from cn (check sts to be worked on

LH needle and work to match)
c6f = place next 3sts on cn, leave at front of work and *either* moss 3 (check sts just knitted on RH needle and work to match) then k3 from cn, *or* k3, moss 3 from cn (check sts to be worked on LH needle and work to match).
This garment is knitted using yarn DOUBLE (ie 2 ends of yarn together) throughout.

BACK
Using 6½mm needles and yarn DOUBLE cast on 79(85:91)sts and knit 4 rows.
Increase row: k3(6:9) *inc k7* 9 times, inc k3(6:9) 89(95:101)sts
Work as follows:
Row 1: k5(8:11) [*p1 k1* twice p1 k3 p1 k1 p1 c2l k5 p1 k5 c2r p1 k1 p1 k3 *p1 k1* twice] *p1 k1* 3 times rep [] again p1 k5(8:11)
Row 2: k5(8:11) [*p1 k1* twice p5 k2 p7 k1 p7 k2 p5 *k1 p1* twice] *k1 p1* twice k1 rep [] again k5(8:11)
Row 3: k5(8:11) [*p1 k1* twice p1 k3 *p1 k1* twice c2l k4 p1 k4 c2r *k1 p1* twice k3 *p1 k1* twice p1] k5 rep [] again k5(8:11)
Row 4: k5(8:11) [*p1 k1* twice p5 k2 p7 k1 p7 k2 p5 *k1 p1* twice] p5 rep [] again k5(8:11)
Row 5: k5(8:11) p1 k1 c6b *see abbreviations* [p1 k1 p1 k2 c2l k3 p1 k3 c2r k2 p1 k1 p1] c6b k1 p1 k5 p1 k1 c6f rep [] again c6f k1 p1 k5(8:11)
Row 6: k5(8:11) [p1 k1 p3 *k1 p1* twice k2 p7 k1 p7 k2 *p1 k1* twice p3 k1 p1] p5 rep [] again k5(8:11)
Row 7: k5(8:11) [p1 k5 *p1 k1* twice p1 k3 c2l k2 p1 k2 c2r k3 *p1 k1* twice p1 k5 p1] *k1 p1* twice k1 rep [] again k5(8:11)
Row 8: k5(8:11) [p1 k1 p3 *k1 p1* twice k2 p7 k1 p7 k2 *p1 k1* twice p3 k1 p1] *k1 p1* twice k1 rep [] again k5(8:11)

Row 9: k5(8:11) [p1 k5 *p1 k1* twice p1 k4 c2l k1 p1 k1 c2r k4 *p1 k1* twice p1 k5 p1] k5 rep [] again k5(8:11)

Row 10: k5(8:11) [p1 k1 p3 *k1 p1* twice k2 p7 k1 p7 k2 *p1 k1* twice p3 k1 p1] p5 rep [] again k5(8:11)

Row 11: k5(8:11) p1 k1 c6b [p1 k1 p1 k5 c2l p1 c2r k5 p1 k1 p1] c6b k1 p1 k5 p1 k1 c6f rep [] again c6f k1 p1 k5(8:11)

Row 12: as row 4

Row 13: k5(8:11) [*p1 k1* twice p1 k3 p1 k1 *p1 k7* twice p1 k1 p1 k3 *p1 k1* twice] *p1 k1* 3 times rep [] again p1 k5(8:11)

Row 14: as row 2

Row 15: k5(8:11) [*p1 k1* twice p1 k3 p1 k1 p1 k5 c2r k1 c2l k5 p1 k1 p1 k3 *p1 k1* twice p1] k5 rep [] again k5(8:11)

Row 16: as row 4

Row 17: k5(8:11) p1 k1 c6b [p1 k1 p1 k4 c2r p1 k1 p1 c2l k4 p1 k1 p1] c6b k1 p1 k5 p1 k1 c6f rep [] again c6f k1 p1 k5(8:11)

Row 18: k5(8:11) [p1 k1 p3 *k1 p1* twice k2 p5 *k1 p1* twice k1 p5 k2 *p1 k1* twice p3 k1 p1] p5 rep [] again k5(8:11)

Row 19: k5(8:11) [p1 k5 *p1 k1* twice p1 k3 c2r *k1 p1* twice k1 c2l k3 *p1 k1* twice p1 k5 p1] *k1 p1* twice k1 rep [] again k5(8:11)

Row 20: k5(8:11) [p1 k1 p3 *k1 p1* twice k2 p5 *k1 p1* twice k1 p5 k2 *p1 k1* twice p3 k1 p1] *k1 p1* twice k1 rep [] again k5(8:11)

Row 21: k5(8:11) [p1 k5 *p1 k1* twice p1 k2 c2r *p1 k1* 3 times p1 c2l k2 *p1 k1* twice p1 k5 p1] k5 rep [] again k5(8:11)

Row 22: as row 18

Row 23: k5(8:11) p1 k1 c6b [*p1 k1* twice c2r c2l *p1 k1* twice k1 c2r c2l *p1 k1* twice] c6b k1 p1 k5 p1 k1 c6f rep [] again c6f k1 p1 k5(8:11)

Row 24: k5(8:11) [*p1 k1* twice p5 k2 p5 *k1 p1* twice k1 p5 k2 p5 *k1 p1* twice] p5 rep [] again k5(8:11)

Row 25: k5(8:11) [*p1 k1* twice p1 k3 p1 k1 p1 c2r k2 c2l p1 k1 p1 c2r k2 c2l p1 k1 p1 k3 *p1 k1* twice p1] *k1 p1* twice k1 rep [] again k5(8:11)

Row 26: as row 2

Row 27: k5(8:11) [*p1 k1* twice p1 k3 p1 k1 p1 k5 c2l p1 c2r k5 p1 k1 p1 k3 *p1 k1* twice p1] k5 rep [] again k5(8:11)

Row 28: as row 4

Row 29: k5(8:11) p1 k1 c6b [p1 k1 *p1 k7* twice p1 k1 p1] c6b k1 p1 k5 p1 k1 c6f rep [] again c6f k1 p1 k5(8:11)

Row 30: as 6, casting on 1st at each end for seam st. Cont as set for cables (12 row repeat) and diamonds (30 row repeat). Change edge sts as follows:

Rows 31–32: k0(1:0) *p1 k1* 3(4:6) times patt 79 *k1 p1* 3(4:6) times k0(1:0)

Rows 33 and 35: k6(9:12) patt 79 k6(9:12)

Rows 34 and 36: p6(9:12) patt 79 p6(9:12)

These 6 rows form edge sts patt. Cont with all patts until work measures 75cm. Cast off in patt.

FRONT

As back until work measures 66cm.

Shape neck: patt 37(40:43), cast off 17sts, patt 37(40:43).

On 37(40:43)sts:

Row 1: patt

** *Row 2:* cast off 2sts patt to end

Rows 3–6: as rows 1–2 twice

Row 7: patt

Row 8: dec patt to end

Rep rows 7–8 to 27(30:33)sts. Cont until work measures 75cm. Cast off.**

Rejoin yarn to rem sts at neck edge and work from ** to **.

SLEEVES

Using 6½mm needles and yarn DOUBLE cast on 41sts and knit 10 rows.

Increase row: k3 *inc k4* 7 times, inc k2 *49 sts*

Change to patt:

Row 1: *p1 k1* 3 times rep [] as row 1 of back *k1 p1* 3 times

This sets panels. Cont as set but work c6b, diamond, c6f and inc each end every 4th row to end working extra sts in moss st bars as at side edge of back. Cont until work measures 41(42:43)cm. Cast off.

POLO COLLAR

Join right shoulder seam. Using 6½mm needles and yarn DOUBLE pick up 19sts from side front neck, 17sts from centre front neck 19sts from

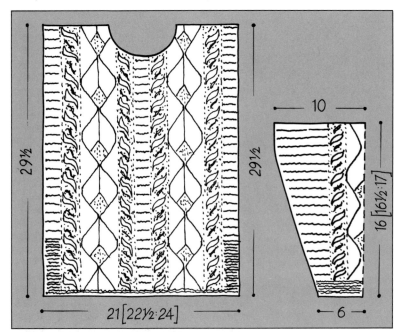

side front neck and 37sts from back neck *92sts*
Work 18cm in k2 p2 rib. Cast off in rib.

MAKING UP
Join left shoulder seam and collar. Join sleeve
seam. Starting from shoulder seam and working
downwards, ease sleeve into position and stitch.
Join side seams leaving first 30 rows unsewn.
Weave in any loose ends.

CARE INSTRUCTIONS
See ball tag and page 172.

*This design, Juniper,
is a thick and heavy
jersey with very
unusual but fairly
complex stitch
details.*

COBRA

T HE CABLES IN THIS DESIGN ARE ACTUALLY MADE TO TRAVEL FROM SIDE TO SIDE BY SHAPING THE OTHER PANELS. THUS BY A SERIES OF ALTERNATING INCREASES AND DECREASES THE FABRIC IS ACTUALLY DISTORTED ON PURPOSE TO GET THIS EFFECT.

Shown on page 142 in cobalt Chandos. This is suitable as a woman's sweater with a shorter sleeve.

See diagram at end of pattern

SIZE cm(in)
To fit bust/chest:

86–94(34–37)	96–104(38–41)	106–112(42–44)

Actual size:

102(40)	112(44)	122(48)

Length from back neck:

71(28)	71(28)	71(28)

Sleeve seam women/men:

42/48(16½/19)	43/51(17/20)	44/52(17½/21)

MATERIALS
Chandos – 50g balls:

23	24	25

1 pair each of 5½mm and 6½mm needles

Cable needle

TENSION
15sts and 20 rows = 10cm square on 6½mm needles over stocking stitch using yarn DOUBLE (ie 2 ends together). See page 9.

ABBREVIATIONS
See page 9.
c6 = place next 3sts on cn, leave at front of work, k3, then k3 from cn
NB This garment is knitted using yarn DOUBLE (ie 2 ends of yarn together).

BACK
Using 5½mm needles and yarn DOUBLE cast on 80(88:96)sts and work 7cm in k2 p2 rib (every row *k2 p2* to end).
Increase row: rib 3(7:11) *inc rib 8* 8 times, inc rib 4(8:12) 89(97:105)sts
Change to 6½mm needles and patt as follows:
Row 1: k16(20:24) p2 k6 p2 k17 p2 k6 *p2 k1* 4 times p2 k6 p2 k16(20:24)
Row 2: p16(20:24) k2 p6 *k2 p1* 4 times k2 p6 k2 p17 k2 p6 k2 p16(20:24)
Row 3: k16(20:24) p2 c6 p2 k17 p2 c6 *p2 k1* 4 times p2 c6 p2 k16(20:24)
Row 4: k18(22:26) p6 *k2 p1* 4 times k2 p6 k21 p6 k18(22:26)
Rows 5–6: as rows 1–2
Row 7: as row 1
Rows 8, 9, 10, 11: as rows 4, 3, 2, 1
Row 12: as row 4
Rows 13–19: as rows 1–7
Row 20: k18(22:26) p6 *k1 inc* 7 times p6 *k1 k2tog* 7 times p6 k18(22:26)
Row 21: k16(20:24) p2 c6 *p2 k1* 4 times p2 c6 p2 k17 p2 c6 p2 k16(20:24)
Row 22: p16(20:24) k2 p6 k2 p17 k2 p6 *k2 p1* 4 times k2 p6 k2 p16(20:24)
Row 23: k16(20:24) p2 k6 *p2 k1* 4 times p2 k6 p2 k17 p2 k6 p2 k16(20:24)
Row 24: k18(22:26) p6 k21 p6 *k2 p1* 4 times k2 p6 k18(22:26)
Rows 25, 26, 27: as rows 23, 22, 21
Rows 28, 29, 30: as rows 24, 22, 21
Rows 31–32: as rows 23–24
Rows 33–35: as rows 21–23
Row 36: k18(22:26) p6 *k1 k2tog* 7 times p6 *k1 inc* 7 times p6 k18(22:26)
These 36 rows form patt rep. Cont in patt until work measures 71cm. Cast off in patt.

FRONT
As back until work measures 62cm.
Shape neck: patt 36(40:44)sts, cast off 17sts,

Following page: The man's jersey, Cobra, is a sensible outdoor design with the added interest of the wavy cables. The girl is wearing a shorter version of Madison also shown on page 158.

patt 36(40:44). On 36(40:44)sts:
Row 1: patt
** *Row 2:* cast off 2sts, patt to end
Rows 3−6: as rows 1−2 twice
Row 7: patt
Row 8: dec, patt to end
Repeat rows 7−8 to 26(30:34)sts. Cont until
work measures 71cm. Cast off. **
Rejoin yarn to rem sts at neck edge and work
from ** to **.

SLEEVES
Using 5½mm needles and yarn DOUBLE cast
on 38sts and work 7cm in k2 p2 rib.
Increase row: rib 2 *inc rib 3* to end *47sts*
Change to 6½mm needles and patt.
Row 1: k3 p2 k17 p2 k6 *p2 k1* 4 times p2 k3
Cont in patt as for back, inc each end of every
4th row to end working extra sts into patt. Cont
until work measures 42:48(43:51:44:53)cm.
Cast off.

POLO COLLAR
Join right shoulder seam.
Using 6½mm needles and yarn DOUBLE pick
up 19sts from side front neck, 17sts from centre
front neck, 19sts from side front neck and 37sts
from back neck *92sts*
Work 18cm in k2 p2 rib. Cast off loosely in rib.

MAKING UP
Join left shoulder seam and collar. Join sleeve
seams. Working downwards from shoulder
seam, ease sleeve into position and stitch. Join
side seams. Weave in any loose ends.

CARE INSTRUCTIONS
See ball tag and page 172.

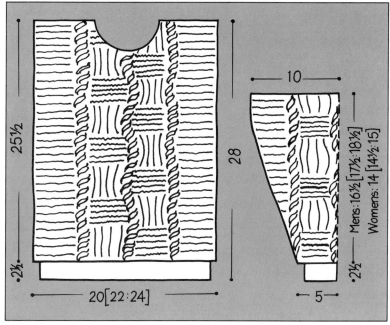

APPLEJACK

THERE IS A PERSONAL REASON FOR RECOMMENDING THIS DESIGN, BECAUSE OF ALL THE JERSEYS I POSSESS, IT IS THE ONE I WEAR THE MOST. AND OTHER PEOPLE SEEM TO LIKE IT A LOT! I THINK IT'S THE LOW V-NECK AND THE BUTTONS WHICH MAKE IT SPECIAL, APART FROM THE YARN ITSELF. AS YOU CAN SEE, IT'S ALL IN STOCKING STITCH SO IT SHOULDN'T PRESENT ANY PROBLEMS TO ANYONE.

Shown on page 147 in charcoal Chicago.
Also shown on page 167 in midnight Chicago.
Sizes are suitable for both men and women, but sleeves should be shortened by 6cm for women.

See diagram at end of pattern

SIZE cm(in)
To fit chest/bust:

89–94(35–37)	96–102(38–40)	104–109(41–43)
Actual size:		
97(38)	104(41)	112(44)
Length from back neck:		
69(27)	69(27)	69(27)
Sleeve seam:		
49(19½)	49(19½)	50(20)

MATERIALS
Chicago – 50g balls:

15	16	17
1 pair each of 5mm and 6mm needles		
5mm circular needle. Stitch holders		
5 buttons		

TENSION
14sts and 20 rows = 10cm square on 6mm needles over stocking stitch. See page 9.

ABBREVIATIONS
See page 9.

BACK
Using 5mm needles cast on 68(72:76)sts and work 5cm in k1 p1 rib.

Change to 6mm needles and stocking st. Cont until work measures 43cm.
Shape armhole: cast off 3(4:5)sts beg next 2 rows. Cont without shaping until work measures 69cm, cast off.

POCKET A (2)
Using 6mm needles cast on 20sts and work 22 rows in stocking st. Leave on holder.

POCKET B (1)
Using 6mm needles cast on 16sts and work 14 rows in stocking st. Leave on holder.

LEFT FRONT
Using 5mm needles cast on 33(34:35)sts and work 5cm in k1 p1 rib.
Change to 6mm needles and stocking st. Work 22 rows.
Place pocket A: k6, place next 20sts on holder, k20 across pocket A, knit to end.
Cont until work measures 28cm.
Shape V neck: dec neck edge on next and every foll 10th row to 24sts. AT THE SAME TIME when work measures 43cm:
Shape armhole: cast off 3(4:5)sts beg next row. Cont without shaping to 53cm.
Place pocket B: place pocket centrally. Cont until work measures 69cm and cast off.

RIGHT FRONT
As left front but reversing all shapings and omitting pocket B.
Place pocket A: k7(8:9), place pocket as above, k6.

SLEEVES
Using 5mm needles cast on 38sts and work 5cm

Following page: The tweedy cardigan to the right is Applejack which is also shown on page 167. The short boxy sweater, Buster, would also work well in any of the bright Chandos colours; the pattern is on page 168.

in k1 p1 rib.

Increase row: rib 2 *inc rib 3* to end *47sts*
Change to 6mm needles and stocking st, inc
each end of every 4th row to 73(75:77)sts. Cont
without shaping until work measures
49(49:50)cm.

Shape sleevehead: cast off 4sts beg next 16 rows.
Cast off.

POCKET TRIMS
With sts from holder and using 5mm needles
work 4 rows in k1 p1 rib. Cast off in rib.

FRONT BAND
Join shoulder seams. Using 5mm circular needle
pick up 44sts from hem to V shaping, 64sts
along V shaping, 20(22:24)sts across back neck,
64sts along V shaping and 44sts from V shaping
to hem *236(238:240)sts*
Work 3 rows k1 p1 rib.
Row 4: rib 2 *yrn dec rib 8* 4 times yrn dec rib
to end. Work 2 more rows in rib. Cast off in rib.

MAKING UP
Join side and sleeve seams. Set in sleeves and
stitch into position. Slipstitch pockets in
position. Weave in any loose ends. Sew on
buttons.

CARE INSTRUCTIONS
See ball tag and page 172.

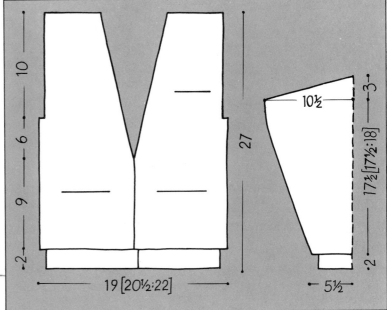

HOPSCOTCH

THIS SNAPPY LITTLE WINTER SWEATER HAS A PANEL OF CABLES AND BASKET STITCH ON THE FRONT. IT WORKS WELL IN THIS SHORT LENGTH AND A BRIGHT COLOUR, BUT OF COURSE YOU COULD KNIT AN EXTRA 15CM BEFORE THE ARMHOLE SO IT WOULD COME, MORE CONVENTIONALLY, TO THE HIP.

Shown on page 150 in bluebell Chandos.

See diagram at end of pattern

SIZE cm(in)
To fit bust:

81–91(32–36)	91–107(36–42)

Actual size:

102(40)	112(44)

Length from back neck:

56(22)	56(22)

Sleeve seam:

47(18½)	47(18½)

MATERIALS
Chandos – 50g balls:

17	18

1 pair each of 5mm, 5½mm, and 6mm needles

TENSION
15sts and 20 rows = 10cm square using 6mm needles over stocking stitch with yarn used DOUBLE (ie 2 ends together). See page 9.

ABBREVIATIONS
See page 9.
c6b = place next 3sts on cn, leave at back of work, k3, then k3 from cn
c6f = as c6b but leave cn at front of work
To clarify the symbols used:
* * = repeat instructions within asterisks as indicated.
[] = sections enclosed within square brackets will be repeated later in the row.
() = sections enclosed within round brackets refer to the second size; the last instruction before the bracket is for the first size only.
eg Row 3, size 1: *p1 k3* 3 times p2 c6f, etc
Row 3, size 2: *p1 k3* 4 times p1 k1 p2 c6f, etc
This garment is knitted using yarn DOUBLE (ie 2 ends together) throughout.

BACK
Using 5mm needles and yarn DOUBLE cast on 77(85)sts and work 22 rows in k1 p1 rib.
Change to 6mm needles and patt as follows:
Row 1: k2 *p1 k3* 18(20) times p1 k2
Row 2: p1 *k1 p3* 9(10) times k1 p1 k1 *p3 k1* 9(10) times p1
Row 3: *p1 k3* 19(21) times p1
Row 4: *p3 k1* 9(10) times p5 *k1 p3* 9(10) times
These 4 rows form patt rep. Cont in patt until work measures 34cm.
Shape armhole: cast off 2(3)sts beg next 2 rows. Dec each end next 4 rows. Dec each end alt rows to 59(63)sts. Cont without shaping until work measures 54cm.
Shape neck and shoulders: cast off 5sts, patt 12(14), cast off 25sts, patt 17(19).
On 17(19)sts:
Row 1: cast off 5sts, patt to end
Row 2: cast off 2sts, patt to end
Rows 3–4: as rows 1–2. Cast off
Rejoin yarn to rem sts at neck edge and work rows 2–5.

FRONT
Using 5mm needles and yarn DOUBLE cast on 77(85)sts and work 21 rows in k1 p1 rib.
Row 22: rib 3 *inc, rib 4* 4 times, *inc, rib 3* 3 times, *inc, rib 1* 5(9) times, *inc, rib 3* 3 times, *inc, rib 4* 4 times 96(108)sts

Change to 6mm needles and patt:
Row 1: k2 *p1 k3* 2(3) times p1 k1(3) p2 k9 [p2 k5 p5 k5 p2] k12 rep [] again k9 p2 k1(3) *p1 k3* 2(3) times p1 k2
Row 2: p1 *k1 p3* 2(4) times k1 p2(0) k2 p9 [k2 p5 k5 p5 k2] p12 rep []again p9 k2 p2(0) *k1 p3* 2(4) times k1 p1
Row 3: *p1 k3* 3(4) times p2 (p1 k1 p2) c6f k3 [p2 k5 p5 k5 p2] c6b c6f rep [] again c6f k3 p2 (p2 k1 p1) *k3 p1* 3(4) times
Row 4: *p3 k1* 2(4) times p3(2) k3(2) p9 [k2 p5 k5 p5 k2] p12 rep [] again p9 k3(2) p3(2) *k1 p3* 2(4) times
Rows 5−6: as rows 1−2
Row 7: *p1 k3* 3(4) times p2(p1 k1 p2) k3 c6b [p2 k5 p5 k5 p2] k12 rep [] again k3 c6b p2(p2 k1 p1) *k3 p1* 3(4) times
Row 8: *p3 k1* 2(4) times p3(2) k3(2) p9 [k2 p15 k2] p12 rep [] again p9 k3(2) p3(2) *k1 p3* 2(4) times
Row 9: k2 *p1 k3* 2(3) times p1 k1(3) p2 k9 [p7 k5 p7] k12 rep [] again k9 p2 k1(3) *p1 k3* 2(3) times p1 k2
Row 10: p1 *k1 p3* 2(4) times k1 p2(0) k2 p9 [k7 p5 k7] p12 rep [] again p9 k2 p2(0) *k1 p3* 2(4) times k1 p1
Row 11: *p1 k3* 3(4) times p2 (p1 k1 p2) c6f k3 [p7 k5 p7] c6b c6f rep [] again c6f k3 p2(p2 k1 p1) *k3 p1* 3(4) times
Row 12: *p3 k1* 2(4) times p3(2) k3(2) p9 [k7 p5 k7] p12 rep [] again p9 k3(2) p3(2) *k1 p3* 2(4) times
Rows 13−14: as rows 9−10
Row 15: *p1 k3* 3(4) times p2(p1 k1 p2) k3 c6b [p7 k5 p7] k12 rep[] again k3 c6b k3 p2(p2 k1 p1) *k3 p1* 3(4) times
Row 16: as row 8
These 16 rows form patt rep. Cont in patt until work measures 34cm.
Shape armhole: cast off 2(3)sts beg next 2 rows. Dec each end next 4 rows. Dec each end alt rows to 76(82)sts.
Cont without shaping until work measures 48cm.
Shape neck: patt 28(31), cast off 20sts, patt 28(31).
On 28(31)sts:
Row 1: patt
Row 2: cast off 3sts, patt to end
Rows 3−6: as rows 1−2 twice
Row 7: patt
Row 8: dec, patt to end
Repeat rows 7−8 until 17(20)sts rem. Cont until work measures 54cm.
Shape shoulder: (wrong side facing)
Row 1: cast off 5sts, patt to end
Row 2: patt
Row 3: cast off 8sts, patt to end
Row 4: patt
Row 5: cast off
Rejoin yarn to rem sts at neck edge and work

rows 2 to 5 (starting shoulder shaping on right side row).

SLEEVES
Using 5mm needles and yarn DOUBLE cast on 41sts and work 15cm in k1 p1 rib.
Increase row: rib 1 *inc rib 1* to end *61sts*
Change to 6mm needles and patt as for back.
Row 1: k2* p1 k3* 14 times p1 k2
Row 2: p1 *k1 p3* 7 times k1 p1 k1 *p3 k1* 7 times p1
Cont in patt, inc each end of every 6th row to 69(71)sts, working extra sts into edge patt. Cont without shaping until work measures 46cm.
Shape sleevehead: cast off 3sts beg each row until 21(23)sts rem. Cast off.

COLLAR
Join right shoulder seam, easing front to back shoulder shapings. Using 5½mm needles and with right side facing, and yarn DOUBLE, evenly pick up 20sts from side front neck, 20sts from centre front neck, 20sts from side front neck, and 34sts from back neck *94sts*
Row 1: *k1 p1 k1 p2tog* to last 4sts *k1 p1* twice. Cont in k1 p1 rib until work measures 18cm. Cast off loosely in rib.

MAKING UP
Join left shoulder seam, collar, side and sleeve seams. Set in sleeves and stitch into position. Weave in any loose ends.

CARE INSTRUCTIONS
See ball tag and page 172.

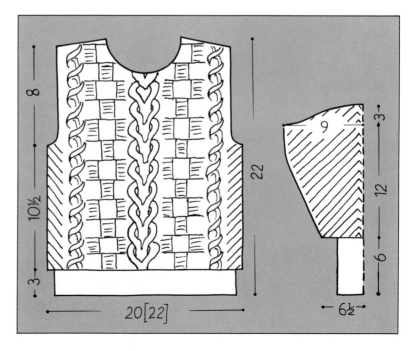

TRISTAN

THE TWEED YARN CHICAGO LENDS ITSELF NATURALLY TO MOSS STITCH WHICH LOOKS VERY EFFECTIVE DIVIDED INTO PANELS AS SHOWN IN THIS MAN'S SWEATER. ONCE AGAIN I HAVE USED THE SADDLE SHOULDER SHAPING WHICH TAKES THE 'DROOPY-SHOULDERED' LOOK OUT OF BIG COUNTRY JERSEYS.

Shown on page 154 in amazon Chicago. Lengthened version shown on page 119 in eskimo Chicago.

See diagram at end of pattern

SIZE cm(in)
To fit chest/bust:

91–102(36–40)	107–112(42–44)
Actual size:	
107(42)	117(46)
Length from back neck:	
Men (short):	
75(29½)	75(29½)
Women (long):	
89(35)	89(35)
Sleeve seam:	
Men:	
50(19½)	50(19½)
Women:	
43(17)	43(17)

MATERIALS
Chicago – 50g balls:

Men (short):	
17	18
Women (long):	
20	21
1 pair each of 5mm and 6mm needles	

TENSION
14sts and 20 rows = 10cm square on 6mm needles over stocking stitch. See page 9.

Following page: Here is a more conventional variation of Tristan which is also shown on page 119 as an extra long sweater. Ellie is wearing a children's version of Richmond which has an oversized cable down the front, although she's got it a bit scrunched up, so have a better look on page 162.

ABBREVIATIONS
See page 9.

BACK
Using 5mm needles cast on 73(79)sts and work 7cm (short) or 20cm (long) in k1 p1 rib.
Increase row: rib 4(8), *inc, rib 8* 7 times, inc, rib 5 (7) *81(87)sts*
Change to 6mm needles and patt as follows:
Row 1: moss 6(9), *p2, moss 9* 6 times, p2, moss 7(10)
Row 2: moss 7(10), *k2, moss 9* 6 times, k2, moss 6(9)
These 2 rows form patt rep. Cont in patt until work measures 42cm (short) or 56cm (long).
Shape armholes: cast off 3(4)sts at beg of next 2 rows. Dec each end of next and every foll alt row to 61(63)sts. Cont in patt until work measures 65cm (short) or 79cm (long).***
Shape shoulders: cast off 4sts at beg of next 6 rows. Cast off 5sts at beg of next 2 rows. On 27(29)sts work further 5cm. Cast off.

FRONT
As back to ***.
Shape neck and shoulders:
Row 1: cast off 4sts, patt 21, cast off 11(13), patt 25
On 25sts:
Row 2: cast off 4sts, patt to end
Row 3: cast off 3sts, patt to end
Rows 4–5: as rows 2–3
Row 6: cast off 4sts, patt to end
Row 7: cast off 2sts, patt to end. Cast off.
Rejoin yarn to rem sts at neck edge and work row 3 to end.

SLEEVES
Using 5mm needles cast on 37sts and work 7cm

in k1 p1 rib.

Increase row: *inc, rib 3* 9 times, inc. *47sts*
Change to 6mm needles and patt as follows:
Row 1: *p2, moss 9* 4 times, p2, moss 1
Cont in patt, inc each end of every 4th row to
73(75)sts, working extra sts into patt. Cont
without shaping until sleeve measures 50cm
(men) or 43cm (women).

Shape sleevehead: cast off 3(4)sts at beg of next
2 rows. Dec each end of next and every alt row
to 59sts. Work 3 rows. Dec each end of next and
every foll 4th row to 51sts. Work one row. Cast
off 4sts at beg of next 4 rows. Cast off 8sts at
beg of next 2 rows. On 19sts work further
12cm. Cast off.

NECKBAND

Join shoulder seams making saddle shoulder (see
page 174), leaving back left shoulder seam open.
Using 5mm needles, pick up 11sts across ½
sleeve, 35(37)sts from front neck, 11sts from ½
sleeve, and 27(29)sts from back neck *84(88)sts*
Work 5 rows in k1 p1 rib. Cast off.

MAKING UP

Join back shoulder seam, side and sleeve seams.
Set in sleeves and stitch into position. Weave in
any loose ends.

CARE INSTRUCTIONS

See ball tag and page 172.

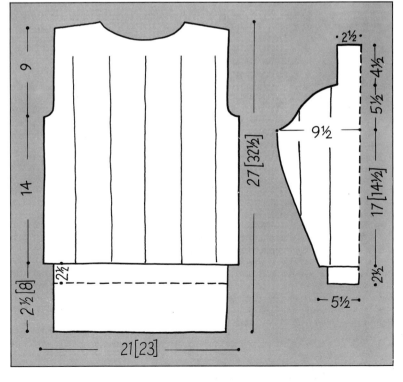

HANOVER

THIS IS A VERSATILE DESIGN, AS I'M SURE YOU CAN ALSO IMAGINE IT IN A LONGER LENGTH TO COVER UP THE LOWER REGIONS. THE CABLES ARE FORMED FROM THE RIGHT SIDE SO THAT THEY APPEAR INTEGRATED TO THE MAIN BODY.

Shown on page 150 in coral Chandos.
Also shown on page 130 in eskimo Chicago
with flannel collar.

See diagram at end of pattern

SIZE cm(in)
To fit bust:

91–97(36–38)	101–106(40–42)
Actual size:	
101(40)	112(44)
Length from back neck:	
59(23)	61(24)
Sleeve seam:	
41(16)	42(16½)

MATERIALS
Chandos and/or Chicago – 50g balls:

coral Chandos:	
17	18
eskimo Chicago:	
14	15
flannel Chandos:	
2	2

1 pair each of 5mm and 6mm needles
Cable needle. 5mm circular needle

TENSION
15sts and 20 rows = 10cm square using yarn DOUBLE (ie 2 ends together) for Chandos or yarn single for Chicago on 6mm needles over stocking stitch. See page 9.

SPECIAL NOTE
When using Chandos in this garment use yarn DOUBLE (ie 2 ends together).

ABBREVIATIONS
See page 9.
c12 = place next 6sts on cn, leave at back of work, k6, then k6 from cn

BACK
Using yarn DOUBLE (Chandos) or SINGLE (Chicago) and 5mm needles, cast on 72(80)sts and work 10cm in k2 p2 rib.
Increase row: rib 0(4), *inc, rib 9* 7 times, inc, rib 1(5) 80(88)sts
Change to 6mm needles and stocking st, and cont until work measures 33(34)cm.
Shape armholes: cast off 3sts at beg of next 2 rows. Cont without shaping until work measures 38(39)cm. Inc each end of next and every foll 6th row to 86(94)sts. Cont without shaping until work measures 54(56)cm.
Shape shoulders: cast off 4sts at beg of next 6 rows. Cast off 9(10)sts at beg of next 2 rows. Cast off 12(13)sts at beg of next 2 rows. Cast off.

FRONT
Using yarn DOUBLE (Chandos) or SINGLE (Chicago), and 5mm needles, cast on 72(80)sts and work 10cm in k2 p2 rib.
Increase row: rib 0(4), *inc, rib 3* 3 times, *inc, rib 1* 4 times, *inc, rib 4* 7 times, *inc, rib 1* 4 times, *inc, rib 3* twice, inc, rib 0(4) 93(101)sts
Change to 6mm needles and patt as follows:
Row 1: k41(45), *p1, k1* 5 times, p1, k41(45)
Row 2: p42(46), *k1, p1* 4 times, k1, p42(46)
Rows 3–6: as rows 1–2 twice
Row 7: k15(19), c12, k14, *p1, k1* 5 times, p1, k14, c12, k15(19)
Row 8: as row 2
Rows 9–14: as rows 1–2 3 times
These 14 rows form patt rep. Cont in patt until work measures 33(34)cm.

Shape armholes: cast off 3sts at beg of next 2 rows.
Divide for neck: patt 43(47), cast off 1st, patt 43(47).
On 43(47)sts:
Dec neck edge on every foll 4th row for 10 decreases, AT THE SAME TIME, when work measures 38(39)cm, inc at armhole edge on next and every foll 6th row for six increases.
Continue until work measures 54(56)cm.
Shape shoulder: cast off 4sts at beg of next and foll 2 alt rows. Work one row.
Cast off 9(10)sts at beg of next row. Work one row.
Cast off 12(13)sts.
NB When casting off over the 12 cable sts, k2tog, then cast off (ie over cable, 2sts = 1 st).
Rejoin yarn to rem sts at neck edge and work to match reversing shapings.

SLEEVES

Using yarn DOUBLE (Chandos) or SINGLE (Chicago), and 5mm needles, cast on 38sts and work 6cm in k2 p2 rib.
Increase row: rib 1, *inc, rib 3* 9 times, inc 48sts
Change to 6mm needles and stocking st, inc each end of every 3rd row to 76(80)sts. Cont until work measures 42(43)cm. Cast off loosely.

COLLAR

Join shoulder seams. Using yarn DOUBLE (Chandos) or SINGLE (Chicago) and 5mm circular needle, with wrong side facing, pick up 61(63)sts from side V neck, 24sts from back neck, 61(63)sts from side V neck *146(150)sts*
Work 9cm in k2 p2 rib. Cast off in k2 p2 rib.

MAKING UP

Join side and sleeve seams, leaving 1cm open to fit armhole. Ease sleeve into armhole. Weave in any loose ends.

CARE INSTRUCTIONS

See ball tag and page 172.

Diagram measurements:
2
8[8½]
9[9½]
4
20[22]
9½[10]
23[24]
14[14½]
2½
4½

MADISON

THERE'S QUITE A LOT OF KNITTING IN THE COAT, BUT IT'S ALL ON BIG NEEDLES, MOSTLY IN STOCKING STITCH AND WELL WORTH THE EFFORT WHEN YOU'VE FINISHED. THIS DESIGN HAS GENEROUS GATHERED SLEEVES AND A DOUBLE-BREASTED FRONT SO THERE'S PLENTY TO WRAP UP IN.

Long version shown on page 158 in charcoal Chicago.
Short version shown on page 142 in blaze Chicago.

See diagram at end of pattern

SIZE cm(in)
To fit bust:

	81–97(32–38)
Actual size:	
	104(44)
Length from back neck	
	long: 97(38)
	short: 61(24)
Sleeve seam:	
	48(19)

MATERIALS
Chicago – 50g balls:

long:	
	22
short:	
	16

1 pair each of 5mm and 6½mm needles

5mm circular needle (longest length)

Cable needle.

Buttons: long – 16; short – 8

TENSION
13½sts and 18 rows = 10cm square on 6½mm needles over stocking stitch. See page 9.

ABBREVIATIONS
See page 9.
c4f = place next st on cn, leave at front of work, k3, then k1 from cn
c4b = place next 3sts on cn, leave at back of work, k1, then k3 from cn

BACK
Using 5mm needles, cast on 75sts and work 3cm in k1 p1 rib.
Change to 6½mm needles and stocking st and cont to 74cm (long) or 38cm (short).
Shape armhole: cast off 3sts at beg of next 2 rows. Dec each end of next and every foll alt row to 57sts.
Cont without shaping until work measures 97cm (long) or 61cm (short), ending on a purl row.
Shape shoulders and neck: cast off 5sts, k16, cast off 15sts, k21.
On 21sts:
Row 1: cast off 5sts, work to end
Row 2: cast off 3sts, work to end
Row 3: as row 1
Row 4: cast off 2sts, work to end. Cast off.
With right side facing, region yarn to rem sts at neck edge. Work from row 2 to end.

LEFT FRONT
Using 5mm needles, cast on 50sts and work 3cm in k1 p1 rib.
Change to 6½mm needles and patt as follows:
Row 1: k16, p2, k9, p2, k21
Row 2: p21, k2, p9, k2, p16
Row 3: k16, p2, c4f, k1, c4b, p2, k21
Row 4: as row 2
These 4 rows form patt rep. Cont in patt until work measures 69cm (long) or 33cm (short).
Place marker at neck edge. Dec at neck edge on

MADISON

next and every foll alt row. When work measures 74cm (long) or 38cm (short).
Shape armhole: cont neck edge shaping AT THE SAME TIME cast off 3sts at beg of next row. Work one row. Dec armhole edge on next 4 rows. Dec armhole edge on next 6 alt rows. Cont decs as before on neck edge until 17sts rem. Cont until work measures 97cm (long) or 61cm (short), ending on a purl row.
Shape shoulders: cast off 5sts at beg of next row. Work one row. Cast off 6sts at beg of next row. Work one row. Cast off.

RIGHT FRONT

Using 5mm needles, cast on 50sts and work 2 rows in k1 p1 rib.
Make buttonhole:
Row 3: rib 14, cast off 2sts, rib to end
Row 4: rib 34, cast on 2sts, rib to end
Cont in rib until work measures 3cm.
Change to 6½mm needles and patt as follows:
Row 1: k21 p2 k9 p2 k16
Row 2: p16 k2 p9 k2 p21
Row 3: k21 p2 c4b k1 c4f p2 k16
Row 4: as row 2. These 4 rows form patt rep.
Cont in patt until work measures 10cm, ending on a purl row.
Make buttonhole: patt 14, cast off 2sts, patt 34. Complete buttonhole as before.
Cont in patt making further buttonholes at 19cm and 28cm (long and short) and at 37cm, 46cm, 55cm and 64cm (long).
Cont in patt as for left front, but reversing all shapings.

SLEEVES

Using 6½mm needles, cast on 26sts. Change to 5mm needles and working in k1 p1 rib, inc each end of every 4th row to 52sts.
Change to 6½mm needles and stocking st.
Increase row: k1, *inc, k3* 12 times, inc, k2
65sts
Inc each end of every foll 5th row to 75sts. Cont without shaping until work measures 48cm.
Shape sleevehead: cast off 2sts at beg of next 4 rows. Dec each end of next 2 rows. Dec each end of next and every foll 4th row to 43sts.
p2tog across row, p1. Cast off.

COLLAR

NB. If your circular needle is not long enough, or you cannot bear to work 351sts at once, work the collar section from marker to marker separately from the button bands and sew together with invisible seam.
Join shoulder seams. Using 5mm circular needle pick up 113sts (long) or 53sts (short) from right

front hem to marker, 47sts from marker to shoulder, 31sts across back neck, 47sts from shoulder to marker on left front, and 113sts (long) or 53sts (short) from marker to hem.
On *351sts* (long) *231sts* (short):
Row 1: k1, p1 rib
Row 2: rib 186 (long) or 126 (short), turn
Row 3: s1, rib 20, turn
Row 4: s1, rib 24, turn
Row 5: s1, rib 28, turn
Cont as set until s1, rib 116, turn
Next row: s1, rib to end
Make buttonholes: rib 241(long) or 181(short), *cast off 2sts, rib 13* 7(long) or 3(short) times, cast off 2sts, rib 3.
NB Check that buttonholes appear level with ones already made.
Next row: cast on 2sts over those cast off in row before.
Rib 2 more rows. Cast off loosely in rib.

MAKING UP

Join side and sleeve seams. Set in sleeves and stitch into position. Weave in any loose ends. Sew on buttons.

CARE INSTRUCTIONS

See ball tag and page 172.

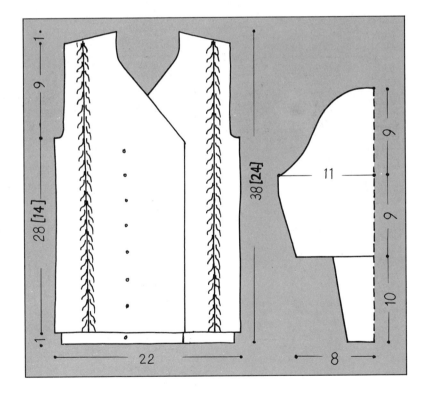

This long tweedy coat, shown here in charcoal Chicago, is also made as a jacket on page 142.

RICHMOND

T HIS DESIGN IS ALL IN STOCKING STITCH, BECAUSE THE CHUNKY CABLE RUNNING DOWN THE FRONT IS ALL FORMED FROM RIGHT-SIDE STITCHES. IT WOULD WORK EQUALLY WELL AS A MAN'S SWEATER, BUT I WOULDN'T RECOMMEND CHANGING THE CABLE PATTERN, AS AN ALLOWANCE HAS BEEN MADE FOR IT TO PULL THE KNITTING IN.

Shown on page 162 in pacific Chicago.
Also shown on page 154 in amazon Chicago.

See diagram at end of pattern

SIZE Child's cm(in)
To fit bust/chest:

1	2	3
61–66(24–26)	71–76(28–30)	81–86(32–34)

Actual size:

71(28)	81(32)	91(36)

Length from back neck:

41(16)	51(20)	61(24)

Sleeve seam:

30(12)	38(15)	43(17)

SIZE Adults cm(in)
To fit bust/chest:

4	5	6
86–94(34–37)	96–104(38–41)	106–112(42–44)

Actual size:

102(40)	112(44)	122(48)

Length from back neck:

66(26)	71(28)	71(28)

Sleeve seam:

46(18)	48(19)	51(20)

MATERIALS
Chicago – 50g balls:

size 1: 7	size 2: 9	size 3:12
size 4:15	size 5:17	size 6:19

1 pair each of 5mm and 6mm needles

Cable needle

TENSION
14sts and 20 rows = 10cm square on 6mm needles over stocking stitch
See page 9.

ABBREVIATIONS
See page 9.
c8 = place next 4sts on cn, leave at back of work, k4, then k4 from cn
c12 = place next 6sts on cn, leave at back of work, k6, then k6 from cn

BACK
Using 5mm needles cast on 50(56:64:70:78:84)sts and work 10(10:14:14:18:18) rows in k2 p2 rib.
Change to 6mm needles and stocking st and cont until work measures 37(47:41:41:45:45)cm.
Sizes 3(4:5:6): inc each end next and every foll 8th row to 74(80:88:94)sts.
Cont until work measures 57(62:67:67)cm.
Shape shoulders: (all sizes) cast off 3(3:4:5:6:6)sts beg next 8 rows. Cast off 3(4:7:5:4:6)sts next 2 rows. Cast off rem sts.

FRONT
Using 5mm needles cast on 50(56:64:70:78:84)sts and work 9(9:13:13:17:17) rows in k2 p2 rib.
Increase row: rib 23(26:29:32:36:39)sts, inc in next 4(4:6:6:6:6)sts rib to end 54(60:70:76:84:90)sts
Change to 6mm needles and work as follows:
Sizes 1–2:
Rows 1–4: stocking st
Row 5: k23(26) c8 k23(26)
Row 6: purl
Rows 7–10: as rows 1–4

Following page:
Here is the grown-up's version of Richmond, which is also shown on page 154 in a child's size. On the right is a sleeveless version of Kimo which is also shown on page 115.

These 10 rows form patt rep. Cont in patt until work measures 15 rows less than back.

Shape neck: (wrong side facing)

Row 1: p23(26) *p2tog* 4 times p23(26)

Row 2: k19(22) cast off 12sts k19(22)

On 19(22)sts:

Row 3: purl

Row 4: cast off 1(2)sts, work to end

Rows 5–6: as rows 3–4

Row 7: cast off 3sts, work to end

Row 8: dec, work to end

Rows 9–10: as rows 7–8

Row 11: cast off 3sts, work to end

Row 12: knit

Rows 13–14: as rows 11–12

Row 15: cast off

Rejoin yarn to rem sts at neck edge and work to match.

Sizes 3(4:5:6):

Rows 1–6: stocking st

Row 7: k29(32:36:39) c12 k29(32:36:39)

Row 8: purl

Rows 9–14: as rows 1–6

These 14 rows form patt rep. Cont in patt until work measures 41(41:45:45)cm. Inc each end next and every foll 8th row to 80(86:94:100)sts. Cont 21 rows less than back.

Shape neck:

Row 1: p34(37:41:44) *p2tog* 6 times p34(37:41:44)

Row 2: k33(35:38:40) cast off 8(10:12:14)sts k33(35:38:40)

On 33(35:38:40)sts:

Row 3: purl

Row 4: cast off 2sts, work to end

Row 5: purl

Rows 6–7: as rows 4–5

Row 8: dec, work to end

Row 9: purl

Rows 10–11: as rows 8–9

Row 12: as row 8

Row 13: cast off 4(5:6:6)sts, work to end

Row 14: dec, work to end

Rows 15–18: as rows 13–14 twice

Row 19: as row 13

Row 20: knit

Row 21: cast off rem sts

Rejoin yarn to rem sts at neck edge and work to match.

SLEEVES

Using 5mm needles cast on 28(28:34:38:38:38)sts and work 9(9:13:13:17:17) rows in k2 p2 rib.

Increase row: rib 0(0:2:2:2:2) *inc rib 3* to end 35(35:42:47:47:47)sts

Change to 6mm needles and stocking st. Inc

each end every 6(6:3:3:3:3) row to 55(59:79:83:83:87)sts. Cont without shaping until work measures 30(38:43:46:48:51)cm. Cast off.

COLLAR

Using 6mm needles cast on 82(82:94:94:98:98)sts. Work 5(5:7:7:7:7)cm in k2 p2 rib. Change to 5mm needles and work 4 rows in rib. Cast off in rib.

MAKING UP

Join shoulder and sleeve seams. Working from shoulder seam downwards, ease sleevehead into position and stitch. Join side seams. Using a flat seam attach collar to garment overlapping collar by 2cm at centre front. Weave in any loose ends.

CARE INSTRUCTIONS

See ball tag and page 172.

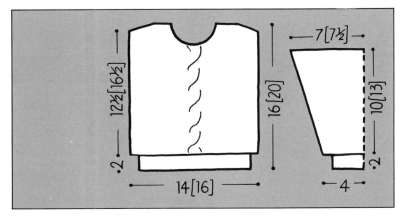

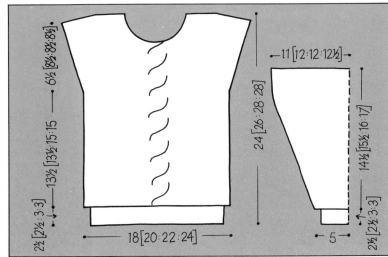

CAPULET

T HIS DESIGN INVOLVES ONLY THE MOST BASIC KNITTING TECHNI-
QUES, BUT THE CABLE DETAILS ON THE SHOULDERS AND POCKET
MAKE IT QUITE DIFFERENT FROM THE REST. IT'S A GOOD SPORTY
SHAPE WHICH WILL TRANSLATE EASILY INTO ANY OTHER COLOUR.

Shown on page 15 in white Chandos.
Child's version shown on page 167 in poppy
Chandos.

See diagram at end of pattern

SIZE Child's cm(in)
To fit chest:

1	2	3
61–66(24–26)	69–74(27–29)	76–81(30–32)

Actual size:

71(28)	79(31)	86(34)

Length from back neck:

46(18)	51(20)	61(24)

Sleeve seam:

30(12)	38(15)	41(16)

SIZE Adult's cm(in)
To fit bust:

4	5	6
84–89(33–35)	91–96(36–38)	99–104(39–41)

Actual size:

94(37)	102(40)	112(44)

Length from back neck:

66(26)	69(27)	71(28)

Sleeve seam:

43(17)	46(18)	51(20)

MATERIALS
Chandos – 50g balls:

Size 1: 6	Size 2: 8	Size 3:10
Size 4:12	Size 5:13	Size 6:15

1 pair each of 3¼mm and 4mm needles

Cable needle. Stitch holders 2(3:3:3:3:3)
buttons

TENSION
22sts and 28 rows = 10cm square on 4mm
needles over stocking stitch. See page 9.

ABBREVIATIONS
See page 9.
c4b = place next 2sts on cn, leave at back of
work, k2, then k2 from cn
c6b = place next 3sts on cn, leave at back of
work, k3, then k3 from cn
c6f = place next 3sts on cn, leave at front of
work, k3, then k3 from cn

BACK
Using 3¼mm needles cast on
78(86:94:102:114)sts and work
10(14:15:15:19:19) rows in k1 p1 rib.
Sizes 3(4:5:6):
Increase row: rib 4(8:12:18) *inc, rib 10* 7
times, inc, rib 4(8:12:18) *94:(102:110:122)sts*
All sizes:
Change to 4mm needles and stocking st.
Cont until work measures
25(34:38:40:41:43)cm
Shape armhole:
Sizes 1–2: place markers each end of next row.
Sizes 3–6: cast off 2(3:4:6)sts beg next 2 rows.
Dec each end next and foll alt rows to
84(88:92:98)sts.
All sizes: cont without shaping until work
measures 40(46:53:58:61:63)cm.
Shape shoulders: cast off 5sts beg next 8 rows.
Cast off 5(8:7:8:9:10)sts beg next 2 rows.
On 28(30:30:32:34:38)sts:
Work 8(8:16:16:16:16) rows. Cast off.

POCKET
Using 4mm needles cast on
18(18:24:24:24:24)sts. Work
16(16:20:20:20:20) rows in stocking st. Leave
on holder.

FRONT

Using 3¼mm needles cast on
78(86:86:94:102:114)sts and work
9(13:15:15:19:19) rows in k1 p1 rib.
Sizes 1 and 2: rib 52(56) *inc rib 1* 4 times, rib
to end *82(90)sts*
Sizes 3(4:5:6:): rib 4(2:1:1) *inc rib 6(7:8:9)*
11 times, inc, rib 4(3:1:2) *98(106:114:126)sts*
Change to 4mm needles and work according to
size as follows:

Sizes 1 and 2:
Row 1: k17(21) *p1 k5* twice p1 k52(56)
Row 2: p53(57) *k1 p4* twice k1 p18(22)
Row 3: k17(21) p1 k1 c4f p1 c4b k1 p1 k52(56)
Row 4: as row 2
These 4 rows form patt rep. Cont in patt until
work measures 29(37)cm placing markers either
end at 25(34)cm.
Divide for neck: patt 43(47) turn (leave 39(43)sts
on holder) on 43(47)sts cont to 33(39)cm.
Place pocket: right side facing k10(12), place
next 22sts on holder, knit across 18sts of
pocket, k11(13) *39(43)sts*
Cont in stocking st until work measures
40(46)cm, ending with a purl row.
Shape shoulders and neck:
Rows 1–3: cast off 5sts, work to end
Row 4: cast off 3(4)sts, work to end
Row 5: cast off 5sts, work to end
Row 6: cast off 3sts, work to end
Rows 7–8: as rows 5–6
Row 9: cast off
Rejoin yarn to rem sts and work to match,
omitting pocket.

Sizes 3(4:5:6):
Row 1: k19(21:23:26) *p1 k7*twice p1
k62(68:74:83)
Rows 2 and 4: p63(69:75:84) *k1 p6* twice k1
p20(22:24:27)
Row 3: k19(21:23:26) p1 k1 c6f p1 c6b k1 p1
k62(68:74:83)
Rows 5–6: as rows 1–2
These 6 rows form patt rep. Cont in patt until
work measures 38(40:41:43)cm.
Shape armhole: cast off 2(3:4:6)sts beg next 2
rows. Dec each end next and foll alt rows to
88(92:96:102)sts.
Divide for neck: (with wrong side facing)
p40(42:44:47), cast off 4sts, patt to end.
On 44(46:48:51)sts: cont in patt until work
measures 47(49:51:53)cm.
Place pocket: k8(9:10:11), place next 28sts on
holder, knit across 24sts of pocket k8(9:10:12)
40(42:44:47)sts
Cont in stocking st until work measures
53(58:61:63)cm, ending with a purl row.
Shape shoulders and neck:
Row 1: cast off 5sts, work to end
Row 2: cast off 4(5:6:6)sts, work to end

Row 3: as row 1
Row 4: cast off 3(3:3:4)sts, work to end
Row 5: as row 1
Row 6: as row 4
Row 7: as row 1
Row 8: cast off 3sts, work to end
Row 9: cast off
Rejoin yarn to rem sts and work to match
omitting pocket.

SLEEVES

Using 3¼mm needles cast on
40(42:44:48:48:52)sts and work
9(13:15:15:19:19) rows in k1 p1 rib.
Increase row: rib 5(6:3:1:1:3) *inc rib 3*
7(7:9:11:11:11) times, inc rib 6(7:4:2:2:4)
48(50:54:60:60:64)sts
Change to 4mm needles and stocking st. Inc
each end 5th and every foll 6(6:5:5:5:5) rows to
68(76:86:96:100:104)sts ending with a right
side row.
Wrong side facing: p31(35:38:43:45:47) *inc
p1* 3(3:5:5:5:5) times p31(35:38:43:45:47).
Change to patt as folls and work according to
size.

Sizes 1 and 2:
Row 1: moss 31(35) k4 p1 k4 moss 31(35)
Row 2: moss 31(35) p4 k1 p4 moss 31(35)
Row 3: moss 31(35) c4f p1 c4b moss 31(35)
Row 4: as row 2
These 4 rows form patt rep. Cont until work
measures 30(38)cm.
Shape sleevehead: cast off 5sts beg next 10 rows.
Cast off 4(7)sts beg next 2 rows.
On 13(15)sts: patt 30(32) rows. Cast off.

Sizes 3(4:5:6):
Row 1: moss 39(44:46:48) k6 p1 k6 moss
39(44:46:48)
Row 2: moss 39(44:46:48) p6 k1 p6 moss
39(44:46:48)
Rows 3–4: as rows 1–2
Row 5: moss 39(44:46:48) c6f p1 c6b moss
39(44:46:48)
Row 6: as row 2
These 6 rows form patt rep. Cont in patt until
work measures 41(43:46:51)cm.
Shape sleevehead: cast off 2(3:4:6)sts beg next 2
rows. Dec each end alt rows to 71(77:73:73)sts.
Dec each and every row to 51(57:53:53)sts.
Cast off 9(10:9:8)sts beg next 4 rows.
On 15(17:17:21)sts: work 32(34:38:40) rows
patt without shaping. Cast off.

COLLAR

Using 4mm needles cast on
101(105:111:117:123:129)sts and work
10(10:14:14:18:18) rows k1 p1 rib.
Change to 3¼mm needles and work
4(4:4:6:6:6) rows rib. Cast off in rib.

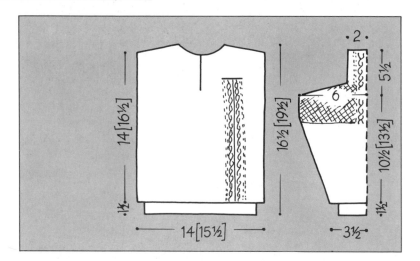

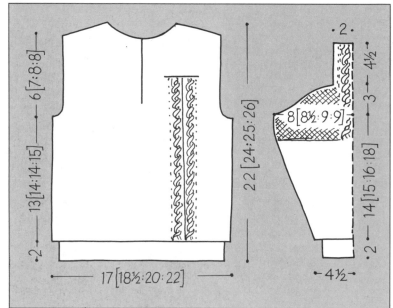

POCKET TRIM
Using 3¼mm needles work 4(4:6:6:6:6) rows
k1 p1 rib from sts left on holder. Cast off
in rib.

Sizes 1 and 2:
BUTTON BAND (Girl LH side, Boy RH side)
Using 3¼mm needles pick up 16(26)sts along
side neck opening, knit 1 row. Cast off.
BUTTONHOLE BAND (Girl RH side, Boy
LH side)
Using 3¼mm needles pick up 16(26)sts along
side neck opening.
Girl: k2 *k2tog yrn k6(7)* once(twice) k2tog
yrn k4. Cast off.
Boy: k4 *yrn k2tog k6(7)* once(twice) yrn
k2tog k2. Cast off.

Sizes 3(4:5:6):
BUTTON BAND (Women's LH side, Men's
RH side)
Using 3¼mm needles pick up 26(26:30:30)sts.
Work 5 rows k1 p1 rib. Cast off.
BUTTONHOLE BAND (Women's RH side,
Men's LH side)
Pick up as for button band. Work 2 rows k1 p1
rib.
Ladies: rib 2(2:4:4) *yrn dec rib 6* 3 times rib
0(0:2:2).
Men: rib 0(0:2:2) *rib 6 dec yrn* 3 times rib
2(2:4:4).
Work 2 more rows rib. Cast off.

MAKING UP
Join shoulder seams (see diagram page 174) and
side seams (on sizes 1 and 2 to markers). Set in
sleeves and stitch. Sew sleeve seams. Slipstitch
pocket to inside and pocket trims to outside.
Using flat seam join cast off edge of collar to
garment. Weave in any loose ends. Sew on
buttons.

CARE INSTRUCTIONS
See ball tag and page 172.

*This little poppy
sweater, Capulet, is
also shown on page
15 in an adult's size.
The man is wearing
Applejack where the
buttons pick out the
different fleck colours
of the tweed, and this
is also shown on page
146.*

BUSTER

THIS IS MEANT TO BE A LIGHT-HEARTED APPROACH TO TRADITIONAL WINTER JERSEYS. IT'S CROPPED OFF AT THE MIDRIFF, AND OVERSIZED EVERYWHERE ELSE SO THAT YOU WEAR IT WITH THE SLEEVES ALL PUSHED UP, AND IT JUST FORMS THE TOP LAYER OF YOUR OUTFIT.

Shown on page 146 in pacific Chicago.

See diagram at end of pattern

SIZE cm(in)
One size only to fit up to:

96(38)

Actual size:

112(44)

Length from back neck:

40(16)

Sleeve seam:

58(23)

MATERIALS
Chicago – 50g balls:

12

1 pair each 5mm and 6mm needles

TENSION
14sts and 20 rows = 10cm square on 6mm needles over stocking stitch. See page 9.

ABBREVIATIONS
See page 9.

BACK
Using 5mm needles cast on 77sts and work 6 rows in k1 p1 rib.
Change to 6mm needles and stocking st. Cont until work measures 40cm.
Cast off.

FRONT
As back until work measures 31cm.
Shape neck: k30, cast off 17sts, k30.
On 30sts:
Row 1: purl

Row 2: cast off 2sts, work to end
Rows 3–6: as rows 1–2
Row 7: purl
Row 8: dec, work to end
Repeat rows 7–8 to 20sts. Cont until work measures 40cm.
Cast off.
Rejoin yarn to rem sts at neck edge and work to match.

SLEEVES
Using 6mm needles cast on 26sts. Change to 5mm needles and working in k1 p1 rib inc each end every 4th row to 52sts.
Change to 6mm needles and stocking st.
Increase row: k1 *inc k3* 12 times, inc, k2 *65sts*
Cont inc each end every 5th row to 75sts. Cont without shaping until work measures 58cm.
Shape sleevehead: cast off 4sts beg next 16 rows.
Cast off.

NECKBAND
Join right shoulder seam. Using 5mm needles pick up 19sts from side front neck, 17sts from centre front, 19sts from side front neck and 37sts from back neck *92sts*
Work 6 rows in k1 p1 rib.
Cast off in rib.

MAKING UP
Join left shoulder seam and neckband. Join sleeve seams. Working downwards from shoulder seam ease sleevehead into position and stitch. Join side seams. Weave in any loose ends.

CARE INSTRUCTIONS
See ball tag and page 172.

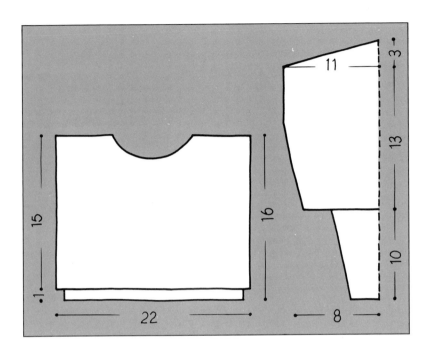

Shown on pages 134 and 167 in poppy Chandos, on page 135 in blaze Chicago, and page 38 in white Chandos.

MATERIALS

Chicago or Chandos – 50g balls:
2

1 pair each of 5mm and 6mm needles

TENSION

14sts and 20 rows = 10cm square on 6mm needles using Chandos yarn DOUBLE (ie 2 ends together) and Chicago SINGLE over stocking stitch. See page 9.

ABBREVIATIONS

See page 9.

SPECIAL NOTE

Chandos is knitted DOUBLE (ie 2 ends together) throughout.

Using 5mm needles cast on 70sts. Work in k2 p2 rib until work measures 10cm.
Increase row: p3* inc p8* 7 times inc p3 *78sts*
Change to 6mm needles and work in stocking st for 22 rows.
Row 23: *k8, k2tog* rep to last 8sts, k8
Row 24: *p7, p2tog* rep to last 8sts, p8
Row 25: k7, k2tog, *k6, k2tog*, rep to last 7sts, k7
Row 26: p6, p2tog, *p5, p2tog*, rep to end
Row 27: k5, k2tog, *k4, k2tog* rep to end
Row 28: p4, p2tog, *p3, p2tog* rep to end
Row 29: k3, k2tog, *k2, k2tog* rep to end
Row 30: p2, p2tog, *p1, p2tog* rep to end
Row 31: k1, *k2tog* rep to end
Cut off yarn and thread through remaining sts, draw up, and secure.
Sew up seam.

CARE INSTRUCTIONS

See ball tag and page 172.

CHUNKY RIBBED SKIRT

Shown on page 150 in coral Chandos and in bluebell Chandos.

SIZE cm(in)
To fit hip:

	89–94(35–37)

Actual size:

	96(38)

Length:

	48(19)

MATERIALS
Chandos – 50g balls:

7

1 pair 6mm needles. Elastic for waist

TENSION
14sts and 20 rows = 10cm square on 6mm needles using yarn DOUBLE (ie 2 ends together) over stocking stitch. See page 9.

ABBREVIATIONS
See page 9.

SPECIAL NOTE
Chandos is knitted DOUBLE (ie 2 ends together) throughout.

BACK AND FRONT (one piece)
Using 6mm needles and yarn DOUBLE, cast on 154sts.
Row 1: k1, *p2, k2* to last st, p1
Cont as set, working in k2 p2 rib until work measures 48cm.
Cast off in rib.

MAKING UP
Join side seam. Thread elastic through top of skirt.
Weave in any loose ends.

CARE INSTRUCTIONS
See ball tag and page 172.

GLOVES

Shown on page 22 in white Chandos on page 139 and page 158 in poppy Chandos.

MATERIALS
Chandos – 50g balls:

2

1 pair each of 3mm and 3¾mm needles

Stitch holder

TENSION
24sts and 31 rows = 10cm square on 3¾mm needles over stocking stitch. See page 9.

ABBREVIATIONS
See page 9.

LEFT GLOVE
Using 3mm needles cast on 45sts and work 20 rows in k1 p1 rib.
Change to 3¾mm needles and stocking stitch.
Work 2 rows.
Work gusset for thumb as follows:
Row 1: k18, inc, k3, inc, k22
Rows 2–4: stocking st
Row 5: k18, inc, k5, inc, k22
Rows 6–8: stocking st
Cont inc as set to 55sts.
Work 5 rows without shaping.
Thumb:
Row 1: k33, cast on 1st, turn
Row 2: p15, turn
Work 18 rows stocking st on these 15sts.
Shape Top:
Row 1: k2tog 7 times, k1
Row 2: purl
Row 3: k2tog 4 times
Break off yarn, and thread through rem sts, pull tight, and sew thumb seam.
With right side facing rejoin yarn and knit up 3sts from base of thumb.
Knit across rem sts.
Continue in stocking st for 13 rows, starting with a purl row.
1st Finger:
Row 1: k29, cast on 1st, turn
Row 2: p15, turn
Work 20 rows stocking st, and shape top as for thumb.
2nd Finger:

Row 1: knit up 3sts from base of 1st finger, k5, cast on 2sts, turn
Row 2: p15, turn
Work 24 rows stocking st, and shape top as for thumb.

3rd Finger:
Row 1: knit up 3sts from base of 2nd finger, k5, cast on 2sts, turn
Row 2: p15, turn
Work 20 rows stocking st, and shape top as for thumb.

4th Finger:
Row 1: knit up 3sts from base of 3rd finger, k5

Row 2: p13
Work 16 rows stocking st, and shape top as for thumb.

RIGHT GLOVE
Work right glove as left but in reverse stocking st (reading k for p, and p for k throughout).

MAKING UP
Sew up with right side stocking st on right side.

CARE INSTRUCTIONS
See ball tag and page 172.

LONG STOCKING STITCH SKIRT

Shown on page 163 in midnight Chicago.

SIZE cm(in)
To fit hip:

84–89(33–35)	91–97(36–38)
Actual size:	
89(35)	97(38)
Waist:	
61(24)	66(26)
Length:	
91(36)	91(36)

MATERIALS
Chicago – 50g balls:

10	11
1 pair each of 5mm and 6mm needles	
Elastic for waistband	

TENSION
14sts and 20 rows = 10cm square on 6mm needles over stocking stitch. See page 9.

ABBREVIATIONS
See page 9.

FRONT
Using 5mm needles, and starting at waistband, cast on 44(50)sts and work 7cm in k2 p2 rib.

Change to 6mm needles and cont in stocking st, inc each end of 3rd and every foll 3rd row 7 times to 58(64)sts. Inc each end of every foll 5th row twice to 62(68)sts.*
Cont without shaping until work measures 93cm. Change to 5mm needles and work 2cm in k2 p2 rib. Cast off.

BACK
Work as front to *.
Cont without shaping until work measures 69cm.
Next row: work 34(37)sts only, to make centre divide on back, leaving 28(31)sts on holder and working last 4sts in moss st to avoid curling.
Cont in stocking st with moss st edge until work measures 93cm.
Change to 5mm needles and work 2cm in k2 p2 rib. Cast off.
Pick up 28(31)sts from holder and cast on 6 extra sts. Work to match other side.

MAKING UP
Join side seams. Fold waistband in half to inside. Slipstitch into position. Insert elastic. Slipstitch top of moss st edging into position. Weave in any loose ends. We recommend that this garment is lined.

CARE INSTRUCTIONS
See ball tag and page 172.

LOOKING AFTER YOUR JERSEYS

There is nothing more devastating than unwrapping your woolly crowd-stopper from its layer of towels over the radiator, and finding a wretched shadow of its former self . . . several sizes smaller, and all felted and matted like a carpet tile. There is no need for this ever to happen to you, if you remember a few rules which can be summed up by the words *heat* and *stretching*. Don't apply either!

Just a few words about machine-washable wool at this point: it is certainly a labour-saving refinement but, in my opinion, it does give a slightly synthetic feel and appearance to pure wool. With untreated wool, such as Chandos and Chicago, you should use a good quality hand-washing solution and soak for a few minutes in cold water as directed. There is no need to get your elbows wet – just squeeze it a bit after the soaking stage. My own method is then to do one rinse in a bath of cold water to get the worst out, and then put the jersey into a pillowcase, or preferably a string bag. This is to prevent it getting tangled and stretched, especially if you are washing more than one at a time. Then put it into a washing machine to do two or three cold rinses, followed by a short spin at 500 r.p.m. None of this requires any great physical effort, and is totally risk free. I don't actually know if any machines which tumble dry do so automatically after rinsing, but, needless to say, this would be a catastrophe. Now is your opportunity to gently pull the knitting out widthways or lengthways if you wish to change the shape at all; also give the ribbing a gentle tug all round if it has become at all stretched-out during wear.

The best way to dry jerseys is on a towel laid over wooden slats in an airing cupboard with the heat turned down to the minimum. If you're going to hang it over a clothes line, make sure that the weight is supported as much as possible; never let the sleeves dangle down or they will stretch, and never hang it with clothes pegs. The alternative, dry-cleaning, is OK but it never really seems to give life to handknitted wool in the way that hand-washing does.

YARN DETAILS

Why do we all bother with yarns of natural fibres, when so many man-made 'easy-care' products are available? The point of wearing cotton, linen, and even viscose in summer, is that you can wear them next to the skin without any fear of allergic reactions, let alone the feeling of wearing a claustrophobic plastic bag which can be induced by acrylics. Cotton slides over the skin without feeling sticky, and is more pleasant to touch. The differences between wool and its man-made imitations are equally pronounced; acrylic fibres in comparison feel like plastic (after all, that's what they are). To me an acrylic yarn feels as if it hasn't been washed for months, even if it's spotlessly clean; whereas wool feels light and springy, not dull and lifeless. Wool is the warmest way to wrap up and yet your skin breathes through it and stays fresh; no other fibre gives you the best of both worlds in this way. It also lasts much longer than acrylic because it is always revived and improved by washing; it was born alive and will always stay alive if you look after it properly.

On to the yarns themselves and their individual merits:

CHANDOS

Chandos has been carefully selected to complement the many different stitch patterns used throughout this book. It has that springy characteristic which shows cabling techniques to their best advantage, and will not let the knitting stretch with age. The yarn is a blend of fine quality merino wool and lambswool, so that it doesn't contain any of the 'tickliness' found in coarser short-fibred wools. As with all luxury wools, you may find that it is prone to 'pilling' with wear. This means it can develop loose balls of fibre on the surface, but these can be easily removed with a strip of sticky tape or with a special 'de-pilling' comb available from most wool shops. Chandos comes in a wide range of colours including the classics – white, walnut, and flannel — as well as original and vivid tones like cobalt, poppy and teal.

CHICAGO
This multicoloured tweed yarn, used in Chapters 3 and 4 of this book, is a traditional English wool spun with flecks of contrasting or toning colours. The result is a beautifully rich effect as the different dyes are blended together. The main characteristic of the yarn is its unevenness; it has thicker and thinner patches which create a nubby effect in the final knitting which complements the colour spots very well.

DRAGONFLY
A combination of cotton and viscose, Dragonfly is a smooth, glossy yarn designed to satisfy the demands of those who would like pure silk but cannot afford either the price or the difficulties involved in washing it. Dragonfly also happens to be much more durable than pure silk knitting yarn.

It is of a lightweight construction so it doesn't weigh you down in the heat and each ball goes a long way. In this book I have used it several times in ivory as a tone-on-tone contrast to white Chandos; the natural sheen of the Dragonfly is an effective complement to the wool, showing up both yarns to their best advantage. Any of the designs in Chandos can also be knitted in Dragonfly, as they both work to the same tension.

KNITTING HINTS

Everybody has their own special labour-saving techniques, and also their individual refinements to get better results. This book is not a technical manual of handknitting; indeed, I have assumed that you already know much more than just how to cast on! Perhaps I should just highlight some areas where people most frequently seem to make mistakes and spoil their hard work:

Tension: is of course the most important thing to get right, as has previously been explained.

Side seams: some people like to slip the first stitch of every row to form a neat edge, but my recommendation is to knit the first and last stitch of every row for an even neater edge. You will find this makes the garment much easier to sew up, and moreover you can't sew up on the right side if you have slipped the edge stitches.

'Block knitting': is when you are changing colour in the middle of a row without carrying strands of yarn, or 'floats', across the back of the work. Always twist the newly introduced colour around the last strand, so that holes do not appear between the colour changes. Depending on the size of the colour 'block', you can work from a strand of yarn, several yards wound round a bobbin or from a separate ball.

Changing colours by the row: if you are doing your own colour pattern, especially when it incorporates textured stitches, the first row of the new colour must always be a knit row regardless, to avoid coloured loops forming where the new colour joins the previous one.

Measuring: you may have heard the expressions 'elastic tape-measure' or 'home-made tape-measure', which are invented for designs which measure 16 inches to the armhole when the pattern states quite clearly 17 inches. When your knitting is all bunched up on the needle, it measures slightly longer than when it is laid out flat. So measure in the centre of the work and push the knitting to each end of the needle so you are measuring a flat bit! Use a row-counter whenever possible and take notes, so that when a pattern says for the front: 'as back to ***', you know how many rows you worked to get to ***. Remember that patterns are written in measurements because people's row tension tends to vary, but you should always try to match your ribs, sleeves and body panels by the exact number of rows you have worked.

Casting on: to my knowledge there are at least six methods of casting on, and everybody seems to do them differently. Suffice to say that the '2 needle' method usually produces a somewhat untidy edge, the 'invisible' method is undoubtedly the best but rather hard to master, and the 'thumb' method is probably the best all round.

Casting off: a very common cause of the finishing touch spoiling the garment is casting off. If a collar is sewn on separately, you should cast off the neck edges and collar edges loosely in rib, or you might not be able to get the jersey over your head. More important are neck edges and cardigan buttonband edges, especially the latter: these must be cast off loosely in rib (i.e. cast off one knitwise, then one purlwise etc, for a 1 × 1 rib) or they will pucker the buttonbands and the knitting will be pulled up in the centre. Sometimes it can also be a help to cast off firmly in knit, for example on shoulder seams, back necks and particularly wide necks. This will then help to stop the knitting stretching and losing its shape. Lastly, it is necessary to cast off on a needle one or two sizes larger for loose edges like buttonbands, and

on the same size needle for firm structural edges.

Shoulders: if you are, for example, casting off 5 stitches 3 times, it is a good idea on the second and third steps to work the last 2 stitches together on the row before the next cast off, then, when casting off, slip the first stitch and cast off 4. This prevents the shoulder from looking like a staircase.

If there is no shoulder shaping, then do not cast off but place back and front onto holding pins or spare needles. Then, with right sides facing each other, slip one stitch from each needle, cast them off together and repeat this.

MAKING UP AND FINISHING

More often than not it is these final details which make the difference between a truly professional result and an amateurish one. Sometimes it is because one is in such a hurry to complete the garment after casting off and sometimes it is a question of technique and practice. I notice that many of the most experienced knitters actually make up the garment as they go along; for example the shoulder seams are finished and the neck knitted before the sleeves are even begun.

In general, your seams should be elastic enough to 'give' with the knitting, but firm on the shoulders to keep the shape of the garment. Start by pinning together the individual pieces, matching up stripes and stitch patterns. Make sure you leave long ends so that there are about 2 inches left to sew in afterwards. Use a blunt needle (a darning needle) and matching yarn. A good idea when sewing up the Chicago tweed is to find a matching colour in an even yarn, so that you are not sewing up with a thick and thin yarn.

Backstitch: this is done from the wrong side with right sides facing each other. It is probably the easiest stitch to do neatly, but it does produce a seam with no elasticity and therefore I would only recommend it for shoulder seams. The technique is to make a loop through both thicknesses, and for the next loop, come back to just after the previous loop.

Backstitch

Oversewing: place the seams together as for backstitch; the sewing up spirals around the edges of the knitting. This stitch tends to be untidy and too bulky and also leaves slight holes in the seam. You can tell it is not my favourite!

Oversewing

Running Stitch or invisible weaving: not only does this produce an invisible seam, but it also has a certain amount of stretch and is thus most suitable for handknitting. Work with both right sides facing you and slip the needle under the loop between the last two stitches in the row, and then under the corresponding loop on the other side.

Running Stitch

The particular advantage of this stitch is that you can do it loosely and then, at intervals, pull the stitches in more firmly. Alternatively you can tug the knitting out a bit if your seam is coming up too tight. If you are sewing stitches (e.g. on a drop shoulder seam) to row ends, the same applies, but on the sleeve slip the needle under the last stitch before the cast off. Running stitch is also the best stitch for sewing ribbing, but instead of going one stitch in from the edge, slip the needle under the loops at the very edge of the ribbing.

Setting in sleeves: on all sleeves you should first pin the centre of the sleeve top to the shoulder seam, and then ease the sleeve along the side seam (on drop shoulders) or into the armhole (on fitted sleeves). If you are gathering the sleeve then run a thread through and pull it in before you start pinning. Here are two diagrams to help you with pleated sleeves and saddle shoulders, both of which occur several times in this book.

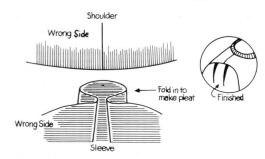

Pleated Sleeve

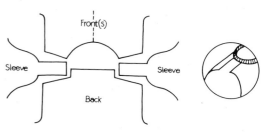

Saddle Shoulder

HELTER SKELTER – Trousers by Sara Sturgeon, dress by Joyce Redding's 'Oui'

PAGES 10/11 – Hat by Phillip Somerville

CLARISSA – Hat from the Hat Shop, skirt from Principles, tights from Liberty

CAPULET – Hat from Accessorize, skirt pattern see page 53, tights from Hennes

EDELWEISS – Hat from the Hat Shop, scarf around the hat from Liberty, shirt by Salvadore Ferragamo, skirt pattern see page 53, tights from Liberty

COLOMBE – Glove pattern see page 170, hat from the Hat Shop, skirt by In Wear Tricot, tights from Hennes, shoes from Jigsaw

GLOUCESTER – Child's hat from Hennes, trousers and boots, model's own

TESS – Hat from the Hat Shop, shirt by Salvadore Ferragamo, skirt by Daniel Hechter, tights by Hennes, brooch by the Hat Shop

BAROCCO – Beret by Marks and Spencer, shirt by Hennes, skirt by Daniel Hechter, tights from Liberty, shoes from Jigsaw

NEVIS & BEAUCHAMP – Hats from the Hat Shop, shirts from Hennes, trousers from In Wear

ELOUISE – Hat from the Hat Shop, shirt by Salvadore Ferragamo, linen shorts from Daniel Hechter

MONTAGUE – 'Hat' is skirt see page 53, secured with hat pin, skirt by In Wear Tricot, gloves see page 170, tights by Liberty, shoes from Jigsaw

Child's – Hat pattern see page 167, brooch from the Hat Shop

SOPHIE – Hat from the Hat Shop, hat pin from the Hat Shop, cashmere scarf from Berk of Burlington Arcade, shirt by Salvadore Ferragamo, trousers by Daniel Hechter

ROSE – Hat from the Hat Shop, brooch from the Hat Shop, skirt pattern see page 53, tights from Liberty

COTESBACH – Hat from the Hat Shop, shirt by Salvadore Ferragamo, skirt by Principles, handkerchief from Liberty

CAVENDISH – Earrings from Accessorize, trousers by Sara Sturgeon

TUTU – Fabric by Liberty

BAROCCO – Silk skirts by Georgina Von Etzdorf

ROSEMOOR – Gloves from Hennes, skirt from Java, tights by Hennes

PRONTO – Gloves by Georgina Von Etzdorf, skirt, antique Victorian, tights by Accessorize

BEAUCHAMP – Skirt by Sara Sturgeon, tights by Liberty

GLOUCESTER – Earrings by Accessorize, fabric by Liberty, tights from Accessorize

MADRIGAL – Trousers by Extravert at Hyper Hyper, tights by Liberty, shoes by Christine Ahrens

BURLINGTON – Dress by Joyce Redding's 'Oui'

SEVILLE – Trousers by Jody Day

ACROBAT – Man's jeans by Hennes, girl's jeans by Radio

COLLAGE – *Left:* Skirt by Pam Hogg, tights by Liberty, shoes by Berk
Right: Skirt by Shirley Wong, tights by Accessorize, shoes by Christine Ahrens

HELTER SKELTER – Earrings from Accessorize, lambswool leggings from Hennes

BRITANNIA – Brooch by Accessorize, linen shorts by Pam Hogg, tights from Liberty, shoes from Berk

GERONIMO – Cycling shorts from The Fitness Centre

KIMO – Hat from Hyper Hyper, skirt on hat from Extravert, at Hyper Hyper, black jersey trousers from Extravert at Hyper Hyper

CAVENDISH – Black velvet beret from the Hat Shop, leggings from Hennes

HERCULES – White shirt and trousers from Hennes

TRISTAN – White shirt from In Wear, leggings from Hennes

CRUSOE – Leggings from Hennes

KALEIDOSCOPE – Earrings from Accessorize, skirt by In Wear Tricot

SPARKS – Scarfs by Monsoon

HANOVER – Trousers and culottes from Java

JUNIPER – Glove pattern see page 170, skirt by In Wear Tricot, tights from Accessorize

COBRA – Black Levi 501's from Hennes

MADISON – White shirt and red leggings from Hennes

APPLEJACK – White polo top from Hennes, jeans from Hennes

BUSTER – Hat from the Hat Shop, shirt from Hennes

HOPSCOTCH – Skirt pattern see page 170, tights from Accessorize

TRISTAN – Shirt and jeans from Hennes

HANOVER – White shirt from Hennes, skirt pattern see page 170, tights from Accessorize

MADISON – Stripy shirt from Hennes, hat from the Hat Shop, glove pattern see page 170, leggings from In Wear

RICHMOND – Tights from Liberty

KIMO – Shoes from Christine Ahrens, shirt from Hennes

CAPULET – Hat pattern see page 169

APPLEJACK – Shirt and jeans from Hennes

The yarns featured in this book are widely available in over 100 shops in the UK and the same number in the USA, as well as a number of shops in Canada and Australia. As the lists of stockists are constantly being updated, it is not practical to give details here. If you do not know of a retail outlet near you, simply send a stamped self-addressed envelope to any of the addresses below or telephone and you will be informed of your nearest source. The yarns are also available by mail-order, but only if you are unable to obtain them locally.

UK
Studio Yarns Ltd.
The Citadel
Blenheim Gardens
London SW2 5EU
(01) 671 7627

USA
Silk City Fibers
155 Oxford Street
Paterson
NJ 07522
(201) 942 1100

CANADA
Lincoln Agencies
76 Dakin Crescent
Cambridge
ONT N1S 3X2
(519) 621 6308

AUSTRALIA
Myer Stores
295 Lonsdale Street
Melbourne 3000
(03) 66 111